LETTING GO

LETTING GO

The Story of Zen Master Tōsui

Tōsui oshō densan

Translated and with an Introduction by
Peter Haskel

University of Hawai'i Press
Honolulu

© 2001 University of Hawai'i Press
All rights reserved
Printed in the United States of America
01 02 03 04 05 06   5 4 3 2 1

Library of Congress Cataloging-in-Publication Data
Menzan Zuiho, 1683–1769.
   [Tosui osho densan. English.]
   Letting go : the story of Zen Master Tosui ; translated and with an introduction by Peter Haskel.
      p.   cm.
   Includes bibliographical references and index.
   ISBN 0–8248–2358–3 (cloth : alk. paper)—ISBN 0–8248–2440–7 (pbk. : alk. paper)
      1. Tōsui, 1605–1683. 2. Priests, Zen—Japan—Biography. I. Haskel, Peter. II. Title.

BQ990.O69 M4613 2001
294.3'927'092—dc21
[B]   2001017449

University of Hawai'i Press books are printed on acid-free paper and meet the guidelines for permanence and durability of the Council on Library Resources.

Designed by Carol Colbath
Printed by The Maple-Vail Book Manufacturing Group

For Maria

Contents

Preface	ix
Acknowledgments	xv
Introduction: Japanese Zen in the Age of Tōsui	1
About the Translation	41

Tribute to the Life of Zen Master Tōsui   43
  by Menzan Zuihō

Biographical Addendum: Tōsui's Story	95
Appendix: *Biography of Master Tōsui (Tōsui oshō den)* by Zōsan Ryōki	121
Notes	
Notes to Text	125
Notes to Poems	153
Bibliography	155
Index	161

Preface

As with so many of the acquaintances who brighten one's life, I encountered Zen Master Tōsui Unkei (d. 1683) quite by accident—much as did the nameless beggars, day laborers, and assorted townsfolk who chance upon him in the pages of his colorful biography, the *Tribute*.[1] In the course of researching the life of the noted priest-poet Taigu Ryōkan (1758–1832), Tōsui's name surfaced as a largely forgotten earlier Zen figure who embodied many of the traits for which Ryōkan was celebrated—a staunch independence and indifference to hardship, a rejection of the monastic world for a life among the common people of Japan, and a keen understanding of Zen combined with an at-times childlike naïveté. Like Ryōkan, Tōsui was a member of the Sōtō school, and undertook long and grueling years of Zen study, receiving the sanction of a distinguished teacher, only to finally abandon the religious establishment. But while Ryōkan returned to settle in his native district of Echigo, where he lived surrounded by patrons, admirers, and friends, Tōsui seems to have been a confirmed loner, a drifter who valued untrammeled freedom above all else and who, even in old age, fought stubbornly to shed all constraints—material, personal, or institutional. So extreme was Tōsui's stance that he has been acclaimed by one modern Japanese writer as unique in the history of Japanese Zen, a history admittedly boasting a great many distinctive characters.[2] Some have likened Tōsui to Saint Francis of Assisi,[3] or even hailed him as the "original hippie" (*hippi no dai sendatsu*) and his biography as a "hippie primer" (*hippi no nyūmon*).[4]

The details of Tōsui's life are arresting indeed. By the time he had reached the pinnacle of his career, he had spent virtually his entire life as a priest, entering the temple as a child, training in monasteries, traveling on pilgrimage to study under a variety of notable teachers, finally receiving his master's sanction of his realization and the transmission of his school of Zen. Having become a Zen master in his own right, he had received abbacy of a temple as well as the patronage of a powerful daimyo and could look forward to a secure and distinguished old age. Yet at this juncture, without any explanations or good-byes, Tōsui suddenly left his temple, his disciples, and his comfortable life as a Buddhist abbot, effectively abandoning his position within the Sōtō school. He seems to have settled for a time at Manpukuji, the chief monastery of the recently established Ōbaku line, whose immigrant Chinese teachers were attracting the notice of many idealistic Japanese Zen monks. But in the end Tōsui left Manpukuji as well and henceforth relinquished temple life altogether and even the outward trappings of a priest, disappearing into the towns and cities of Japan to eke out a hand-to-mouth existence as an itinerant beggar, vendor, and day laborer. Pursued by anxious disciples, who discovered him living in Kyoto, homeless, ragged, and unkempt, Tōsui refused all pleas to resume his role as teacher and declined to accept any material assistance that might circumscribe his cherished freedom.

Once having left the temples, Tōsui never turned back. Right to the end, he fiercely maintained his independence, rejecting any help that was not completely unconditional, that might leave him beholden to any person or group. Yet for all its solitude, poverty, and physical discomfort, Tōsui never regarded his way of life as a form of trial or penance, but purely as a source of delight, a manifestation of what the *Tribute*'s author extols as "oneness with the principle of cosmic play" (*yugyōzanmai*). When Tōsui died in Kyoto, operating a vinegar stand in the city's northern suburb of Takagamine, his final poem expressed only the sense of a lifetime of joy and of the beauty of the autumn evening that shimmered before him.

As it has come down to us, Tōsui's life as a Zen master hidden *in* the world rather than *from* it seems not merely the record of an exceptionally free-spirited and uncompromising personality, but a silent rebuke to the Zen of his day, and even a challenge to that of our own. In particular, it suggests that Zen practice and enlightenment need not depend on a temple establishment, a priesthood, or any external organization but can be integrated seamlessly and often invisibly with one's daily life. Perhaps, Tōsui's story implies, this is itself the most direct form of Zen teaching.

Unfortunately, Tōsui, unlike Ryōkan, left behind no written legacy. That we know about him at all is largely because of a single biography, the *Tribute*, composed some fifty years after Tōsui's death by the Sōtō

Zen master Menzan Zuihō (1683–1769). Menzan had spent years collecting information about Tōsui, interviewing monks who had known the Master firsthand and others who had heard stories about him from colleagues and teachers who had themselves been his disciples and associates. The resulting facts and assorted anecdotes Menzan assembled in rough chronological order to produce a sort of impromptu biography. Of Tōsui's actual views regarding Zen, Zen practice, and the various issues confronting the Zen monks of his day, Menzan's account records nothing apart from a handful of verses and a few, albeit telling, offhand remarks. Yet what survives in the accumulated vivid detail of Menzan's record is something far more compelling than words or thoughts, namely Tōsui himself. Tōsui's life, as we have it, the *Tribute* makes plain, was his ultimate teaching, his true Zen legacy.

Tōsui's biographer, Menzan, was the most celebrated Sōtō scholar of the Tokugawa period (1600–1868) and at the time of his death possibly the leading figure in the Sōtō school. The author of more than fifty sectarian works, including textual studies and biographies of Dōgen Kigen (1200–1253), Japanese Sōtō Zen's founder, Menzan was also an ardent practitioner and an active Zen master, principal heir to the early Tokugawa movement that sought to renovate the Sōtō temples by establishing an orthodoxy inspired by Dōgen's original teachings. Indeed, the Sōtō sect as it exists in Japan today is in many respects the creation of Menzan and his colleagues in this movement, which became the prevailing force in Sōtō Zen.

Menzan tells us in his introduction to the *Tribute*[5] that he had often heard about Tōsui from Kohō Ryōun (d. 1717), who was not only Menzan's early teacher but also Tōsui's nephew and the heir of Sengan Rintetsu (n.d.), one of Tōsui's Dharma brothers.[6] Tōsui seems to have guided his nephew's spiritual development, bringing him at age ten to train under Sengan and later sending him to study at Manpukuji under the émigré Zen master Kao-ch'üan. Kohō, in turn, revered Tōsui and had intended to honor him with a formal biography but died before undertaking the task, which Menzan resolved to complete in his late teacher's place. Menzan also states that he was anxious to expand the available accounts of Tōsui's life, which he regarded as hopelessly inadequate, an apparent reference to the brief and nearly identical profiles included in two collections of Sōtō priests' biographies published in the first decades of the eighteenth century.[7]

But aside from setting the record straight and showing respect to his first teacher, the preface makes clear that Menzan wished to convey something of his own heartfelt enthusiasm for Tōsui and that he deliberately presented the Master's story in a way that he felt would appeal not only to Zen monks and nuns but to ordinary lay men and women. Tōsui's biography was one of the few popular works Menzan composed in the course of his long and prolific career. It is not only written in an easily readable, unvarnished, and occasionally colloquial style, but provided with illustrations in the form of twenty woodblock prints depicting various episodes from the text. The *Tribute*, to my knowledge, is the earliest biography of an Edo-period Zen priest to be published with narrative illustrations.

As a quintessential "establishment" figure, Menzan might seem an unlikely champion for a maverick like Tōsui, who essentially turned his back on the Sōtō temples and his position as a Sōtō abbot. But whatever Menzan's sectarian concerns and convictions regarding Sōtō orthodoxy, his remarks in the *Tribute* leave one in no doubt that he felt Tōsui's story had something of real value to say about Zen and that he hoped to see the work disseminated as widely as possible both inside and outside the temples.

The *Tribute*, as noted before, is not just the best account of Tōsui's life but the only account, for all practical purposes. The two earlier, capsule biographies, though they have at least the virtue of having been compiled shortly after Tōsui's death, are uncritically assembled patchworks of fact, legend, and hearsay, offering little more than fragments of often dubious or garbled information. Subsequent biographies of Tōsui, including those that have appeared in the modern period, are based entirely on the two early accounts and the *Tribute*, and essentially add nothing to the record, apart from occasional unsupported speculation. The best of these works, Tanaka Shigeru's 1939 *Beggar Tōsui (Kōjiki Tōsui)*, exposes various baseless assertions marring the other Tōsui biographies, both modern and premodern, but then proceeds to introduce undocumented speculation of its own.

Menzan's work itself, for all its pleasures, suffers from a variety of imperfections. The *Tribute*'s narrative consists for the most part of anecdotes grouped roughly by period and suggesting an ordered chronology; but the actual placement of the stories within each grouping is often, as Menzan concedes, purely random. The *Tribute* supplies few fixed dates,[8] and Menzan confesses that for the latter part of Tōsui's career there is no way of knowing where the Master was at a given time. Yet the text repeatedly offers figures for the number of years covered by various periods in Tōsui's life—five years, six years, thirty years, and so forth—numbers that, in the context of the narrative as a whole, fail to add up in any coherent fashion.[9] All in all, present-day scholars may justifiably carp at the chronological contradictions and inconsistencies that reveal themselves in Menzan's account. But it should be borne in mind that while often failing to match the needs of modern historical research, the *Tribute* fully accords with the actual purposes for which its author intended it. Menzan's aim in the work was not so much to provide a careful and consistent chronology of Tōsui's career as to offer a "tribute" (*san*) to Tōsui's character as revealed in various episodes from the Master's own life, a tribute that might serve, in turn, as inspiration to both Zen monks and laypeople.

Because the *Tribute* is itself primarily a biography and the basis for nearly all we know of Tōsui's life, in introducing the text I have deliberately refrained from doing more than touch on the broad outlines of the Master's singular career. To do otherwise, to discuss Tōsui's story in greater detail, would not only be repetitious but anticlimactic, anticipating and inevitably diminishing the original's lively and entertaining account. Readers interested in an extended examination of Tōsui's life as represented in the traditional sources are referred to the biographical essay that follows the translation.

No personality, however original, exists in a vacuum, and distinctive as Tōsui was in many respects, he remains very much a man of his period, the seventeenth century, itself a peculiarly colorful time in the history of Japanese Zen. Because we lack virtually any record of Tōsui's own religious practice or outlook, it is not possible to relate him directly to any of the movements or trends in the Zen temples of his day or to know to what extent he was influenced by the many famous priests whom the *Tribute* tells us he sought out and studied under. We can, however, delineate something of the atmosphere of Tōsui's world by examining certain of the forces that shaped Tokugawa Zen and, in particular, by focusing on those Tokugawa teachers whom Tōsui himself is said to have encountered. By adopting such an approach in the introduction, I have tried both to fill in background pertinent to the *Tribute* and to call attention to personalities, issues, and institutions that may have informed Tōsui's own development as a Zen master.

At the same time, the special character and flavor of Zen in Tōsui's period cannot be conveyed without some sense of Japanese Zen in the period immediately preceding, that is, the late Middle Ages. Nearly all of Tōsui's teachers shared a sense that Japanese Zen had failed during the previous centuries and needed to be revived, even reinvented. This attitude seems to have been a reaction to particular developments in late-medieval Japanese Zen, and for this reason, the introduction begins with an overview of certain features of the still only dimly understood Zen of this period, including the distinctive, and at times bizarre, forms of koan study and secret transmission prevalent in the late-medieval Rinzai and Sōtō temples.

It is, of course, perfectly possible to enjoy Tōsui's story purely on its own terms, and the forthright, untrammeled spirit revealed in the *Tribute* speaks to us clearly across the centuries. But I believe that appreciation of Tōsui is greatly enhanced by viewing him within the broader context of the Zen of his time, of the figures and forces that animated the Zen temples in early Tokugawa Japan.

Acknowledgments

My labors on the present book were considerably lightened by the assistance and encouragement of a number of individuals and organizations. I am especially grateful to Professor Ryuichi Abe of Columbia University's Department of Religion, who freely gave of his time, wisdom, and experience in helping me find my way through nettlesome patches of the text and in advising me on countless other technical and historical questions that arose in the course of following Tōsui's trail. I am also deeply appreciative of the efforts of Reverend Shokau Okumura of the San Francisco Soto Zen Education Center and Arthur Braverman, both of whom generously aided in aspects of the book's preparation. Maria Collora, Michael Hotz, Robert Lopez, and John Storm read over the final manuscript and offered numerous helpful suggestions, while Peeter Lamp supplemented my rudimentary computer skills. Columbia University's Starr East Asian Library was an invaluable resource, and in the course of my research I benefited from the assistance of Mihoko Miki, the Starr's Japanese research librarian; Alexander Brown; Kenneth Harlin; D. John McClure, and other members of the staff. I would also like to thank Sharon Yamamoto and Patricia Crosby, my editors at University of Hawai'i Press, for their resourcefulness, patience, and sensitivity and to express my appreciation to the book's copy editor, Joanne Sandstrom, and to the press's managing editor, Ann Ludeman. Finally, I would like to thank the First Zen Institute of America in New York City for making available to me its computer facilities and library.

INTRODUCTION

Japanese Zen in the Age of Tōsui

Although the Zen schools in Japan tend to emphasize their medieval[1] origins, Japanese Zen as we know it today, which is to say the modern Sōtō and Rinzai sects, is to a great extent the product of the more recent Tokugawa, or Edo, period, which spanned the years 1600 to 1868. It was during these critical two and one half centuries that the current identities of the Zen schools were created, or perhaps more accurately, recreated, in large part as an attempt to restore the integrity of the teachings of the medieval founders.

In the Rinzai school the revival of the teaching was the work of Menzan Zuihō's contemporary, Hakuin Ekaku (1686–1769), whose teaching line and brand of energetic koan study still dominate virtually all Japanese Rinzai temples.[2] Generally speaking, the koan (C. *kung-an*) method is a teaching device by which the student, under a teacher's guidance, attempts to penetrate selected "cases," consisting of the often paradoxical sayings of various early Chinese Ch'an (J. Zen) masters. The method reached maturity during the Sung dynasty (960–1279), and along with seated meditation (C. *tso-ch'an;* J. *zazen*) was the principal form of Ch'an practice brought from the continent to medieval Japan. Hakuin's forebears included many famous exponents of koan Zen, among them the Sung master Hsü-t'ang Chih-yü (1185–1269) and the Japanese teacher Shūhō Myōchō (Daitō Kokushi, 1282–1337), founder of the Kyoto headquarters temple Daitokuji. Drawing inspiration from these celebrated predecessors, Hakuin and his successors systematized a method of study that involved completion of a series of cases, a process that aimed at deepening and testing the student's grasp of Zen and emphasized a vigorous intuitive approach. "Hakuin Zen" swept the Rinzai temples in the late eighteenth and early nineteenth centuries and remains the standard form of Rinzai Zen in Japan today.

While reform in the Rinzai school centered on a single personality, the Zen master Hakuin, and a single practice, koan study, the resurgence of the Sōtō school in the Tokugawa period took the form of a sectarian revival movement.[3] This movement was exemplified by Menzan Zuihō's writings on Sōtō history and doctrine and by the campaign of Menzan's preceptor Manzan Dōhaku (1635–1714) and his colleagues to regularize the procedures for Dharma transmission according to their reading of *Shōbōgenzō*, the masterwork of the sect's founder, Dōgen. Dharma transmission, in both Rinzai and Sōtō Zen, refers to the manner in which the teaching, or Dharma, is passed from a Zen master to his disciple and heir. The procedure establishes the disciple as a transmitting teacher in his own right and successor in an unbroken line of teachers and disciples, a spiritual "bloodline" (*kechimyaku*) theoretically traced back to the Buddha himself. Succession is attested by a written certificate, commonly referred to in Rinzai Zen as *inka* and in Sōtō Zen as *shisho*.

During the late Middle Ages,[4] Menzan maintained, Dharma transmission in the Sōtō school tended to be treated as the property of a particular temple rather than of an individual teacher, and most Sōtō temples permitted only teachers of their own temple's lineage to serve as abbots. To circumvent the problems posed by this system, and to welcome qualified outsiders, new abbots automatically received transmission within the lines of all the various temples where they served, so that an abbot might be obliged to change lines as often as he changed temples. This change could be simply effected through an accommodating master or his proxy, or even by paying one's respects before the pagoda of a deceased teacher in the temple's line. In either case, the inevitable result was a tangle of lineages and the progressive attenuation of the ideal of a direct personal bond between master and disciple.[5] It was to rectify these problems, which had continued to plague the Sōtō temples, that Manzan spearheaded a movement to restore what he regarded as the sect's authentic mode of transmission.[6] Based on their interpretation of Dōgen's *Shōbōgenzō*, Manzan and his colleagues contended that a Sōtō student could legitimately receive Dharma transmission only once, from a single teacher who must sanction the student directly in a face-to-face encounter. According to Manzan, this not only represented Dōgen's original method of Dharma transmission, received from his Chinese master T'ien-t'ung Ju-ching (1163–1228), but was the method still universally observed in the Japanese Rinzai school.[7]

Various Sōtō teachers disputed Manzan's assertions, some defending the legitimacy of the status quo, others attacking what they regarded as Manzan's one-sided emphasis on formal considerations. Manzan's Sōtō colleague, the Zen master Dokuan Genkō (1630–1698), for example, openly questioned the necessity of written acknowledgment from a teacher, which he dismisses as "paper transmission." "Those nowadays who claim to be Dharma heirs," Dokuan argues, "are merely receiving paper Zen."[8] The only genuine transmission, Dokuan insists, is the individual's independent experience of Zen enlightenment, an intuitive experience that needs no external confirmation: "What is called Zen enlightenment is not dependent on another's enlightenment. It is only what you realize for yourself, attain for yourself, just as you know when you've eaten enough rice to satisfy your hunger, or drunk enough water to slake your thirst."[9] Ultimately, however, Manzan and his supporters prevailed in the transmission debate, and their descendents became the principal force shaping the development of the Sōtō school.

As suggested above, during the Tokugawa period Japanese Zen was transformed through efforts within each sect to reestablish and revitalize the teachings of its early founders, efforts that continue to determine the character of the modern Rinzai and Sōtō schools. In a sense, then, Japanese Zen as we know it today is Tokugawa Zen, a teaching that looks back to its medieval roots but does so through the prism of its own special concerns. Even so, real consensus within the Zen sects was not forged until at least the eighteenth century. By contrast, the early Tokugawa period, roughly synchronous with Tōsui's life, was a time when the identity of both the Sōtō and Rinzai schools was relatively fluid, a period of lively debate, experiment, and self-examination unparalleled in the history of Japanese Zen. Perhaps as a consequence it was also a period populated by a host of original and vivid Zen personalities, not the least of whom was Tōsui himself.

• • •

When Ieyasu, the shogunate's founder, inaugurated Tokugawa rule by vanquishing his rivals in 1600 at the Battle of Sekigahara, Zen had been an active force in Japanese religious life for some four hundred years. Indeed, on its arrival in Japan during the Kamakura period (1192–1333), Zen already had a rich and lengthy history on the Asian continent. A distinctive Chinese form of Buddhism that emerged during the Tang (618–906) and Five Dynasties (907–960) periods, Ch'an emphasized meditation practice combined with the realization and manifestation of enlightenment (C. *wu;* J. *satori*), the direct intuitive experience of original, unconditioned "Buddha Mind." According to Ch'an, this was the truth realized by the Buddha himself and transmitted to his disciple Mahakashyapa, a "special transmission outside the scriptures," passed down through an unbroken chain of enlightened teachers and disciples. Often the Buddha Mind was demonstrated in lightninglike give-and-take between Ch'an adepts, the characteristic Ch'an "dialogues" (*wēn-ta;* J. *mondō*), which might include various forms of shouting, pushing, and beating that underlined the dynamic, earthy character of the exchanges. It was these often puzzling episodes that formed the basis of the *kung-an* (J. *kōan*) that later Ch'an teachers assigned as problems to students.

> A monk asked Yün-mēn,[10] "What is the Buddha?"
> Yün-mēn said, "A shit-wiping stick."[11]

> A monk asked Chao-chou,[12] "Why did the patriarch come from the West?"[13]
> Chao-chou said, "The cypress tree in the garden."[14]

While the details of practice in the early Ch'an communities remain unclear, *kung-an* study seems to have taken shape largely after Ch'an's golden age, the Tang and Five Dynasties periods, and by the Southern Sung dynasty (1126–1279) had become a feature of both the leading Ch'an schools, the Lin-chi (J. Rinzai) and the Ts'ao-t'ung (J. Sōtō). Sung masters anthologized *kung-an* in collections, adding comments in poetry or prose as a kind of individual appreciation. The shortest of these comments, known as *hsia-wu* (J. *agyo,* "offered words") or *cho-yü* (J. *jakugo,* sometimes translated "capping phrases"), were often as cryptic as the original *kung-an* themselves. They might be the Sung teachers' alternative responses or critical comments on the cases and drew freely upon poetry, proverbs, and contemporary slang, including a variety of shouts and imprecations—a distinct genre that represented a marriage of Ch'an and Chinese literary and popular culture.

The Lin-chi and Ts'ao-t'ung Ch'an that was transmitted to Japan[15] was this Southern Sung teaching, often carried by Japanese monks who had completed their studies on the continent and become successors in their Chinese masters' lines. Among the most famous of these Japanese teachers were Nanpo Jōmyō (Daiō Kokushi, 1235–1308), founder of the Rinzai line that leads directly to Hakuin and modern Rinzai Zen; and Dōgen Kigen, the Sōtō school's founder, from whom Tōsui and all present Japanese Sōtō masters trace their descent. After receiving the sanction of his Chinese teacher, Ju-ching, Dōgen returned to Japan, establishing the country's first Sung-style Zen meditation hall at his temple, Kōshōji, near Kyoto. In 1243 for reasons still uncertain, he left with his followers to found Eiheiji, the temple in the mountains of Echizen (present-day Fukui Prefecture) where he remained till his death, completing *Shōbōgenzō* and presiding over a strict, isolated, and austere monastic community. Together with an emphasis on regular meditation practice, Dōgen's teachings, like those of Nanpo, reflect the importance of koan study, which in one form or another remained a feature of Sōtō Zen throughout the medieval period.

Zen was also reaching Japan in the thirteenth century with émigré Chinese masters, who at the invitation of the country's military rulers established Sung-style monasteries in the shogunate's capital, Kamakura. These teachers, nearly all members of Lin-chi lines, also served as bearers of contemporary Chinese culture, especially literary culture. At Kenchōji, for example, Japanese-style clothes were forbidden, while at Engakuji, applicants vying for admission had to compete in an examination in Chinese poetry composition.[16] Henceforth, along with their duties as abbots and teachers, Zen masters in medieval Japan's great urban temples frequently performed an additional role, as custodians of aristocratic Chinese culture. This cultural component, in turn, attracted to Zen not only the socially ambitious military elite in Kamakura but also the palace and court aristocrats, who helped to establish the teaching in Kyoto, the imperial capital. The two leading Rinzai temples of Tōsui's period, Daitokuji and Myōshinji, were founded in the early fourteenth century in part through the patronage of the emperor and court; imperial support for Zen continued throughout the Middle Ages and into the Tokugawa period, and it was not uncommon for medieval Japanese emperors to undertake Zen study with masters of the Kyoto temples.

Patronage by the warrior elite also contributed to the prominence of the Kyoto Zen monasteries, particularly under the Muromachi shogunate (1333–1573), which ruled its domains from the imperial capital and had close connections with the city's Zen temples. Under the Muromachi shoguns, a system of official ranking for select Zen temples was observed, the so-called Gozan, or "Five Mountains" system, "mountain" in East Asia being a metaphor for Buddhist temples. Despite its name, the Gozan's leading institutions were actually six Kyoto Rinzai temples that enjoyed the extensive material support of the feudal government, and five parallel, albeit less powerful, temples in Kamakura.[17] In the system's prime, between the last quarter of the fourteenth century and the first quarter of the fifteenth, the lavish patronage of the ruling elite and revenues from vast provincial holdings combined to endow the Gozan temples with enormous wealth and prestige, augmented by the presence of tonsured members of the court and military aristocracy among the temples' abbots.

Due in part to these aristocratic connections, the atmosphere in the leading Gozan temples seems to have become increasingly bureaucratic and effete, with an emphasis on cultural and particularly literary pursuits at the expense of Zen practice. Classical Chinese culture, and particularly the composition of poetry in Chinese, consumed the attention of many Gozan monks, and Chinese literary specialties became the focus of the curricula at the various subtemples, or *tatchū*, which formed the basis of the large official Zen monasteries. Another aspect of Gozan Zen was the ready incorporation of practices associated with Esoteric Buddhism (Shingon, or Mikkyō), which since the Heian period (794–1192) had remained a powerful force in Japanese religious life and was closely identified with the court and aristocracy.

By contrast, those Zen groups not included in the Gozan system tended to preserve a dedication to the rudiments of Zen practice, such as *zazen*, koan study, and *angya*, the traditional pilgrimage in which a Zen monk tests and matures his realization by traveling to study under a variety of masters. Sometimes referred to by the collective term *"rinka,"*[18] these outsider groups, chief of which were the Daitokuji and Myōshinji lines and the Sōtō school of Dōgen, became a magnet for idealists fleeing the enervated "literary Zen" of the Gozan temples. However, with the Gozan virtually monopolizing official patronage in the capital, the *rinka* organizations tended to develop actively in provincial Japan, where they garnered the support not only of farming communities—in the case of the Sōtō school—but also of members of the "new" classes, including provincial warlords, merchants, and masters of Noh, poetry, and tea. These social groups became increasingly prominent in the late Muromachi period as the authority of the central government in Kyoto eroded and economic and military power shifted to the provinces. In the process, the Gozan found itself critically weakened, with Kyoto riven by warfare between contending provincial generals, many of them the patrons of *rinka* lines. By the sixteenth century, following their warrior patrons to power, the Zen groups that had formerly been outsiders had become insiders. Daitokuji and Myōshinji, which successfully cultivated the support of the new generation of warlords, enjoyed a rapid expansion in the provinces. The Sōtō school, too, experienced extraordinary growth throughout Japan, centering on Sōjiji, the headquarters temple established in Noto (Ishikawa Prefecture) by Dōgen's descendent Keizan Jōkin (1268–1325), revered as the Sōtō school's "second founder." Under Keizan's disciple Gasan Jōseki (1275–1369) and Gasan's heir Tsūgen Jakurei (1322–1391), Sōjiji branched out across Japan, adapting itself to the needs of its provincial patrons by performing funeral services, holding precepts and meditation retreats for laypeople, and incorporating local religious beliefs involving exorcism, divination, and the worship of popular Buddhist and Shinto deities.[19] It was this Sōjiji Tsūgen line that was the driving force behind the sect's growth during the sixteenth century and the line from which Tōsui traced his descent. In this way, during the fifteenth and sixteenth centuries *rinka* organizations like the Rinzai Myōshinji line and Dōgen's Sōtō school moved from a marginal role outside the official temple system to a place at the center of Japanese Zen, a position they commanded into Tōsui's period and have maintained up to the present.

Such apparent continuity, however, belies the fact that the Zen actually practiced by the *rinka* schools during their ascendancy in the late Middle Ages differed from that advocated by their founders or practiced in the Sōtō and Rinzai temples of our own, or even of Menzan's, day. Formed as they were under such similar circumstances and accommodating similar sets of patrons, the medieval *rinka* groups developed certain common approaches to Zen study even while maintaining their discrete organizational identities. Koan practice remained a key element in virtually all the *rinka* lines. But it often assumed the character of a formal initiation in which the "secrets" of the koans were transmitted by the teacher to the student, to be recorded in private manuals or memoranda.[20] The contents of many of these texts, which have survived for all the major *rinka* lines, center on the *agyo,* the special phrases referred to earlier, employed in the classic Chinese koan collections: "Heaping snow in a silver bowl"; "The pine is straight, the brambles bent"; "One thief recognizes another."[21] In each teaching line, particular *agyo* were transmitted as "answers" to certain koans, and these together with the teacher's explanations and comments were recorded by the student. In this context, *inka* (literally, "seal of approval"), the Zen master's written sanction of a student's enlightenment, came to signify receipt of a line's transmission of *agyo* and associated comments.

Judging by the anguished complaints of contemporaries, this formalized approach to the koan, sometimes referred to as *missan* ("secret study"),[22] seems to have become popular in the *rinka* temples by the late fourteenth century,[23] though its roots may go back to the Kamakura period.[24] While preserving the forms and conventions of Sung-style koan Zen, including private interviews between master and student (J. *sanzen* or *dokusan*) and the use of dialogue and arcane phrases, this method was at times closer in spirit to the secret oral transmissions traditionally associated with Japanese Esoteric Buddhism. This influence is reflected in the names for many of the *missan* transmission documents[25] and at times in their contents as well. Often Esoteric Buddhism is presented in a curious form that draws on yin-yang–type beliefs, in which the idea of original being is given a literal, physiological interpretation occasionally incorporating sexual symbolism. Thus, one Rinzai *missan* document identifies the famous case "Hsiang-yen's 'Man Up a Tree' "[26] as "the *a-hum* koan of the Shingon (Esoteric) school, . . . the answer that we make at birth to the question of why the Patriarch came from the West."[27] And a Sōtō transmission contains a large diagram of the Sanskrit letter *a*—in Shingon the symbol of the cosmic Buddha Mahavairocana—bearing the inscription, "The letter *a* is the original form of the human being within the womb. . . . It is the koan Chao-chou's dog."[28] Other diagrams in the same work are constructed upon a fanciful numerology that links various groups of numbered items, such as "fours"—for example, the four directions, four seasons, and "four streams." In Sōtō Zen, the commentary notes, this last is interpreted as the waters of yin and yang, in which the yin represents the mother's vagina, indicated by the color red, and the yang, the father's semen, indicated by white.²⁹ Still other syncretic Sōtō transmissions are couched in a traditional dialogue *(mondō)* format. One such text offers what appears to be script and stage directions for the private interview between a *missan* teacher and his disciple. Much of the exchange centers on the explanation of various esoteric symbols, such as the black *manji*³⁰ contained in a red circle.

> Within a red circle is a black *manji*. This is called the right-sided *manji* diagram. It is the state existing even before the empty *kalpa*.³¹
> The teacher asks, "What is the significance of the diagram?"
> The student comes forward, covers his head with his robe, and seating himself, says, "This expresses the state before birth. Within this placenta, everything is present. This is the great *manji*, representing the perfection of all virtues."
> The teacher says, "The black color of the *manji* symbolizes the state of nondiscrimination, the state before east and west were distinguished, when you were in the realm of undifferentiated existence *(konton)*. Thus, this very instant is none other than the black *manji*."³²

Such bizarre syncretic interpretations may have originated in the sixteenth century,³³ but they persisted, in certain Sōtō temples, at least, well into the mid-Tokugawa period, when they were denounced by Menzan Zuihō.³⁴ While no doubt representing the radical extremes of Rinzai and Sōtō *missan* traditions, they suggest just how far this form of Zen might deviate from the Sung-style teachings of the schools' Japanese founders.

There were, in fact, isolated protests against the worst abuses of the *missan* system. The eminent Daitokuji master Ikkyū Sōjun (1394–1481) broadly satirized the mechanical manner in which koans were being transmitted at the temple, their answers reduced to formulas that could be recorded and preserved by ignorant lay followers in exchange for donations. "Whether it's a man or a dog, a fart or a turd," Ikkyū complains in 1455 of Daitokuji's current abbot, "he's ready to cajole them, selling koans and then calling it transmission."³⁵ And another critic, the Shōkokuji abbot Keijo Shūrin (d. 1518), deplores the numbers of Zen priests "selling Rinzai and Sōtō, falsely labeling this the authentic transmission. . . . Calling themselves teachers, their instruction to students consists in having them study koans by finishing one and moving on to the next, just as though they were piling up [the stories] of a pagoda."³⁶

Such dissenting voices notwithstanding, by the late sixteenth century, *missan* study pervaded nearly all the lines of Japanese Zen, even penetrating many of the Gozan temples of Kyoto and Kamakura.³⁷ Tamamura Takeji, one of the first modern scholars to explore this phenomenon, has even argued that with the final ascendancy of the *missan* system, Zen, as such, ceased to exist in late-medieval Japan.³⁸ However, our understanding of the nature and development of *missan* Zen still remains highly imperfect and may not justify such a severe assessment. Aspects of traditional Zen practice and training seem to have been preserved in many *rinka* temples during the late Middle Ages, comfortably coexisting with the pursuit of *missan* study. In the Sōtō school, for example, *kessei ango*, the biannual three-month intensive meditation retreats standard in Zen temples, were apparently maintained throughout the sixteenth century, and portions of Dōgen's written legacy continued to be passed on, albeit in the form of a *missan*-style transmission.³⁹ But while Tamamura may be overstating the case for the negative effect of the *missan* system, his low opinion of late-medieval Zen as a whole would have been shared by many of Tōsui's most celebrated teachers and contemporaries, Zen monks coming of age in the early seventeenth century who looked back on the preceding era as a time of spiritual stagnation and decay that had left the teaching nearly defunct.

• • •

The unification of Japan under the Tokugawa ushered in an era of peace that lasted more than 250 years and left a profound mark on the character of Japanese life.⁴⁰ From its capital in Edo (present-day Tokyo), the Tokugawa military government, or Bakufu, presided over a feudal order whose ruling principle was the regulation and control of all levels of Japanese society. The Bakufu sought to enforce a rigid four-tiered class system, dominated by the the samurai, the hereditary warrior caste. The farmers, who formed the broad mass of the population and the country's principal tax base, were next in the social order, followed by the craftsmen, and finally, the merchants. In practice, however, the Tokugawa class system was considerably more porous than is sometimes appreciated. Despite the Bakufu's repeated injunctions to "know one's place," a certain amount of social mobility did occur. Early Tokugawa merchant families, for example, originated not only in already existing merchants groups, but with samurai who relinquished their military calling to pursue trade and peasants who had abandoned the land to try their luck at commerce in the cities and towns. Similarly, though illegal it was not unheard of for wealthy merchants to receive samurai status, whether through marriage or adoption into a samurai family or simply on their own merits. Merchants might also recycle their profits into agricultural industries and reclaimed farm land, blurring the distinctions between themselves and wealthy peasant landowners.[41] Although technically relegated to the bottom of the social ladder by a Confucian-inspired bias against commerce, the merchants, or townspeople (*chōnin*), enjoyed considerable prosperity throughout the Tokugawa period, and their lively urban culture was a conspicuous feature of Tōsui's day. Tōsui himself, the *Tribute* tells us, was born into a merchant family, and many of his most devoted patrons and followers, people such as the nun Chihō and the townsman Suminokura, shared similar commercial backgrounds.

Although not included among the four classes that made up Tokugawa society, Buddhist priests occupied a privileged position, below the rank of samurai but above that of commoner. While noble birth clearly enhanced one's prospects in the Buddhist clergy, even a priest of humble extraction could distinguish himself by virtue of his wisdom, piety, or administrative or artistic accomplishments and be considered worthy to visit the local castle or even the imperial palace. At the same time, the Buddhist sects were strictly regulated by the feudal government. During the sixteenth century, many of the Japanese Buddhist organizations had fielded armies that rivaled the forces of the leading warlords, and soon after its establishment, the Tokugawa shogunate acted to curb the power of the Buddhist temples. Unlike the Shingon, Tendai, True Pure Land, and Nichiren schools,[42] the Zen schools had never assembled monastic armies or played an active military role in the wars of the sixteenth century; but they maintained important patrons among the court and military elite, including various groups hostile to the Tokugawa, and were subjected to Bakufu control in the same manner as the more militant Buddhist sects.

Generally speaking, the Buddhist organizations were brought under government control by integrating them within the structure of the feudal system, establishing clear lines of authority, and therefore of responsibility, within each sect and between the sects and the Bakufu. Superintending the entire religious establishment were samurai commissioners known as *jisha bugyō* (magistrates for temples and shrines). These were assisted in turn by priest officials called *furegashira* (chief spokespersons), eminent clerics who acted as intermediaries between the Bakufu and the individual Buddhist sects, conveying orders from the government to the temples and representing their sects in matters coming before the shogunal commissioners. Within the Buddhist sects themselves, authority was enforced through the main-and-branch (*honmatsu*) temple system. Between 1632 and 1633, the Buddhist sects were obliged to submit registers, known as *honmatsuchō*, that precisely defined their various temples' standing within the sect's hierarchy, the major temples being confirmed by the Bakufu as main temples (*honji*) and the subordinate temples ranked as branch establishments (*matsuji*). In fact, the system was highly complex, with three grades of main and three grades of branch temples, so that every temple, with the exception of the main headquarters temples (*sōhonzan*) and the least of the branch temples, had one main and several branch establishments. Various methods were followed in determining a temple's status as the branch of a particular main temple. In the Sōtō school, for example, a temple could qualify as a branch temple only if it had been established by the main temple's founder or by one of his descendants. The founder was thus the key to the Sōtō temple's status, further emphasizing the importance of the temple line over the particular teaching line of the temple's current abbot.

Determining which temples were main and which subordinate was occasionally a problem. Temples wrangled over their respective positions, and the system was not truly completed till the institution of a revised, comprehensive register in 1692. In several of the Buddhist sects multiple headquarters temples were designated by the Bakufu, a recognition of these temples' traditional authority and prestige and of the rivalries that had at times divided them. Thus, in the Sōtō school, both Eiheiji and Sōjii were named headquarters temples, as were both Daitokuji and Myōshiji in the Rinzai school.

The main headquarters temple played a powerful role in the life of each sect. It held power over the appointment of abbots in the branch temples and was authorized to discipline, dismiss, and even expel abbots and monks. Additionally, it approved and confirmed all ecclesiastical honors and appointments and supervised the teaching of the sects' priests, who, in the Zen schools, for example, had to be authorized by the headquarters temple's officers before becoming teachers in their own right. The Bakufu enjoined on the branch establishments absolute obedience to the rulings of their headquarters temple on sectarian matters, and refusal to submit could result in confiscation of a temple's estates.

Even while carefully regulating the Buddhist establishment, the Tokugawa Bakufu found it a convenient tool in its campaign to root out Christianity. Introduced to Japan in the sixteenth century by Portuguese and Spanish missionaries, the new faith enjoyed a certain initial success, even attracting a number of daimyo and their retainers, but was finally outlawed by Ieyasu, who regarded it as a subversive foreign belief. The Bakufu's persecution of Christianity began in 1612 and continued throughout the Tokugawa period. Converts who refused to renounce their faith were ruthlessly pursued and executed, but those who formally recanted and apostatized were generally pardoned. The Bakufu was especially concerned over the existence of "hidden" Christians, and local officials and Buddhist priests were enlisted in ferreting out secret believers, so that something of a witch-hunt mentality informed many of the government's anti-Christian activities.

As proof that they were not Christians, all Japanese were required to maintain membership in a parish temple (*dannadera*) and to obtain each year from the temple's priest a certificate (*tera'uke shōmon*) affirming that they were parishioners in good standing. In turn, parishioners were expected to contribute regularly to the temple's support. While a degree of freedom could be exercised in choosing one's parish temple, the fact remains that for the first time in Buddhism's history in Japan, parishioners, temples, and priests were legally bound to one another. Temple funerals, for example, which had become increasingly popular in the Middle Ages, were now compulsory and formed a staple of the parish temple's economy, with the priest required to inspect the corpse, administer the tonsure, and assign a posthumous Buddhist name.[43] Parishioners were even expected to open their household altars to the priest for inspection, recalling the humorous scene in the *Tribute* in which the pack-horse drivers urge Tōsui to hang a Buddha image in his shack lest he incur suspicion of being a Christian.

By 1660, every household was required to register in a periodic religious census known as *shūmon* (or *shūshi*) *ninbetsuchō* (registry of religious affiliation). The process called for each family to present its certificate from the parish temple, which the headman would record in a register to be copied and forwarded to the province's daimyo. A sample preamble from one such register contains an affidavit that states in part,

> We have checked thoroughly, and no Christians are to be found in our village or any persons under suspicion [of being Christians].... All the men and women of the village have presented certificates from their parish temples.... Any denunciations suggesting that someone may be a Christian have been investigated in person by the temple's chief priest and the local leaders.... None of our parents, wives, or other relations are Christians, and those persons who were formerly Christians but have apostatized are honestly stated as such, with no attempt at concealment.... Anyone who seems in the least suspicious will in future be duly reported without delay as will anyone who disposes of a deceased person himself and fails to request the temple to do so.[44]

Following this appear the names of each household head, accompanied by detailed information on family members, place of birth, permanent domicile, and sect and location of parish temple. Such registers, which bore the seals of both the village officials and the parish temple, served not only to extend the Bakufu's anti-Christian policy to the local level but assisted the government in tracking the country's rural population, determining who could be taxed and restricting the farmers to their villages.

The parish system (*danka seidō*) demonstrated the subordination of the Buddhist sects to the Tokugawa government, which obliged the priests to perform what were essentially police functions, appropriating the clergy as a tool for official surveillance over the population. Economically, however, the system represented a windfall for the Buddhist establishment, offering the parish temples and priesthood virtually guaranteed support, and as such it contributed to a tremendous growth in the number of Buddhist temples and priests in seventeenth-century Japan.

The aim of Tokugawa religious policy was not to suppress Buddhism, but to control it and to use it in combating the perceived menace of Christianity. Nevertheless, during the seventeenth century many both in and out of office openly opposed Buddhism itself and counseled the government to adopt an aggressively anti-Buddhist stance. Foremost among these critics were various Confucian scholars who attacked Buddhism on economic, political, and theoretical grounds.[45] Sung Neo-Confucianism had expanded in influence in Japan during the sixteenth century, and under the Tokugawa shogunate had assumed the role of a semiofficial orthodoxy. The hundred years preceding Tokugawa rule had been a time of traumatic disorder and upheaval, with a constant shifting of fortunes and alliances as power changed hands among contending warlords. Not surprisingly, the victorious Tokugawa stressed the Confucian virtues of loyalty and filiality, and the concomitant duty to fulfill one's allotted role within the social order, as crucial to the hierarchy of relations that bound society together at every level and enabled it to function harmoniously.

Confucianism perceived itself as rational, practical, and human-centered, concerned with establishing norms of ethical conduct and with fostering enlightened governance, social stability, and the welfare of the common people. In turn, it often faulted Buddhism for seeking a way outside the real world and for advocating a vision that was, in its view, not only nonhumanistic but also frequently irrational, embracing as it did beliefs in miracle-working priests, rebirth, and transmigration as well as the existence of various heavens and hells. Buddhism, its Tokugawa Confucian detractors tended to argue, offered no practical benefit to ordinary men and women and was worse than useless, since the tax-exempt temple establishment absorbed valuable lands and revenues, depriving the domains of income and the farmers of desperately needed cropland. In addition, Buddhism was frequently denigrated as a foreign belief, presumably because it had originated in India—although Neo-Confucianism itself was hardly an indigenous teaching, having been introduced to Japan from China and Korea, in many cases through the efforts of sympathetic Zen priests.

Among Buddhism's leading Japanese critics was Kumazawa Banzan (1609–1691), a Confucian scholar and samurai who served as adviser to the daimyo Ikeda Mitsumasa (1609–1682) and was the principal theorist behind a series of anti-Buddhist policies instituted in Ikeda's domain of Okayama (present-day Okayama Prefecture). In his writings, Banzan depicts Buddhism as devastating Japan's economy. The priesthood, Banzan contends, is a wholly unproductive sector, eating but not working, its temples taking up arable land meant to support farmers and their families, many of whom are consequently left destitute.[46] Much of the problem, he claims, is attributable to the parish system, which offers the clergy a guaranteed living and has spawned an enormous growth in the numbers of temples and priests.[47] The result is that the nation's wealth is increasingly sapped for Buddhism's support—as if Japan had been reduced to a vassal state, sending a quarter of its wealth in yearly tribute to India.[48] Vast amounts of gold and silver are wrung from the common people by the priests, who play on the masses' superstitious fears of the afterlife, while the swelling ranks of the priesthood itself deprives the domains of a significant source of corvée and farm labor as well as tax revenue. No less critical was the depletion of the country's natural resources as a consequence of unbridled temple construction. A proto-ecologist of sorts, Banzan repeatedly alleges that the nation's forests are being ravaged for temple building materials, denuding the hillsides and drying up streams.[49]

Among the solutions Banzan proposes are a century-long moratorium on new temple construction[50] and a thirty-year ban on ordinations, with the current population of monks forcibly returned to lay life to resume their original status as farmers, artisans, or merchants.[51] Japanese priests, Banzan asserts, have long since ceased to observe the precepts,[52] and he compares them unfavorably with priests of the past, who supported themselves by mendicancy, freely sharing any surplus alms among beggars and other outcasts.[53] (Tōsui is seen to do just this in the *Tribute*.) Even the virtuous priests of Banzan's acquaintance acknowledge that most of their brethren are thieves and urge that they be returned to lay life, if only to cleanse Buddhism of its current evil reputation.[54]

The Zen sect, for Banzan, represents a particular disappointment. Chinese Ch'an masters, in his view, had originally rejected all magical or superstitious "Indian" practices; in addition, he says, masters of former times had maintained strict standards, insisting that students experience genuine realization. By contrast, Banzan finds the current crop of Zen teachers prepared to "flatter any daimyo, millionaire, or rascal" and proclaim him to be enlightened. Other Zen priests exploit their supposed enlightenment as an excuse to indulge in arrogance and licentiousness, insisting that the enlightened can do whatever they want.[55]

Banzan's discussion of Buddhism is clearly a partisan attack rather than a scrupulous, balanced assessment of the religion's shortcomings.

Abuses certainly existed in the temples, but whether the problems were as entrenched or as pervasive as Banzan claims is by no means evident from his writings or from those of other anti-Buddhist intellectuals of the day. Except in a handful of domains, such as Okayama, the specific, radical policies urged by the Confucians to suppress or restrict the influence of Buddhism were rarely adopted by the nation's rulers. Yet in many ways, throughout the seventeenth century, Japanese Buddhism seems to have been placed on the defensive as a result of the Confucians' critiques, and their anti-Buddhist rhetoric remained a familiar feature of the early Tokugawa period. Not since the time of its introduction from the continent more than a thousand years before had Buddhism in Japan been forced to justify and defend itself to such an extent. The constant calls among seventeenth-century Zen masters for renovation and reform, as well as their frequent stress on Zen's practical value to ordinary laypeople, can be seen in part as a response to the Confucians' challenge. Similarly, Tōsui's implied rejection of the wealth and ostentation of the temples, his simplicity, frugality, and willingness to work to pay his own way rather than depend, like so many of his colleagues, on the support of parishioners and powerful patrons may be seen to reflect contemporary attacks like Banzan's on the degeneration of the priesthood.

Buddhist reaction to the Confucian assaults was generally muted, at times almost apologetic. Perhaps because of Confucianism's role as the guiding moral standard of the regime, there were virtually no Buddhist attempts to mount a counterattack that questioned Confucianism's basic teachings, which seem to have been generally accepted within the Tokugawa Buddhist establishment. While Buddhist teachers freely rejected Confucian condemnations of Buddhism itself, their response to Confucian accusations that the Japanese priesthood had grown morally and spiritually corrupt frequently took the form of intense self-criticism. Many notable seventeenth-century Zen teachers could be as vehement as their Confucian counterparts in denouncing the debased state of Buddhism, with the Rinzai master Shidō Mu'nan (1603–1676) castigating professional priests as the "worst sort of evil there is, thieves who get by without having to work."[56]

Such problems notwithstanding, the early Tokugawa period was a time of remarkable growth and activity for Buddhism, and the vituperative attacks of critics such as Banzan may simply articulate frustration over Buddhism's continued success. The temples, it is true, were hemmed in by various government restrictions and deprived of much of the autonomy they had enjoyed during the Middle Ages. But if the Tokugawa shoguns made themselves the overlords of the Buddhist establishment, they were also among its leading patrons. The Tokugawa family dispersed huge sums to the priesthood for sundry purposes and founded and patronized large numbers of temples. Buddhist ceremonials were performed for the reigning shogun, and deceased shoguns were interred in Buddhist mausoleums and assigned posthumous Buddhist names. A series of eminent priests served as trusted advisers to the early shoguns, and several Tokugawa rulers evinced a personal interest in Buddhism. The Tokugawa's daimyo retainers were also conspicuous patrons of Buddhism, founding and restoring numerous temples in their domains and inviting distinguished priests to serve as abbots.

For the Zen sect, in particular, Tōsui's period was a time of signal prosperity, especially for the Sōtō school and the Rinzai Myōshinji line, both of which continued to benefit from the expansion of their organizations during the late Middle Ages. In a nationwide survey of temples' sectarian affiliation conducted by the Bakufu in 1632–1633,[57] Zen temples constituted the largest single group, 44 percent of the total, Sōtō temples making up 28 percent, and Rinzai temples 16 percent.[58] In terms of patronage, too, the Zen school enjoyed a distinct advantage, remaining identified with Japan's military elite and building on the links forged with powerful warrior clans during the fifteenth and sixteenth centuries. Of the 259 Tokugawa daimyo, for example, 167, some 65 percent, were affiliated with Zen temples.[59] Throughout the Tokugawa period, new Zen temples were erected by the daimyo and their families, not only within their domains but in Edo, where, after 1635, the feudal lords were obliged to reside during regular alternate terms. (In the *Tribute*, Tōsui's brother monk Unpo is accompanying the train of his daimyo patron to Edo for such a period of alternate attendance when he comes upon the aged Tōsui peddling straw horseshoes in the street.)

Yet despite its material success, its multitude of temples, and the continuing support of powerful samurai patrons, Zen in the early Tokugawa period was, in the view of many priests, in deep spiritual crisis. Teachers in both Rinzai and Sōtō temples had begun to repudiate the legacy of late-medieval Zen, to critically examine the present condition of the teaching, and to ponder what direction it should take. The *missan* system of koan transmission persisted in various Sōtō monasteries and in certain Rinzai temples like Daitokuji and Engakuji,[60] making the seventeenth century a particularly active period in the production of *missan* documents. These included the class of texts referred to earlier that mingle Zen with bizarre interpretations drawn from Tantric and yin-yang traditions. But elsewhere, Sōtō and Rinzai temples witnessed a forceful reaction against the Zen of the late Middle Ages, accompanied by a surge of idealism aimed at restoring the authentic teachings of the school's founders.

While never numerous, such idealists were significant and frequently influential figures and a conspicuous feature of early Tokugawa Zen. Though advocating varied methods and approaches, they shared a common conviction that Zen had been corrupted, leaving the teaching seriously endangered. The Myōshinji scholar priest Mangen Shiban (1626–1710) expressed a common view when he wrote in 1703 that the authentic Zen transmission in Japan had failed to survive beyond the first five or six generations of teachers, having languished for the previous two hundred years. It had only lately been revived, Mangen insisted, by a group of outstanding Myōshinji masters: Gudō Tōshoku (1579–1661), Ungo Kiyō (1582–1659), Daigu Sōchiku (1584–1669), and Isshi Bunshu (1607–1645).[61] These four were among the most celebrated Zen teachers of their day, and the *Tribute* records that Tōsui, during his years of pilgrimage, studied with all except Isshi Bunshu, though he did study under Isshi's original teacher, the Daitokuji master Takuan Sōhō (1573–1645). All of these priests, of course, were Rinzai masters. It is interesting to note that despite Tōsui's being a Sōtō priest, the Zen teachers the *Tribute* tells us he visited in the course of his travels are, with one exception—Suzuki Shōsan—members of the Rinzai school.[62] Nor was Tōsui's choice of Rinzai teachers unusual. A host of famous Sōtō priests of the early Tokugawa period studied under Rinzai masters (including the Ming masters of the Ōbaku school),[63] though the reverse seems to have been relatively rare. This suggests not only a telling absence of sectarian bias, but also a sense on the part of many noted seventeenth-century Sōtō priests that the authenticity of their own school's transmission had been compromised, while in the Rinzai school certain masters had managed to preserve something of the traditional core of Zen practice and enlightenment.

At least some of Tōsui's contemporaries thus believed that even if the Zen transmission had failed during the preceding period, in their own age enlightened, "clear-eyed" (*myōgen*) masters had appeared in Japan once again. Others, however, were decidedly less sanguine about the current state of the teaching. Repeatedly one hears the lament that true Zen has ceased to exist in Japan and enlightened teachers are no longer to be found.[64] At issue for those who held such views was the problem of how to proceed given what they regarded as the long rupture in the authentic transmission and the accompanying deterioration in the quality of the priesthood. If Zen, as its tradition asserted, depended on an unbroken mind-to-mind transmission preserved through numberless generations of masters and disciples, what were sincere students to do in an age when, they believed, the transmission had been defunct for nearly two centuries and there remained no masters competent to pass on to others the essence of the teaching or to certify students' experience of Zen?

For some, the only alternative in such desperate circumstances was to win realization on one's own and to sanction one's own enlightenment, to strive independently as, in the end, the historical Buddha himself had done. It seemed to many Zen monks of Tōsui's day that the only authentic legacy remaining from the past was the original mind of enlightenment itself. In the present period of decline, they believed, it was this mind alone, not the paper sanctions of unrealized teachers, that linked them with the buddhas and patriarchs of earlier times. "In today's Zen temples," Dokuan Genkō observes, "they transmit the robe and bowl [i.e., the symbols of the teacher's transmission]; but while the name continues, the reality [of enlightenment] has long ceased to exist. Those who carry on the wisdom of the buddhas and patriarchs rely on themselves, being enlightened independently, without a teacher; so that even though the name has ceased, the reality itself continues."[65]

One of the most striking features of early Tokugawa Zen is the number of celebrated priests who achieved realization on their own, who were what was at times referred to as "self-enlightened and self-certified" (*jigo jishō*), or as Dokuan says, "enlightened independently without a teacher" (*mushi dokugo*).[66] The roster of self-enlightened teachers included such notables as the Myōshinji masters Daigu, Ungo, and Isshi[67] and the Sōtō priest Suzuki Shōsan.[68] Thus, of the four early-Tokugawa teachers cited by Mangen for having revived the Zen teaching after its two-hundred-year decline, all but one, Gudō Tōshoku, fall within the "independently enlightened" category. And of the six Zen teachers with whom we are told Tōsui studied during his years of pilgrimage, fully half—Daigu, Ungo, and Shōsan—can be considered self-enlightened and self-certified.

The need felt by such priests to struggle toward enlightenment on their own in the absence of a vital tradition and awakened masters forced on them an independent and at times highly individual, even eccentric, approach. Although the exact nature and extent of Tōsui's studies with Daigu, Ungo, and Shōsan is not known, his relentless and uncompromising search for autonomy and authenticity was itself characteristic of many of the Zen independents of his period.

The careers of Daigu and Ungo, in particular, offer dramatic illustrations of the self-enlightened, self-certified phenomenon. As teachers, the two were very different individuals: Daigu, an explosive and outspoken personality; Ungo, a modest and retiring priest who espoused a synthesis of Zen and Pure Land Buddhism. Both, however, were colleagues who, as young priests, had studied and traveled together, and their search for enlightenment shared certain common features. Although each received his teacher's sanction and was a recognized master in the Myōshinji line, both later found themselves questioning their attainment and setting out once more in middle age on the quest for realization.

Daigu entered the temple as a child and while still in his twenties was awarded office at Myōshinji and succeeded to the line of his teacher, Itchū Tōmoku (1522–1621), known as "Itchū the Stick" for his liberal use of the same on his students. According to Daigu's biography,[69] his spiritual crisis was prompted when a woman came to his temple and asked him to perform the funeral service for her dead child. Daigu agreed, but when the mother begged him to tell her where her child had gone, he found himself unable to answer, and the woman went off, sobbing in despair. Shaken by this incident, Daigu is said to have recognized the shallowness of his understanding, and, feeling no longer competent to serve as abbot, he abandoned his temple and at age forty set out once more on pilgrimage. After six years of wandering, Daigu finally realized enlightenment when the rotted well-crib on which he customarily passed the night meditating gave way, plunging him into the water. Convinced, however, that no master existed in Japan qualified to testify to his experience, he turned instead to the "buddhas and patriarchs," praying to them to confirm whether or not his enlightenment was genuine, and if they found it to be false to punish him on the spot.

Although Daigu was regarded in his day as one of Myōshinji's leading figures, he seems to have maintained a reputation for impulsive and often abrasive behavior. Despite the Buddhist prohibition against liquor, for example, he is said to have been inordinately fond of sake, and in his cups would lash out at whoever happened to be nearby. Not surprisingly, many of Daigu's relations with authority were fraught with difficulty. During a stay in Edo, two concubines belonging to a certain daimyo fled to Daigu's temple, and the master gave them refuge. The upshot was that Daigu was denounced for keeping concubines and as punishment was forbidden to visit Myōshinji for seven years. He is also said to have fled the capital to avoid repeated invitations from the shogun Iemitsu (1604–1651) and declined a summons from the retired emperor Gomizuno'o (1596–1680), a prominent patron of Buddhism, declaring that it was not his way to appear before noble personages. When Gomizuno'o suggested in reply that this was simply a bit of posturing on his part, Daigu retorted, "Not at all! Since I just give free rein to my tongue and say right out whatever leaps to mind, your Majesty, not having a profound faith in Buddhism, is sure to become angry and stop me. That is why I have refused."

Despite his stated aversion to the powerful and pedigreed, Daigu's last years were spent in a temple in Echizen provided by a devoted daimyo benefactor. Sensing that death was imminent, Daigu brushed a final poem—

> The true heir of the West [India]
> The bedrock of the East [China]
> Always I've followed
> The path of nonduality

—but then added at the close that the death verse was written three days too soon, a prediction that proved correct. To the end, Daigu is said to have remained true to character. Whenever he wanted to write something, he would call to his attendant for paper, and when the attendant tried to hand it to him, Daigu would give him a slap for his trouble.

The story of Ungo's enlightenment, as recorded in the biography of his heir Daiki Kin'yō (1629–1697),[70] is similar to Daigu's in many respects. The son of an important samurai retainer of the Ichijō clan, Ungo entered the temple at age eight. Like Daigu, he became a disciple of the Myōshinji master Itchū, and after studying under Itchū for six years, set out on a famous pilgrimage, during which he visited many of the leading teachers of the day.

Having completed his Zen studies, Ungo became Itchū's successor and was appointed abbot of Myōshinji. But despite his accomplishments, Ungo found himself at age fifty beset by concerns that his understanding of Zen was merely intellectual and superficial. He was debating how to resolve his doubts when, early that autumn, the bodhisattva Kannon[71] appeared to him in a dream, declaring that Ungo would realize enlightenment if he climbed Mount Ochi in Echizen (Fukui Prefecture) and undertook a period of solitary practice.

Mount Ochi had been a sacred peak since the Nara period (710–794) and remained a center of popular worship focused on the shrine of its Shinto avatar, or *gongen*. When Ungo reached the mountain in late fall of 1631, snow had already blanketed the slopes and passes, and the priest-custodian of the shrine attempted to discourage him from proceeding with his retreat. Ungo, however, would not be dissuaded and, climbing to the shrine, began seven days of intensive practice, sustained only by a small supply of boiled beans carried to him by the anxious shrine priest. By evening of the sixth day, the beans had been exhausted, and the following morning at dawn Ungo at last experienced enlightenment, suddenly perceiving the truth that "all things are unborn." However, once having realized enlightenment, Ungo, like Daigu, was now confronted with the problem of how to confirm his experience.

> "In the Zen school," the Master reflected, "if one experiences enlightenment, if he fails to meet a clear-eyed teacher and receive his sanction, it is called 'being enlightened independently without a teacher' (*mushi dokugo*). Such a one, moreover, is considered a heretic.[72] However, for two hundred years now the Zen of our land has been divorced from the true Dharma, so that no more clear-eyed teachers remain. While there are many people in the world of Zen, there is none able to sanction my own present experience of enlightenment."[73]

Like Daigu, Ungo was forced to conceive of an alternative to sanction by one of his own contemporaries. His enlightenment, he reasoned, had been due to the spiritual assistance of the gods and buddhas. It was to them, therefore, that he would turn for some sign that his realization was genuine. Holding aloft his *hossu*, the ceremonial whisk that is the symbol of the Zen master's authority, Ungo prayed to the gods and buddhas, "If my enlightenment is genuine, as proof, return this *hossu* to my hands. If it is false, let me never again behold it!" He then hurled the *hossu* a "thousand fathoms" into the valley below and descended the mountain.

Some fourteen years later, Ungo was on his way to Kyoto to Myōshinji when he stopped for the night at a temple near Mount Ochi. The abbot came to pay his respects and brought with him a *hossu*. He reported that it had been found by a woodcutter abandoned on the floor of the valley and returned it to Ungo, saying, "I believe this once belonged to Your Reverence." Tearfully receiving the *hossu* from the abbot, Ungo was overcome by gratitude to the gods and buddhas for having finally acknowledged his realization.[74]

Following his enlightenment on Mount Ochi, Ungo found himself swamped by eager students and dedicated supporters. But declaring himself disgusted by the hypocrisy of the Buddhist clergy, he exchanged his priest's garb for a plain threadbare robe, bamboo hat, and straw sandals and, reminiscent of Tōsui, took to the road as a simple beggar, mingling freely with the common people. The year 1633 found Ungo living incognito at Katsuoji, an old Shingon temple in Settsu.[75] Here he earned a reputation for undertaking the most menial tasks, hulling and cleaning rice, gathering firewood, and hauling water. At his request, the temple's abbot assigned Ungo a small hut, where the master hoped to end his days. But Ungo's whereabouts were discovered by his old friend Daigu, and in 1636, at the repeated urging of his fellow teachers at Myōshinji, Ungo reluctantly accepted an invitation from the powerful Date clan of Sendai to serve as abbot of Zuiganji in Matsushima.[76] Eager to mount a suitable reception for the temple's distinguished new abbot, the daimyo ordered the domain's monks, laymen, and samurai to line the road to welcome Ungo. He also dispatched one of his leading retainers to position himself on horseback at the head of the throng and personally conduct the master to the castle. The samurai waited expectantly, but no one passed by apart from a solitary and decidedly unprepossessing traveler in plain cotton robe, straw sandals, and bamboo hat and staff. Informed after a time that Ungo had already arrived, the embarrassed retainer realized his error, and, wheeling his horse, tried to overtake the shabby figure, but Ungo had already reached the castle unescorted.

To the end, Ungo's simple and unpretentious way of life never changed. In 1645, he was honored with a second term as abbot of Myōhsinji, but when journeying to and from the great Zen temple, he refused to provide himself with funds, traveling as an ordinary penniless monk and begging his way to Kyoto and back. If money were forced on him, Ungo would distribute it to any beggars he encountered or else leave it by the roadside and simply walk away.

When he died in late summer 1659, Ungo was once again living in a secluded hermitage, on the summit of Mount Tsunagi in Sendai.[77] At twilight, he climbed the mountain's eastern slope, rang the evening gong himself, and then sat in meditation until midnight, when he summoned his disciples and announced that he was about to depart the world. Begged for a final verse, Ungo laughed and replied, "The streams, the birds, the trees and woods, all these are my verse. Why are you asking for something more?" And so saying, he quietly passed away.[78]

The stories of Daigu and Ungo, like much of Tōsui's own story, often smack more of legend than of history. But they convey the sense of these figures' staunch independence and articulate fundamental questions about the nature of realization and transmission that were being ardently debated in many quarters of the Zen world of early Tokugawa Japan. While perhaps not always factual in the ordinary sense, such stories, in common with others that typically surround famous Zen masters, are not just stories, but themselves an integral part of the history of Zen, one that has influenced and inspired successive generations of students and teachers.

While Daigu and Ungo bemoaned the absence of awakened masters in the Japan of their age, other Zen priests despaired even of finding good students. The Daitokuji-line teacher Takuan Sōhō, for example, whom the *Tribute* says Tōsui visited in Edo, steadfastly refused to appoint a successor, despite pleas from such prominent patrons as the shogun Iemitsu and the retired emperor Gomizuno'o.[79] For a Japanese Zen master to decline to name a successor was, and remains, highly unusual. Yet so adamant was Takuan about having no heir that he reiterated his intention in the final instructions (*yuikai*) he left his students. "I have no disciple who has succeeded to my Dharma [i.e., teaching]," Takuan wrote. "After I am dead, if anyone says he is my heir, that person is a Dharma thief. Report him to the authorities and see that he is punished severely!"[80]

Some two hundred years earlier, at Daitokuji, in almost identical terms, Ikkyū Sōjun had declared his refusal to bestow on anyone his *inka,* or formal sanction,[81] and Takuan's testament is clearly meant to express a similar pessimism about the Daitokuji Zen of his own day. Seeing no students qualified to carry forward the teaching, Takuan apparently preferred to let it lapse temporarily and to cut off his line. "That which is the Dharma cannot be passed on," Takuan muses in *Tōkai yawa,* a collection of his writings on Buddhism and other topics. "That which can be passed on is not the Dharma.... When the Dharma obtains suitable men, it is revealed; when it does not, it is concealed. When concealed, it is like the sun; when revealed it is also like the sun."[82] The Dharma, like the light of the sun, can never be extinguished, Takuan insists, but it can become temporarily obscured. It need not depend on an unbroken transmission from teacher to disciple; it is always waiting to be rediscovered, by the right man at the right time. This combination of pessimism about the state of Japanese Zen as a whole with optimism about the individual's potential to experience enlightenment and revive the teaching seems to have characterized many of the teachers with whom Tōsui came into contact and contributed to the distinctive atmosphere of early Tokugawa Zen.

It is tempting to question some of the more extreme criticism that Zen priests in Tōsui's period directed against their contemporaries. Was the situation of Japanese Zen in the seventeenth century truly as dire as its detractors claimed? Were there really no enlightened masters? Had the teaching, in fact, degenerated hopelessly over the previous two hundred years? Clearly there were some Zen priests whose own experience was at variance with this picture. Gudō Tōshoku, who regarded himself as the principal bulwark of orthodoxy within Myōshinji and the true heir of the temple's medieval founders, is said to have experienced great enlightenment after exhaustive study under his master, Yōzan Keiyō (n.d.); Gudō also produced numerous Dharma heirs of his own, among them Shidō Mu'nan, whose disciple Dōkyō Etan (1642–1721) was the teacher of the great eighteenth-century Rinzai Zen master Hakuin. Moreover, while our information on precisely how Zen was studied in the temples of seventeenth-century Japan remains limited, we know that many teachers continued to advocate koans and *zazen,* practices that had traditionally formed the basis of Zen training. In the Sōtō school, for example, Tōsui's biographer Menzan Zuihō was renowned even in old age as an ardent meditator;[83] and the early Sōtō reformer Gesshū Sōko (1618–1696), regarded as one of the founders of the Tokugawa Sōtō revival, mentions having assigned koans to the monks at his temple.[84] Whether, as many priests maintained, enlightened masters and students had long since ceased to exist in Japan is a qualitative, "Zen" question of the sort that inevitably lies beyond speculative analysis. At best, we can simply register the early Tokugawa Zen world's perceptions of itself.

If the Zen teachers of early Tokugawa Japan were often skeptical of the quality of the priesthood, many evinced a distinct confidence in the ability of lay Japanese men and women to grasp and put to use the fundamentals of Zen practice. Indeed, many of those masters most critical of the Zen priests of their day became active purveyors of "popular" Zen. The approach of these masters was popular in the sense that they sought to simplify and disseminate Zen not by diluting its teachings, but by clarifying them, reducing them to their essentials and presenting them in a manner that was at once familiar and direct. Such popular teachings often tend to stress the dynamic functioning of the mind, the mind in action in the world, the practical application of Zen in the details of one's ordinary activity.

There are several likely explanations for the emergence of this particular brand of popular Zen in the Tokugawa period. For one, the teachings of many Tokugawa Zen priests reflect the feudal ethic of the day, with its emphasis on group cohesion and the importance of wholeheartedly fulfilling one's allotted role in the social order. Much of the popular Zen teaching of the period seems a response to such concerns, focused as it is on the daily-life circumstances of ordinary people and on the ways in which Zen can enable one not only to surmount personal and spiritual problems but also to become a better neighbor, parent, farmer, tradesman, samurai, and member of society as a whole. At the same time, Japanese culture generally in Tōsui's age was changing, becoming more accessible, open, and democratic. The works we now view as the cultural high points of the early Tokugawa period were also the popular culture of the day, enjoyed, supported, and created by the common people themselves. The dramas of Chikamatsu Monzaemon (1653–1724), the tales of Ihara Saikaku (1642–1693), the poetry and prose of Matsuo Bashō (1644–1694) and his disciples, the prints of Hishikawa Moronobu (d.1694)—all were representative of this new popular culture. It is probably not unreasonable to suggest that this atmosphere extended to the area of religion and that Zen, previously confined, like poetry and the fine arts, largely to the appreciation of an intellectual and social elite, was now being "democratized" as well.

Among the earliest and most celebrated of the Tokugawa popularizers of Zen were the Daitokuji master Takuan Sōhō and the Sōtō teacher Suzuki Shōsan. Takuan, who has been mentioned previously, was one of the last famous Daitokuji masters, a well-known figure in his period and today one of the few Zen priests whose name, linked with the affectionate suffix *san* (mister), is familiar to many ordinary Japanese.[85] Takuan, it is true, had extensive connections with leading members of the court and military and was a favorite of the third Tokugawa shogun, Iemitsu, who erected a temple, Tōkaiji, for Takuan in Edo to insure his presence in the capital. But the patronage Takuan enjoyed at the shogunal court did not prevent him from becoming an exponent of popular Buddhism, teaching commoners at Tōkaiji and composing a number of vernacular works. Among the latter are *Tōkai yawa*[86] and *Ketsujōshū*,[87] collections of writings touching on miscellaneous topics, and *Fudōchi shinmyō roku*,[88] a treatise focusing on Zen and swordsmanship.

Characteristic of Takuan's popular approach to Zen is an emphasis on enlightened mind as a principle to be put to work in one's actual daily affairs. Takuan particularly stresses immediacy and directness of response, the active functioning of mind that, flowing unhindered, freely pervades one's whole being. When one interferes with this natural flow, artificially constricting the mind by stopping or fixing it in a particular place, mental or physical, one loses the original freedom and becomes deluded. For this reason, the mind, Takuan says, must be free of thought, of all conscious intention. However, to willfully try not to think, or to artificially restrain the mind through constant vigilance, only stiffens it, obstructing its intrinsic spontaneity.

> It's just as when you get a baby sparrow, and then have to keep the cat always tied tightly to its leash, never letting it loose. When you keep your mind, like the cat, on a tight leash, making it unfree, it can't function spontaneously. However, once you have the cat well trained, you can untie it and let it go wherever it likes, so that even if it's right next to the sparrow, it won't grab it. To practice like this ... means that in using your mind you let it go free, as if you were turning loose the

cat, so that even though it goes wherever it pleases, the mind doesn't attach anywhere.[89]

This insistence on the mind's freedom and naturalness, on letting go, lies at the heart of Takuan's practical expositions of Zen. It is the substance of Takuan's advice to the swordsman confronting his opponent, to the rider saddling a shying horse, to anyone attempting to deal with the familiar human problems of anger or emotional distress.[90]

The stress on the operation of enlightened mind in the midst of daily life is especially prominent in the teachings of another famous popularizer of Zen whom Tōsui met in the course of his travels, Takuan's contemporary, Suzuki Shōsan. Unlike Tōsui, Takuan, and the other Tokugawa teachers discussed above, Shōsan was not a career priest, but a samurai, who had fought under the Tokugawa and only entered the priesthood in middle age.[91] Though formally affiliated with the Sōtō sect, he was a colleague of the Rinzai masters Daigu, Ungo, and Gudō and seems to have been primarily an independent, whose teaching style remained highly personal.

Settling in 1648 in a small hut in Edo's Asakusa district, Shōsan regularly instructed both priests and lay students and composed a number of vernacular works dealing with Buddhism, among them *Mōanjō*, *Banmin tokuyō*, and *Nenbutsu sōshi*.[92] Generally speaking, Shōsan's writings are popular in both style and approach, incorporating stories, poems, and cautionary tales, and they enjoyed a wide readership in his day, becoming best sellers of a sort. Shōsan's appeal is not hard to understand. In his teaching Shōsan stressed that it is not necessary, or even desirable, to become a priest or to live in a temple to study Buddhism or Zen. In fact, given what he sees as the pitiful state of the Buddhist clergy in his day, Shōsan asserts that those with a genuine feeling for Buddhism feel compelled to *leave* the temples.[93] In any case, the most effective way to practice Buddhism, according to Shōsan, is in the world, while performing one's allotted tasks, whether as a samurai, farmer, tradesman, or merchant. This radical merger of Buddhism and secular activity was, Shōsan maintained, his own original creation.[94]

Largely dismissing such contemplative methods as koan study and formal *zazen*, Shōsan sought to substitute what he regarded as more active and dynamic forms of Zen practice. To a great extent, Shōsan's approach to this problem was conditioned by his samurai background, and the ideal of the warrior spirit animates much of his teaching. Shōsan urges Zen students to develop what he refers to as *yūmōshin*, the spirit of daring and valor, the dauntless, intrepid mind, and to foster an intense awareness of death, akin to what the soldier experiences on the battlefield, by placing the character for death (*shi*) on their foreheads.[95] When Shōsan does recommend *zazen*, it is a warrior-style meditation, "battle cry (*toki no koe*) *zazen*."[96]

Shōsan devised a distinctive practice embracing all these concepts, focused on the Niō, the twin guardian kings of wrathful aspect whose life-size wooden images were often placed at the gates of Buddhist temples. Shōsan's students were encouraged to study the images of the Niō and to take them as their model in meditation, imitating precisely the deities' fearsome attitudes, eyes wide open and glaring, fists clenched, teeth gnashing fiercely. Not only samurai, but ordinary commoners, men and women alike, were encouraged to perform this practice, which Shōsan would demonstrate personally.[97] To a visiting samurai, Shōsan explains:

> "It is good to practice doing *zazen* in the midst of pressing circumstances. For the samurai, particularly, it is essential to practice the sort of *zazen* that can be put to use in the thick of battle. At the moment when the guns are blazing, when lances cross, point to point, and the blows of the enemy rain down, amid the fray of battle—here is where he must practice, putting his meditation immediately to work. In a spot like this, what good is going to be the sort of *zazen* that calls for a quiet place? However much a samurai claims to love Buddhism, if it doesn't do him any good when he finds himself on the battlefield, he'd better give it up. That's why you've got to constantly cultivate the mind of the Guardian Kings."[98]

Despite the doubts voiced by various seventeenth-century priests concerning the viability of Japanese Zen, teachers like Daigu, Ungo, Takuan, Gudō, and Shōsan attracted an enthusiastic following. Certain of these teachers saw themselves, and were regarded by others, as reviving Japanese Zen after centuries of protracted decline. Some Zen students, however, remained dissatisfied and looked to masters from outside Japan, from the continent, the teaching's original homeland.

For many of those who despaired for the future of Japanese Zen, the arrival of a number of distinguished Chinese masters in the mid-seventeenth century offered a glimmer of hope, a timely answer to the problems posed by the teaching's alleged degeneration. In contrast to the Kamakura period, when monks like Dōgen and Nanpo had freely visited the mainland to seek out Chinese teachers, Tokugawa Zen monks were prevented from studying abroad by the shogunate's 1635 ban on foreign travel. Isshi Monju, for example, unable to find a Japanese teacher competent to certify his enlightenment experience, had sought to journey to the continent to obtain the sanction of a Chinese teacher, but his hopes were dashed by the Bakufu's "closed country" (*sakoku*) policy, which made overseas travel a capital offense.[99] Hence, the appearance on Japanese shores of a new generation of Chinese teachers in the mid-seventeenth century created a considerable stir in both Rinzai and Sōtō circles. Japanese priests flocked to the Chinese teachers' temples, some abandoning their original affiliations to become the teachers' disciples, others simply drawn by curiosity about this exotic import in an age when foreign contact of any sort was severely restricted.

Acceptance of the newcomers, however, was by no means uniformly enthusiastic. The somewhat syncretic Ming-style teaching of the seventeenth-century Chinese masters differed from the Sung Ch'an introduced to Japan in the Kamakura period and was rejected by certain members of the Japanese priesthood, even while others, like Tōsui, succumbed to its appeal. Zen had by this time an extensive history of its own in Japan, and there were those who believed that the teaching in China had long since decayed, fallen away from the ideals of the noted Sung-dynasty teachers from whom the principal Japanese Zen lines proudly traced their descent.[100] In any event, few of the leading Zen priests of the day were untouched by the arrival of these later Chinese masters, who constituted the last transmission of continental Zen to Japan and provided a colorful stimulus to the world of early Tokugawa Zen.[101]

In the early years of the Tokugawa shogunate a sizable Chinese merchant community had been allowed to settle in Nagasaki, since the end of the sixteenth century a center for trade with China and from the 1630s the only Japanese city where foreigners—limited to Chinese and Dutch nationals—were permitted to reside and the only legal port of entry for foreign shipping. Here the Chinese had established their own

Buddhist temples, inviting priests from the mainland to serve as abbots. In part, this was a response to the requirements of the Bakufu's anti-Christian campaign and specifically the parish system, which was binding on the Chinese resident in Nagasaki. But the temples also played an important role in the social life of the Chinese community, offering prayers for calm voyages and funerals for those who died abroad or at sea. As with many modern overseas Chinese associations, the Nagasaki temples were established, supported, and patronized by groups originating in particular localities. Thus, in 1620, Kōfukuji was founded by a group of families from Nanking (and hence was referred to at times as the Nankinji, or "Nanking temple"), and in 1628, merchants from Changchow in Fukien established Fukusaiji. A third temple, Sōfukuji, established the following year by families from Foochow, completed the triad of what came to be called the "three good fortune temples" (*sanpukuji*), a reference to the character *fuku* (good fortune) that appears in the name of each.

The first generations of priests who assumed office at the Nagasaki temples were not especially noteworthy, restricting their activities entirely to the immigrant Chinese communities they had been brought to serve. It was only with the arrival of Tao-che Chao-yüan in 1651 that the temples began to attract broader attention as centers for the practice and propagation of contemporary Chinese Ch'an. In that year, Sōfukuji had invited a disciple of the celebrated master Yin-yüan Lung-ch'i to assume the temple's abbacy, but the priest had been drowned in a shipwreck, and when Tao-che arrived on a merchant vessel, he was installed as abbot in the priest's place.

As with Yin-yüan and other noted Chinese teachers who would follow, Tao-che's precise reasons for coming to Japan are unclear. The mid-seventeenth century was a turbulent period in China, which had witnessed the Ming dynasty's fall to invading Manchu forces from the north and the victor's inauguration of a new dynasty, the Ch'ing (1644–1912). For many Chinese, these events were something of a national trauma, and conditions for a time remained unsettled, particularly in the south, where groups of loyalists continued to resist rulers they considered foreign barbarians. Manchu troops entered Yangchow in 1645, massacring the city's population, and during the 1650s, Fukien's coast was effectively ruled by the half-Chinese, half-Japanese Cheng Ch'eng-kung (1624–1662), a merchant-freebooter turned Ming loyalist whose forces routinely harassed the Manchus in south China.[102] It is possible that in traveling to Japan some of the Chinese masters sought to escape the turmoil in their homeland, carrying their teaching to an island nation that in the past had shown itself receptive to émigré Ch'an monks.[103]

Tao-che spoke no Japanese, and by his own account, communication with his Japanese students was conducted entirely by writing.[104] (Classical Chinese was the language of the Buddhist and Ch'an scriptures imported to Japan, and most Japanese Zen priests would have had some facility with written, though not spoken, Chinese.) Despite the language barrier, Tao-che quickly attracted a large and enthusiastic following among both Sōtō and Rinzai priests; and perhaps at a loss to explain the sudden popularity of the temple, a Chinese visitor at Sōfukuji was heard to remark that the Japanese must be coming in such large numbers because they were hungry.[105] Ultimately, Tao-che returned home after only eight years, but he exerted an important, if fleeting, influence during his stay, numbering among his followers many who would become leading figures in Tokugawa Zen, including Gesshū Sōko and Bankei Yōtaku.

Tao-che was a member of the same Ch'an lineage as Yin-yüan, who landed in Nagasaki some three years later. Like Yin-yüan, Tao-che's teacher was an heir of the noted Lin-chi master Fei-yin T'ung-jung (1593–1661), abbot of Wan-fu ssu (Myriad Good Fortune Temple) in what is now Fukien Province. In Japan, the line established by Fei-yin's descendants came to be referred to as the Ōbaku school, after the Japanese reading for Huang-po shan (J. Ōbakusan, or Ōbakuzan), the mountain in Fukien where Fei-yin's temple stood, and as such it constituted a distinct, if relatively minor, school of Japanese Zen, which still survives. In China, however, Fei-yin's line had never existed as a separate school, and styled itself simply the "authentic Lin-chi school" (*Lin-chi chen-tsung;* J. *Rinzai shōjū,* a.r., *shōshū*); the title "Ōbaku" it received in Japan merely identified it as a late Ming and early Ch'ing brand of Zen imported in the mid-seventeenth century.

Ming Ch'an, which continues to influence Chinese Buddhist practice, combined traditional Ch'an teaching with elements of Pure Land belief and an emphasis on strict observance of the full Buddhist precepts (250 commandments for priests, 348 for nuns). Certain forms often associated with Esoteric Buddhism were also commonplace: Yin-yüan's liturgy for his Japanese temple, Manpukuji, for example, included the performance of mantra, dharani, and mudra.[106] Like the use of mantra and dharani and the stress on precepts observance, the incorporation of Pure Land belief was not new to Ch'an, but it became a conspicuous and nearly universal feature of the teaching during the Ming dynasty. A particular staple of Ming Ch'an was use of the *nien-fo* (J. *nenbutsu*, recitation of the phrase "Hail to the Buddha Amitabha!") as a koan-type technique, the so-called *nien-fo kung-an*: "Who is it reciting 'Hail to the Buddha Amitabha'?"[107] Pure Land influence is reflected in *Ōbaku shingi*, the monastic code devised in Japan by Yin-yüan and his disciples, which calls for recitation of Pure Land chants and of praises to Amitabha.[108] Such syncretism was not wholly unknown among Japanese Zen teachers. Esoteric Buddhist elements, it will be recalled, had been incorporated in late-medieval koan transmissions, and esoteric rites (*kitō*), too, had been performed by various medieval Zen priests, both those affiliated with and outside the official temples. In Tōsui's own day, Pure Land practice was championed by Ungo Kiyō, who advocated it to his lay followers, and rigorous observance of the precepts was actively promoted by Ungo's fellow Myōshinji master Isshi Monju.[109]

Yin-yüan[110] was already an important figure in Chinese Ch'an when he arrived in Nagasaki in 1654 aboard a merchant vessel. He wore his hair long, carried a large wooden staff, and was accompanied by some two dozen Chinese priests, half of whom would return the following year. Yin-yüan had come to Japan at the invitation of Kōfukuji's Chinese patrons, but he created an instant sensation in the broader Japanese Zen community. Almost from the moment of his arrival, he was swamped by throngs of Sōtō and Rinzai priests, and Kōfukuji became the temporary setting for a Zen "boom" of sorts.

Other Japanese, however, in both the Zen priesthood and the government, received Yin-yüan with a marked suspicion and hostility that was tinged strongly with xenophobia. The Bakufu, always wary of foreign penetration and concerned that it might serve as a cover for intrigue by outside powers, kept a watchful eye on all the Chinese priests arriving in Japan and carefully restricted their movements. Yin-yüan himself was suspected by the shogunate of being a spy, and even when he was finally allowed to travel outside Nagasaki to stay at a Japanese disciple's temple in Settsu, he was kept under virtual house arrest. The Bakufu's wariness of Yin-yüan was shared by the Confucian scholar

Kumazawa Banzan, whose anti-Buddhist views were touched on earlier. Not only would the arrival of Chinese priests like Yin-yüan add to the ranks of an already bloated and parasitic Japanese priesthood, Banzan warned, but it threatened to bring in its wake the victorious Manchu armies—just as the arrival of Chinese Ch'an teachers during the Kamakura shogunate had been followed by an attempted Mongol invasion of Japan.[111]

In the Zen school, opposition to Yin-yüan was centered at Myōshinji, spearheaded by Gudō Tōshoku, Daigu Sōchiku, and others who took exception to what they regarded as an alien and inferior mode of Zen practice.[112] When not merely petty or scurrilous, works articulating the views of the Myōshinji anti-Ōbaku faction often seem to reflect essentially cultural problems. There are complaints, for example, that the Chinese priests wear hats, that their walking meditation is so rapid it amounts to sprinting, that their style of chanting lacks the authenticity and decorum of the Japanese version—introduced, it is claimed, from Tang China by Kūkai.[113] Yin-yüan himself is attacked as arrogant, deceitful, and mean-spirited. Gudō expresses outrage that the Chinese teacher did not immediately come to pay his respects to him, as Japan's foremost Zen master; had Gudō visited China, he would have paid his respects to Yin-yüan.[114] Yin-yüan is further accused of feigning ignorance of the Japanese language with visitors while speaking it fluently with his Japanese students and of intercepting and destroying Tao-che's *inka*, which had been forwarded from China by Tao-che's teacher.[115]

Rivalries of a more overtly political nature also seem to have played a part in fueling anti-Ōbaku sentiment at Myōshinji. A number of Myōshinji priests had gone to study with Yin-yüan,[116] among them the Zen master Ryōkei (a.r., Ryūkei) Shōsen (1602–1670), Myōshinji's abbot at the time of Yin-yüan's arrival, and the temple itself was bitterly divided between those sympathetic to the Chinese teacher and those, like Gudō, who opposed him.

Various Myōshinji priests continued, nevertheless, to travel to Nagasaki to sample and scrutinize Yin-yüan's Zen, reporting their impressions to their colleagues. One such account, contained in a letter from the Myōshinji-line priest Kirei (a.r., Kyōrei) Ryōkaku (1600–1691) to his Dharma brother Tokuō Myōkō (1611–1681),[117] describes a 1654 training period held by Yin-yüan at Kōfukuji. Kirei states that some seventy Japanese and twenty Chinese priests participated. The two groups, he writes, mingle freely at the temple, though language difficulties remain to be overcome. Regular meditation periods are observed, and monastic regulations, while varying from those in Japanese temples, are strictly enforced. Mealtimes, for example, are different, Kirei reports, with the Chinese priests eating as many as six or seven times a day, so that they tend to become paunchy, in contrast to their Japanese counterparts. At the close of morning and evening meditation, the assembly chants the nenbutsu. While acknowledging the splendor of certain of the Chinese rites, Kirei finds others less impressive than their Myōshinji equivalents. He expresses interest in the style of the Chinese chanting, with its distinctive use of bells and drums, but believes it is not really suitable for Japan; at times, he confesses, the noise is almost deafening. In spite of this, he finds the meditation practice at Kōfukuji to be admirable and insists that, while externally Pure Land, the core of Yin-yüan's teaching is authentically Zen. On the negative side, Kirei notes that Yin-yüan's entourage includes few outstanding figures,[118] and comments several times on the arrogance of certain of the Chinese priests, a quality, he adds, that, despite their accomplishments, makes them distasteful to the Japanese.

Other Myōshinji priests who visited Yin-yüan were openly contemptuous of the syncretic practice in his assembly, as witnessed in the following statement by Teki Shuso (n.d.), a priest of the temple who was a contemporary of Kirei's:

> I am presently in residence at this temple [i.e., Myōshinji]. Having had a thorough look at the Zen master Ingen [Yin-yüan], when the summer training period came to a close, I was ready to leave. When you observe the style of teaching in his temple, it's *mondo* and lectures, just like Zen; but before you know it, they're chanting "Namu Amida Butsu!" just like the Pure Land school; then all of a sudden, they're performing mudras, drawing signs with their fingers, just like Shingon. Basically, it's like someone who's operating a variety store. One does not find here the ancient and revered practices of our school.[119]

Such criticism notwithstanding, Yin-yüan continued to attract an enthusiastic and loyal following at Myōshinji, and Ryōkei Shōsen even led a movement to welcome him at the temple. This effort was ultimately unsuccessful; but Ryōkei remained a staunch supporter of Yin-yüan's, and although himself a Zen master who had served two terms as Myōshinji abbot and was a teacher of the retired emperor Gomizuno'o, in late middle age Ryōkei joined Yin-yüan's assembly, becoming his first Japanese Dharma heir. Predictably, Ryōkei's act was denounced by many at Myōshinji as a betrayal of his original lineage, as well as an affront to the temple's founder and traditions. It was voted to expunge from the temple register the names of Ryōkei and any other Myōshinji priests who followed teachers of other lines, though Yin-yüan's partisans at the temple protested that far from being a threat to the founder's Zen, Yin-yüan's teaching offered an incomparable opportunity to rescue Myōshinji from the disastrous effects of a centuries-long stagnation and decline.[120]

The Bakufu, in the meantime, had begun to ease the restrictions placed on Yin-yüan, and he was finally permitted to travel more freely. In 1658, Yin-yüan obtained an audience in Edo with the reigning shogun, Ietsuna (1639–1680), and appears to have made a favorable impression, as the following year (1659) he received official approval to erect a temple at Uji, south of Kyoto, the Bakufu ultimately donating both the site and a regular temple stipend. The temple, dubbed Manpukuji, the Japanese reading for Wan-fu ssu, Yin-yüan's temple in Fukien, served as the headquarters for Yin-yüan's line. Like the Nagasaki temples earlier, Manpukuji quickly became a magnet for curious Sōtō and Rinzai priests, numbers of whom flocked to Uji, Tōsui among them. Additionally, the shogun's active support for Yin-yüan's organization attracted the patronage of many Tokugawa daimyo, and several hundred Ōbaku temples eventually sprang up across Japan, some newly erected on the sites of earlier temples, others conversions of temples belonging to other lines, including branch establishments of Myōshinji.

The atmosphere at Manpukuji was distinctly Chinese. Its early abbots were limited to Chinese teachers,[121] and its buildings' design and decoration faithfully reproduced those of continental temples. Initially, even the monks' robes and manner of eating followed current Chinese style. Besides its role as a monastery devoted to Zen practice, Manpukuji, like certain of the early Kamakura Zen temples, also became a center for the diffusion of contemporary Chinese culture—in this case, the culture of the late Ming and early Ch'ing dynasties. Through the Ōbaku temples, recent developments in Chinese architecture, painting, calligraphy, and medicine reached Japan, and even the quasi-shamanistic practice of spirit-writing, by which the Ōbaku monks claimed to communicate with the legendary Taoist immortal Chen Tuan.[122]

It is difficult to assess the effect of the Ōbaku masters on Tokugawa Zen. Particular aspects of their teaching such as the emphasis on the precepts and the strict observance of monastic regulations embodied in *Ōbaku shingi* seem to have stimulated and encouraged certain Japanese masters of similar bent. In the Sōtō sect, for example, the Chinese teachers influenced the monastic codes of reformers like Gesshū Sōko and Manzan Dōhaku who had studied under Ōbaku masters.[123] In the Rinzai sect, the émigré monks have even been credited with generating interest in the founder Lin-chi I-hsüan's (d. 866) original Ch'an, as represented in the classic *Lin-chi lu* (J. *Rinzai roku*).[124] But whether, beyond this, the Ōbaku masters had any profound effect on Japanese Zen remains unclear. The frequently reiterated belief that their arrival was the crucial stimulus that roused Japanese Zen from the lethargy that had afflicted it since the late Middle Ages[125] seems questionable at best. Even before the arrival of Tao-che and Yin-yüan, as we have seen, an assortment of dynamic and dedicated priests were striving to revive the teaching of Zen in Japan. Many Japanese practitioners, like Tōsui and Dokuan, joined the Chinese teachers' assemblies for a time; but others like Gudō were openly critical of Ōbaku Zen, and some, like Bankei, who were initially drawn to Ōbaku masters, later became disillusioned.[126] Clearly, the Ming brand of Buddhism brought by the Ōbaku priests exerted an influence on Tōsui and numbers of his contemporaries in both the Sōtō and Rinzai temples. But it is by no means certain whether this influence was basic to the revitalization of Zen that occurred in early Tokugawa Japan or merely one of the varied ingredients that contributed to the curious atmosphere attending it.

• • •

The history of Zen in seventeenth-century Japan is a complex, still evolving study, and the foregoing pages are intended only to highlight certain aspects of the subject that offer some context to Tōsui's tale. It is difficult, however, to treat any period of Zen's development in Japan without at least some reference to the school's medieval origins. This is particularly true of Tōsui's time, when Zen priests frequently viewed the difficulties confronting their school in terms of its history during the previous four centuries, exalting the teachings of the early Japanese founders while decrying what many perceived to be the subsequent decline of Zen practice.

In describing the Japanese Zen of Tōsui's own period, I sought to focus on those noted teachers with whom the Master is said to have associated, and through these figures to suggest something of the varied character of early Tokugawa Zen, of the very different teaching styles and personalities to which Tōsui was exposed. The extreme individualism of many of these teachers, as depicted in their traditional biographies, is itself a common element that unites them with one another and with Tōsui. The Zen master Daigu's irascibility, for example, his unwillingness to defer to wealth or power, call to mind the aging Tōsui's stubborn refusal to accept any assistance that would threaten his cherished sense of freedom and independence. Ungo's abandoning his followers to live in seclusion, his insistence on traveling as a simple beggar and performing the most menial temple chores parallels Tōsui's decision to relinquish the trappings of a Zen abbot for the existence of an itinerant laborer toiling in Kyoto and its environs. Similarly, Takuan's and Shōsan's interest in popular teaching, in putting Zen to use in people's actual daily lives, seem to anticipate elements of Tōsui's merger with the secular world, his life as a Zen master who disappeared into the fabric of urban Japan, camping among beggars, working as a porter, weaving straw sandals, and hawking vegetables. This aspect of Tōsui's career, in turn, seems to respond obliquely to Confucian accusations that Buddhism was alienated from the workaday existence of ordinary men and women, a burden on the Japanese people and state that was no more than a pretext for organized exploitation and parasitism.

Finally, Tōsui's connection with the famous masters mentioned in his biography points up a conspicuous feature of Zen in his day, the ready contact among teachers and students of the different Japanese Zen schools. As noted earlier, all the teachers whom the *Tribute* tells us Tōsui sought out were, with the exception of the Sōtō priest Shōsan, members of Rinzai organizations. Like Tōsui, many Sōtō priests of the period studied under Rinzai teachers, including Chinese masters at the temples of the newly imported Ōbaku line. Tōsui himself, we are told, spent many years at the Ōbaku headquarters temple, Manpukuji, and entrusted two of his close disciples to the temple's fifth-generation abbot, Kao-ch'üan. Tōsui was even buried at Kao-ch'üan's temple, Bukkokuji, and the Chinese master officiated at Tōsui's funeral service.[127] The very fact that the details of Tōsui's diverse connections with Ōbaku and Japanese Rinzai masters are first recorded by Menzan, a revered champion of Sōtō orthodoxy, is surely significant in itself. Generally speaking, among the principal Japanese Zen groups in the early Tokugawa period, there appears to have been considerably more fluidity and less sectarian feeling than is sometimes realized.

Taken together, these aspects of Tōsui's world, it is hoped, suggest a broader setting for some of the episodes depicted in Menzan's biography. But Menzan's account is above all the presentation of a single headstrong and uncompromisingly eccentric personality, a figure who stands out even in this boisterous period in the history of Zen as a master quite unlike any other.

About the Translation

Tribute to the Life of Master Tōsui (*Tōsui oshō densan;* full title, *Rakuhoku Takagamine Tōsui oshō densan* [Tribute to the life of Master Tōsui of Takagamine, on the northern outskirts of the imperial city]) was compiled by the Sōtō scholar Menzan Zuihō in 1749 and published in an illustrated woodblock edition in 1768, the year before Menzan's death. The work consists of a brief preface *(jō)* in *kanbun,* classical Chinese read in Japanese transliteration; a dedicatory essay, *Tōsui oshō densan shojutsu innen* (How I came to write the life of Master Tōsui), in *kana majiri,* Chinese characters mingled with the Japanese *kana* syllabary, in which Menzan explains how he compiled Tōsui's record as an offering to his own late teacher, Kohō Ryōun, who is briefly recalled along with Tōsui's teacher, Igan Sōtetsu; the main text, also in *kana majiri,* including twenty narrative illustrations commissioned by Menzan, each paired with a short poem Menzan composed in praise of Tōsui. The twenty poems, written in *kanbun* in a style known as *shichigon hakku* (eight lines of seven characters), appear as they did in the 1768 edition, placed together with their illustrations on separate pages. The *Tribute's* text and illustrations are included in volume 17 of *Sōtōshū zensho* (Complete works of the Sōtō school), pages 327–364. Although in the original, Menzan's preface and essay precede the main text, in the present translation they follow it. Compared to the narrative itself, both are formal, even "formula" pieces of hagiography, and while the essay contains some interesting information on Kohō and Igan, overall, these sections seemed to mute the effect of the main story for modern readers, and therefore better placed at its conclusion. Menzan's intertextual notes to the *Tribute* have been set off in a smaller typeface as is usual in Japanese printed texts.

    Names of Chinese priests living in Japan appear in their Japanese readings, the form in which they would have been known to Tōsui as well as to Menzan and his readers; Chinese readings are supplied in the

41

footnotes and are employed in the introduction and biographical essay. At times in the *Tribute* Menzan refers to Tōsui directly by name, at other times simply as "the Master" (*shi*), and the translation follows the particular usage in the text. Ages are given in the traditional Japanese style, whereby a child is considered to be one year old at birth. Thus, when the *Tribute* speaks of Tōsui's being "age seven," this would be roughly equivalent to six years old by modern Western reckoning. Finally, on the question of style: Readers may note the occasionally jarring contrast between the formal, even reverential tone of the narrator's voice and the lively, colloquial ring of some of the dialogue portions of the *Tribute*. This contrast is a characteristic of Menzan's text that contributes to the work's particular flavor, and the attempt has been made, whenever possible, to preserve it in the translation.

Tribute to the Life of Master Tōsui

(*Tōsui oshō densan*)

Menzan Zuihō

A Child Clutches the Buddha

Though an infant, he transcends the causes of secular existence
Still unable to tell east from west, already he recognizes the truth
He clutches the Buddha, a treasure in his sleeve
Hurling away a thousand coins into the dust beneath his feet[a]
As mud sends forth the auspicious lotus and the lotus grows more and more fragrant
As stone yields white jade and the jade becomes ever more luminous
Henceforth his reflected radiance will impart a perfume
He is about to awaken the people of the world lost in their dreams

Tribute to the Life of Master Tōsui of Takagamine, on the Northern Outskirts of the Imperial City

The Master's formal name was Unkei, his common name Tōsui.[1] He was a native of the castle town of Yanagawa[2] in Chikugo Province, the child of a merchant family. His family belonged to the Pure Land sect.[3] His father and mother were both devout believers, taking care to see that there were always incense and flowers on their Buddhist altar.

The Master's mother had a strange dream and became pregnant. From the time he was born, the child was fond of Buddhist images, having no interest in other toys. Once, seeing him leave the house with the statue of Amida from the household altar clutched in his arms, his mother ran after him.

"Here," she said, holding out some coins, "take this money instead and give Mother back the Buddha."

"I don't want those!" the Master replied, throwing the coins on the ground and running off clasping the Buddha to his breast.

Things like this happened all the time so that the Master's parents decided that their child was not suited to becoming a merchant. Therefore, at age seven, he was given up [to become a priest]. He was packed off to Master Igan[4] of En'ōji in Hizen Province,[5] and Igan had the Master's head shaved. Later, Igan left to become abbot of Ryūchōin in Higo Province.[6]

The Master was diligent in his studies and quick-witted. From the age of thirteen or fourteen, his cleverness manifested itself. On one occasion, during the rainy season,[7] a layman who was a patron of the temple noticed the Master standing on a bridge holding a hollyhock and asked him, "What flower is that?"

The Master replied, "Can't you see it's a hollyhock?"

A Novice's Sharp-Witted Reply

Plucking a flower, he ambles alone over the bridge
A layman, happening by, seeks to test his quick wits
Instead the novice strikes back and reverses the situation
The arrow shot to the east turns and goes back to the west
Endowed by heaven, his wisdom encompasses the knowledge acquired from practice in previous lives
His accomplishment acknowledged, his wisdom gradually unfolds
With a single stroke who can suggest the feeling of a thousand miles?
The marvelous feather of his arrow is about to leave far behind the dust of the world

The patron said, "If it's a hollyhock [*aoi*, also the Japanese word for "blue"], how come the flower is red?"

The Master replied, "This is a bridge [*hashi*, also the Japanese word for "side"], but you're crossing it down the middle."

The layman was left speechless.

• • •

From age fifteen or sixteen, without anyone's telling him to do so, the Master undertook various practices, acting entirely on his own. He would fast for three days; remain standing all night in the garden reciting sutras and dharani; or stay alone deep in the mountains without returning to the temple for as many as two or three nights. At other times, he would practice *zazen* all day and night on the banks of a large stream. Such things happened on countless occasions, and what others saw and heard of Tōsui led them to wonder at this novice who was so different from ordinary people. Igan, it is said, did not subject the Master to any test of his attainment, simply calling him "madman."[8]

• • •

Igan once instructed his assembled disciples: "The Buddha admonished his followers that monks must be dedicated above all to freeing themselves from the five desires. The five desires are the desires for sex, food, sleep, fame, and wealth. To free oneself from the first three of these desires is easy for one who has become a monk; but to free oneself from the two desires for fame and wealth is hard even for a monk. If, as you attain seniority, people come to revere you, [the desires for] fame and wealth will grow more and more powerful. Then, after the fact, you will find excuses for glorying in fame and wealth, and that is why, I believe, the ancients warned us to guard against these [desires] above all. You who would call yourselves my disciples should know that your wisdom and realization are [the result of] what you achieve in your own practice. Just take care at all times to free yourselves of these two desires."

Igan's instruction was detailed and thorough. [When he had finished,] all of those present remained silent. Only the Master, it is said, grumbled that he was being lectured about obvious matters as if they were things of real importance.

Traveling on Pilgrimage with Staff and Bamboo Hat
In the east he begs for the Dharma, in the south he travels to
    consult with teachers—the free life of a pilgrimage monk
Following in the fragrant footsteps of the masters of old, he
    carries his bag on his back
To the pavilions of wisdom beyond the steep mountains he
    journeys thousands of steps
And with one snap of his fingers penetrates Maitreya's innermost
    gate
Looking up from under his bamboo hat he sees Mount Fuji's
    peak, sheer, soaring, covered in snow
His straw sandals are soaked from Lake Biwa's boundless waves
The Sōtō and Rinzai temples of Japan are filled with lazy fellows
One must realize thoroughly what it means to carry the Zen
    monk's wisteria staff

• • •

After age twenty, the Master traveled on pilgrimage to the Kantō,[9] staying for a time at Kichijōji in Edo.[10]

While the Master was in Edo, he stayed at a temple in Shitaya[11] that had used several hundred wooden memorial tablets to fence off its grounds.[12] Worse yet, the Master often noticed that the fertilizer the temple's servants threw on the vegetable garden would splatter the tablets. This troubled him, and every day he would go out in the streets to beg, using whatever money he received to purchase planks of wood, which he brought to the temple, replacing the tablets with a new fence he made from the planks. The Master then carried the memorial tablets to the Sumida River[13] and set them adrift as he chanted sutras.

When the temple's abbot was inspecting the vegetable garden, he noticed the new fence. Accusingly questioning one of the monks from the kitchen about this, he was told, "That monk who recently came to stay at the temple used his own money, purchased planks and set them up, taking the memorial tablets from the old fence and tossing them into the river."

The abbot was mortified.

Word that the tablets from the old fence had, one and all, been thrown into the river and a tall new fence put up in their place was bruited about everywhere. As a result, it is said that at that time, the use of memorial tablets for fences in the Sōtō-school temples in Asakusa in Shitaya ceased.

• • •

The Master continued his pilgrimage through the provinces, studying with all the famous teachers of the day. He participated in the assemblies of Daigu, Gudō, Ungo, Shōsan[14] and others and visited Takuan[15] in Edo. He met Ingen[16] in Nagasaki and later spent seven or eight years in residence at Mount Ōbaku,[17] during which time he established close ties with Mokuan and Kōsen.[18]

Learning that Igan was serving as abbot of Ryūchōin, the Master returned to see him and served as his attendant for more than ten years. The Master was appointed head monk of Daineiji in Chōshū,[19] and on the eleventh day of the seventh month of the third year of Meireki

Plunging the Wooden Stupas into the River

One should recognize what is lofty and exalted, the dignity of a
   stupa
Revealing the tathagata's five wisdoms[b]
Even erecting a single wooden stupa brings posthumous benefits
   to the deceased
Instantly demolishing the great prison of hell and sparing one
   from the sea of transmigration
Those who are blind to the working of cause and effect will bind
   together [wooden stupas] to make a fence
Those who can distinguish truth from falsehood will untie the
   stupas and hurl them into the stream
When the stream's waters enter the ocean, the limitless virtue of
   this deed
Will surely delight the dragon king[c] and save the creatures of the
   deep

(1657), he entered Igan's chambers and completed his studies by becoming his teacher's Dharma heir. The following year he underwent the abbacy ceremony at Sōjiji in Noto and then assumed abbacy of Jōsuiji in Nangō in Higo.[20]

● ● ●

On one occasion, the Kumamoto monks Kōrin[21] and Daiyū[22] together made a long journey of more than ten ri[23] to see how the Master was faring. When they arrived at sundown, the Master was delighted and told them: "Having come such a distance you must be famished. I had better straightaway prepare your evening meal. Why don't you just rest."

When the Master went into his room, the monks heard the sound of something or other being pounded in a mortar. Time passed and it was already the fourth hour of the night,[24] but though they waited, the Master did not emerge from his room. Curious about what he was making, Daiyū peeked through the sliding door and saw the Master putting something into an earthenware mortar and pounding it with a wooden pestle. Mystified, Daiyū asked from behind the door, "What is your Reverence making?"

The Master, still pounding away intently at the barley, replied, "I ran out of the rice I got as alms. Since the village is a long way off and it's nighttime, there was nothing to be done, so I'm taking the barley I received from my begging and grinding it to make barley rice[25] in order to offer you something to eat. I wanted to do it quickly, but it seems I'm getting nowhere."

Exchanging sympathetic smiles, the monks, disarmed by the Master's innocence, whispered to one another, "If he's still grinding that barley now, how will he ever have it ready for dinner?" They then made the Master stop, and resigning themselves to their hunger, spent the whole night listening to his Dharma talk.

Kōrin and Daiyū stayed the following day, and used their own money to buy a small amount of food, which they offered to the Master before returning to their home temples. It is said that, afterward, the two monks recounted this as a once-in-a-lifetime experience.

Kōrin served as abbot of Hōonji in Kumamoto. Daiyū was a disciple of Igan and abbot of Chishōin.[26]

Ingenuousness in a Quiet Retreat
A worn-out robe and five copper coins—a distinctly individual hospitality
It is hard to hastily explain to others the Master's everyday mind
His body at ease like the drifting scraps of cloud reflected in the valley stream
His mind bright like the moon's radiance illumining the mountains
Horse barley is sufficient to sustain his life, a result of his karmic conditions
Like a honey-bee among flowers he diligently busies himself entertaining his guests
He just clutches the bowl that has been passed down in unsullied purity through the generations
And having no bottom it swallows up all within the ten directions

∙∙∙

When Master Sengan[27] was third-generation abbot of Ryūchōin

His formal name was Rintetsu. He was Igan's successor as abbot and Tōsui's Dharma brother, as well as the ordination teacher of Ryōun[28],

the Zen teacher Tetsugen[29] delivered lectures on the Lotus Sutra. The Master was among those present. He would sit by himself just outside the reception hall behind a clothes stand on which he had draped the worn-out altar cloth he used as a robe.[30] One day the sky suddenly turned overcast, and the Master, barefoot and wearing his dilapidated robe, rushed off carrying buckets of manure, which he proceeded to spread on the vegetable garden.[31] Seeing this, Sengan rebuked him angrily. "Imagine doing such filthy work!" he scolded. "As a Buddhist monk, how can you touch excrement! Stop that immediately!"

The Master replied calmly, "If that's the case, then one can't even wipe one's ass in the toilet. Everyone uses the same hands they wipe their ass with to pray, but I never heard of the buddhas or bodhisattvas taking offense. And manuring the vegetable garden probably isn't even as filthy as that. I only did it because I thought the eggplants were looking skinny." He said nothing more.

This was heard by all the men and women assembled to listen to the lecture on the Lotus [Sutra]. Some laughed, it is said, but others were moved.

∙∙∙

The Osaka Hōganji had been repeatedly robbed, and no one could be found to serve as abbot. As the position had remained vacant, one of the temple patrons who knew the Master offered him the post, and, accepting the invitation, the Master assumed the temple's abbacy.

Never liking to be tied down, the Master made a singular abbot. It frequently happened that he was away from the temple for as much as ten days at a time, locking the door behind him and leaving only a servant as caretaker. This irked the temple patrons, but, concerned that if they offended the Master he would leave for good and go someplace else, they went out of their way to please him and urged him to remain as permanent abbot.

Nurturing the Vegetable Garden
Because his garden is sweet-scented and wishes to repay its
    indebtedness to the Three Treasures
The Master nourishes the purple eggplants in the rain
Seizing the initiative and casting aside all conventional concerns
At the two ends of his shoulder pole the Way itself exists
The forest's trees are wrapped in mist, further enhancing their
    beauty
Shouting and roaring, the mountain spring crashes over rocks
The human and heavenly beings that everywhere follow him all
    prepare to enter
As the Master throws open wide Vimalakirti's gate of nonduality[d]

The Master had served only two years as abbot when [the following incident occurred]. A certain Hirano, a samurai from Kumamoto in Higo, had been the recipient of a large stipend, but for various reasons became a masterless samurai and moved with his entire household to Osaka. With no residence for his retirement immediately available, he went to Hōganji to visit the Master, whom he knew. The Master was delighted and told him, "It's good to see you! Stay as long as you like." The upshot was that some twenty people, including male and female followers, were accommodated. Every day they would noisily bustle off to go sightseeing and visit temples and shrines all over the city.

This came to the attention of the town constable, who reported to the authorities that some apparently high-ranking samurai, along with a large party of male and female followers, were staying at Hōganji, and that every day they went off on excursions. "This requires looking into," the authorities declared. The result was that [the abbots of] all the Osaka Sōtō-school temples were without exception summoned to appear the following day at the magistrate's headquarters.

That evening a meeting was held at the temple of the *furegashira*.[32] Everyone said: "This time the abbot of Hōganji's freewheeling behavior has finally gone too far! It has always been a strict rule in the city of Osaka that when persons armed with lances or halberds are staying in the town, the local officials must be notified in advance, and must inform the city magistrate.[33] In the case of temples, the *furegashira* must always be notified, and then inform the city magistrate. However, without any such notification, these visitors stayed at the temple for several days, with the result that when this came to the authorities' attention, it incurred their censure. To have all the [abbots of the] Sōtō school [in Osaka] summoned by the authorities like this—there's never been such a scandal!

"As to tomorrow's investigation by the magistrate, since *we* failed to notify [the authorities of this matter], *they* have called a general meeting, so there's no way we can avoid dealing with this now. However, let us do our best under the circumstances. How many days altogether have these guests been staying at the temple?"

The Master replied, "These samurai are people from Kumamoto—there's nothing in the least disreputable about them. That's precisely why I let them stay. They arrived sometime after the middle of last month, so I think they've probably been with me thirty-two or thirty-three days."

[Hearing this, the abbots] all declared, "No wonder the constable

Meeting with a Reprimand at Government Headquarters
At Osaka the Master absents himself from his temple, shutting the brushwood gate
By chance he meets up with an acquaintance from home and welcomes a layman
At the monk's dwelling, compassion commands sympathy for a friend's situation
At the official's quarters, a harsh rebuke excoriates the Master's error
For a time storm-clouds gather and thunder peals
But an instant later the rain is gone and the sun is shining brightly
He has never been bothered by idle concerns
What a pity that in our world the awakened are so rare!

found out! If you give that sort of explanation, it's going to be serious, so you'd better let us do all the talking. You just bow low and keep absolutely quiet the whole time."

The Master agreed to do as he had been told, and everyone left.

Sure enough, the following day, when the assembled abbots presented themselves at the magistrate's headquarters, the magistrate himself questioned them directly.[34]

"It has recently come to my attention," he said, "that samurai armed with lances and halberds have been staying secretly at Hōganji together with their followers, some twenty persons in all. This has been brought to my notice by the constable. I understand that these persons have been at the temple for a considerable time.

"Abbot of Hōganji!" the magistrate thundered, "tell me plainly and truthfully: how long have they been there?"

Tōsui remained silent, without answering, while the *furegashira* said, "It has not been so long a time as your Lordship heard. I have ascertained it to be merely the last day or two. Indeed, all the abbots have ascertained this to be the case."

Whereupon every one of the assembled abbots promptly swore that, as had been stated, it was a matter of no more than one or two days, so there had not been time to inform the *furegashira*.

Hearing this, the magistrate once again questioned the abbots. "Let me caution you," he said. "Persons reported seeing the visitors at Hōganji during the last part of the previous month, so that *two or three* days is surely closer to the truth. Slight though the difference may be, this is an official matter, and if anyone is lying, there will be no leniency shown, even for priests. Isn't there a small discrepancy in your account?"

The *furegashira* declared, "With all due respect, there is no discrepancy whatever in what I have stated."

Tōsui then raised his head and said, "What the *furegashira* has just told you is what we'd decided at our secret conference last night. But to be perfectly truthful, my guests arrived in the middle of last month and only left yesterday, so that altogether they stayed thirty-four or thirty-five days."

When he heard this, the magistrate appeared amused and declared, "Very well, very well. It's over with, so we'll leave it at that. But don't let it happen again! Now all of you, go!"

The abbots then departed, let off without any further charges, and the case was closed.

On the way home all the abbots, laughing sardonically, berated the Master: "Really, Hōganji,[35] how could you have said such a thing to the authorities! You're absolutely pathetic!"

Only the Master seemed pleased, as if congratulating himself. "The magistrate threatened that if we didn't tell the truth, he'd show no leniency, even if we were monks," he said. "And look! By telling the truth everything turned out all right!"

• • •

During this period, a monk named Ejō,[36] a disciple of Zen master Unpo,[37] learned that the Master was abbot of Hōganji and visited him there, paying his respects. He remained at the temple for half a year, serving as the Master's attendant.

When Ejō begged the Master for a gatha[38] to express his teaching, the Master offered the following verse:

> Ejō, let your wisdom and meditation be clearly illuminating
> And then and there you'll let things go
> Let go! Let go even of letting go
> Then what will be left to let go of?
> Drink your tea, eat your rice
> Don't go looking anywhere else
> Ejō, let your wisdom and meditation be clearly illuminating
> And the ten thousand things will all come to rest

During the Master's abbacy at Hōganji, he would go out begging every day, accompanied by no more than one or two attendant monks. He would take whatever raw rice he received, cook it, and use it to make as many rice balls as he could. Then promptly at dusk he would bring the rice balls to the place where the beggars gathered and personally distribute them to each of the beggars. With whatever cash [he received from begging], he would buy rice cakes and give them to the beggars' children. He would do this as often as ten times in a single month. The merchants were moved on learning of this, and in increasing numbers they would wait for the master and add copiously to his bowl.

• • •

When the Master returned to his native Yanagawa, the monks and laypeople of the area thought it a precious opportunity and entreated him to remain for a while and deliver sermons. In response, the Master lectured on the Final Teachings Sutra[39] as a transfer of merit to his deceased parents.[40] A large audience assembled to listen; offerings were plentiful, and all were donated to the temple holding the lectures on the sutra. This came to the notice of the local officials, and they begged the Master to settle permanently in the province. But saying that he never had any intention of settling in his native district, he went to stay at Seiunji[41] in Shimabara in Hizen.[42]

At that time, the lord of Shimabara, the daimyo Kōriki Sakon,[43] invited the Master to assume the abbacy of Zenrinji in Ninji.[44] The previous abbot had had a passion for flowering shrubs. He had planted peonies in terraces all over the garden, and when they were in bloom he would hold banquets and invite guests. The first thing the Master did on becoming abbot was to dig up the garden, wielding the mattock with his own hands. Bringing tea plants from Takezaki[45] in Hizen, he planted them instead. Among those who saw or heard this, some praised the Master and others condemned him. But the great patron [Lord Kōriki] declared, "He is a true monk!"

● ● ●

The Master had been abbot of Zenrinji for some five years when he held a winter retreat.[46] More than 120 monks attended, including Kengan,[47] Gūhaku,[48] Unpo, Echū,[49] and Gakuryū.[50] At that time, the Master lectured on the *Shōshūsan*,[51] instructing the assembly.

The following spring, on the day when the retreat came to a close,[52] the monks of the assembly went to the abbot's quarters to bid [the Master] farewell. But though an attendant searched for him, the Master could not be found. Nor was there any sign of the Master's satchel[53] or his staff. At the entrance to the abbot's quarters was affixed a single sheet of paper, on which the Master had written in his calligraphy:

> Today the retreat comes to an end
> The assembly arrives to bid farewell
> This old monk has gone ahead
> To the east, to the west, wherever his spirit leads

Destroying the Flower Beds with a Mattock
Each grain in his bowl is five Mount Sumerus[e]
One must be firm in upholding Buddhist practice and
    scrupulously avoid the seven evil acts[f]
What is the love of flowers but to pass the days in idleness
How much more so to be addicted to wine, spending one's time
    intoxicated
Go and dice are the mind of the fighting demon
Dance, music, and song are likewise aspects of hell dwellers
Extirpating such things that offend the Dharma
The temple is made pure and even one's dreams become
    auspicious

The assembly scrambled after him in pursuit, but in the end no one could discover where the Master had gone. On learning of this, the daimyo was greatly alarmed and commanded that departures be halted at all the ferry crossings. But the Master, he was informed, was nowhere to be found. This was the beginning of the Master's life among the ordinary people of the world. He is said at this time to have gone to visit the graves of his parents at Yanagawa, traveling directly from there via the Chūgoku[54] road to a boat that brought him to Osaka.

• • •

The Master had three disciples whom he personally ordained. The first was named Zekan, the second, Chinshū, and the next Chiden.[55]

> Zekan was a native of Kumamoto in Higo. His ordination took place when the Master was staying in Nangō. Later, Zekan returned to his native province and served as abbot of Ryūchōin in place of the Venerable Master Sengan, dying there at the temple. On the eleventh day of the tenth month of the second year of Kanbun (1662), Tōsui bestowed on Zekan *jōza*,[56] the written transmission[57] of the Bodhisattva precepts.[58] When I[59] was a novice at Ryūchōin, I found [the above-mentioned document] at the home of one of Zekan's relatives. I requested it from them, and to this day have preserved it carefully, a rare Dharma treasure that allows me to feel close to the Master's teaching.

Having always been at the Master's side, Chinshū and Chiden knew how eccentric he could be, and they set out in search of him, traveling to Kyoto. Each day they would split up and look for the Master in every quarter. Summer passed, and when mid-autumn arrived, Chinshū finally discovered the Master among a throng of beggars behind the Yasui Imperial temple, below Kiyomizudera in Higashiyama.[60]

Observing him discreetly, Chinshū saw that the Master's hair had grown wild and his whiskers long. A threadbare robe barely clung to his shoulders, and on his back he carried a reed mat. In his right hand he held a broken wooden bowl, in his left a shabby satchel. He mingled with all the other beggars, chatting in a friendly manner.

Torn between joy and grief, Chinshū went directly before the Master, prostrating himself and weeping. He could only sob unrestrainedly, unable to utter even a single word.

Remaining composed, the Master told Chinshū, "Novice, you had no business in coming here looking for me. Now go away, I don't care where. We won't be seeing each other again in this life."

Expounding the Dharma, Teaching Disciples

The Dharma banner flaps in the wind, beckoning all from the
   four directions
Even the barbarians crowd around the throne of the King of the
   Brahma Heaven[g]
The Master discourses on the buddhas' and patriarchs' *Tribute to
   the Authentic School*
Clearly revealing how in the East [China] and West [India] the
   teaching was secretly passed on to the great
An accomplished Zen monk, a paragon of wisdom, where can he
   have fled?
The eyes of human and heavenly beings instantly spring open
An arrow released from the bowstring, the Master's verse for
   those who come to bid farewell
With lightning speed he makes his escape, and no one can catch
   him or bring him back

So saying, the Master strode off briskly up the mountain.

Chinshū pursued him, declaring as he walked that he had no wish to go anywhere without the Master; his only desire was to stay by his side for as long as the Master lived, and only afterward determine what to do with his own life.

But despite his insistent pleading, the Master would not even turn to look back and strode quickly along, saying, "Mind your own business!"

Chinshū scrambled after him, and when they entered the mountains, the Master turned and said, "Novice, didn't you hear me tell you to mind your own business? We belong to different worlds, so you can't come along. Even if you force yourself on me, you'll only find later that you can't stand it and have to drop out. It's useless your begging to join me—go back!"

With these words, the Master strode off.

His eyes filled with tears, Chinshū followed the Master, continuing to plead with him, sobbing loudly and declaring as he had before, "I won't leave you, even if it means ending my life here and now!"

Thereupon the Master told him, "Very well, then, have it your way. But I doubt you'll manage to stay with me even ten days. By that time, you'll learn your lesson!

"All right," he ordered Chinshū, "give me your satchel." And taking all of Chinshū's belongings, he threw them into a beggar's hut by the side of the road and then made Chinshū carry the reed mat on his back.

"Now," the Master said, "I have business to attend to in the direction of Ōmi.[61] Nightfall is approaching, so hurry up!"

They reached Ōtsu[62] and then headed toward Sakamoto.[63] At a small shrine in the midst of a forest they spread the reed mat, and teacher and disciple passed the night together. The whole evening, the Master did not say a word about the past or future. Instead, Chinshū overheard him reciting a gatha to himself:

> This is what my life is like
> This is what it's like, broad and free
> A worn-out robe, a broken bowl
>   —how peaceful and calm!
> When hungry, I eat, when thirsty, I drink
> That's all I know
> I've got nothing to do with the world's "right and wrong"

A Beggar Gives Instruction

Our view of others is muddied by questions of rank and honors, fame and wealth
A sudden spiritual transformation leads the Master to mingle with the dust of the world
His life freer than the empty sky
He permeates the vast universe, smiled upon by all the buddhas
Exhausting filial devotion, his disciple searches for him
And the old man, moved by his follower's sincerity, expounds the meaning of benevolent kindness
The upshot is that, henceforth, the disciple will stick to him like a magnet
Lodging in the fields, sleeping in the mountains, and sharing a bed of grass

At the first light of dawn, they went to beg in the town of Sakamoto, and then headed toward Katada.⁶⁴ An old beggar had fallen dead by the side of the road, and seeing him, the Master told Chinshū, "Go to the hut at the entrance to that village over there and borrow a mattock. If they ask you why you need it, say, 'A friend of mine died, and I want to bury his corpse. I'm afraid if I just left it lying there, the stench would offend the travelers going by.'"

Chinshū did as he was told and returned with a mattock.

The Master then took the mattock and buried the body with his own hands.

Watching this, Chinshū exclaimed, "Ah, how pitiful!"

To which the Master replied, "Why is it only this corpse you find pitiful? From the emperor and shogun down to this dead man, all of us come into the world without so much as a single thread or a grain of rice. So when we leave it naked and starving, isn't it an even deal? Even if you amass a million *koku*⁶⁵ of rice, when it comes time to die you won't be able to swallow so much as a smidgen of gruel.⁶⁶ Even if your storehouse is bursting with clothes, in the end you'll be wearing a single burial robe. Those who fail to realize this imagine that death for the emperor, the shogun, and the daimyo, the wealthy and important, is somehow different. How foolish!"

With these words, the Master took the half-eaten vegetable-and-gruel hodgepodge left beside the corpse's head and devoured half of it with great zest. Bestowing the remainder on Chinshū, the Reverend Master commanded, "Eat this!"

Chinshū managed to choke down two or three mouthfuls.

Then, seeing that the disciple was unable to go on, the Master said, "What's the matter? You don't like it? Give it back to me!" And taking the food, his Holiness gobbled it all up, down to the last morsel.

Before long Chinshū began to vomit. His face turned pale, his eyes swam in his head, and staggering to the side of the road, he collapsed.

Seeing this, the Master declared, "That's why I told you right from the start that you couldn't come along. But because you were so determined, you wouldn't take my advice. Now go back! I left word at the house where we were yesterday that in around ten days' time I'd send back the novice who left his satchel and have him come to pick it up. So go collect your things right away. Then find out your brother novice's whereabouts, and the two of you go together to see Kōsen at

Master and Disciple Travel Together
Journeying eastward past Yamashina,[h] they let themselves drift according to circumstances
Staff and straw sandals, master and disciple—what's it all about?
At Ōtsu's post station, travelers rein in their horses
At Miidera,[i] at the sound of the evening gong, fishermen tie up their boats
On the waters of Lake Biwa ripples appear as the wind stirs
Mount Hiei's peaks rise precipitously deeply shrouded in fog
By luck, at the side of the road is a rustic shrine
All through the night, even in his dreams the Master puts to rest the dreamy mind

Bukkokuji.[67] Tell him, 'The two of us are Unkei's[68] disciples, and in accordance with his instructions, we've come to serve as your attendants.' Then stay at his side forever. And once you're there, don't look back, even if the training is harsh enough to kill you! This is as far as we go together. Just put me completely out of your minds, even in your dreams. Then you'll both be filial disciples. Farewell!"

So saying, the Master strode off briskly in the direction of the lake.[69]

Chinshū, left utterly speechless, returned to the place he had been the day before and retrieved his satchel, and then having discussed things with Chiden, [the two went to Bukkokuji]. They followed Master Kōsen for life and became his Dharma heirs.

> Ryōun[70] heard this account directly from Master Chinshū, and I have set it down just as I heard it during [Ryōun's] tea talks. Later, Chinshū founded Tōgen'an.[71] He passed away on the twenty-eighth day of the first month of the third year of Hōei (1706). Chiden founded Shōshūan,[72] and passed away on the twentieth day of the fifth month of the sixth year of Hōei (1709). They are buried together at Bukkokuji beneath an oval tombstone.[73]

After this, the Master traveled to Ise,[74] where he mingled with the beggars in the vicinity of the inner and outer shrines.[75] He also spent time in Nagoya in Owari,[76] and in Nara,[77] where he worked at such jobs as sweeper at the Daibutsu.[78] Later, he hired on as a servant in Kusatsu[79] and even worked as a *kago*[80] carrier. In Kyoto, it is said that he associated with pack-horse drivers and the like in Awadaguchi.[81] However, he would never remain a full year doing the same thing in any one place, but would move freely about, changing his location, his occupation, and his appearance.

● ● ●

When he was living in Ōtsu, the Master made sandals and straw horseshoes[82] and would go out selling them every day. But later all [his customers] would [come to] place their orders and wait for them to be finished. People spoke of "the old man of Ōtsu's shoes."

The Master's rented dwelling was a vacant space of no more than six or seven *shaku*,[83] between two merchant storehouses. He roofed over the area with thatch, but used the space only for sleeping, and did not keep any cooking utensils. Here he made the straw horseshoes and sandals, and with the proceeds would buy rice cakes and such. He spent some two years in this manner.

Burying the Dead and Offering Instruction

Emperor and commoner, both end in the grave

The affairs of the world: a foolish tangle of confusion

We are hopelessly deluded by the physical body, impermanent as the dew on a blade of grass

We cling forcibly to the illusion of our existence, evanescent as a cloud in the sky

Poison and ghee,ʲ are these two different tastes?

The body of Dharma and stinking flesh, right from the start there is no distinction

However, if you haven't yet realized this in your daily activity

From here on you've got to practice hard in order to garner the prize of wisdom

Once, when some pack-horse drivers and *kago* porters were gathered at the Master's quarters, they said to him, "Old man, there's no Buddha in your place. They say that not having a Buddha means you're a Christian. Why haven't you installed a Buddha here?"

The old man replied, "Even Buddha can't stand a place where they never cook food!"

Everyone burst out laughing.

The following day, one of the pack-horse drivers brought an Ōtsu-style[84] hanging scroll depicting Amida Buddha and gave it to the Master, saying, "Here, old man, this is for you. Use it as your personal Buddha."

"I don't need a Buddha," the Master protested, but the pack-horse driver pressed it on him, and grumbling that his place was small enough already, the Master took the scroll and hung it up.

When the Master went out, his neighbors noticed that a Buddha scroll had been hung up and that something that looked like writing had been scribbled across the top. When they examined it, they found a comic poem inscribed in cinder ink:[85]

> Cramped though your lodgings are, Amida, sir
> I'm going to ask you to let me stay
> Just don't think I'm depending on you
> To help me in the life after this[86]

• • •

The Zen master Gyōgan Unpo,[87] founder of Tenpukuji in Kakihara in Higo,[88] was a teacher of great virtue. Vice Commander Lord Hosokawa Tsunatoshi[89] became his disciple. When Unpo delivered sermons in Bungo[90] he converted adherents of the heretical teaching,[91] leading them all to take refuge in the Three Treasures.[92] By dint of his virtue, he founded Nō'ninji in Takada in Bungo[93] and Tenpukuji in Higo, along with more than ten branch temples, and between Bungo and Higo, he established some thirty new temples. His last years were spent at Tenpukuji, where he passed away on the eighth day of the twelfth month.[94]

I had the opportunity to meet Unpo when I was young. He was very tall, and had a strange look in his eyes. From the middle of his forehead curled a white tuft of hair,[95] which seemed to extend some two

Hanging a Buddha Scroll and Weaving Straw Horseshoes
A buddha comes, but if the Master won't display him, what will happen?
Weaving straw horseshoes by the roadside, he helps the pack-horse drivers
He's on the best of terms with ostlers and grooms
Although managing to avoid Maitreya's assistance, he still ends up getting help from Amitabha[k]
The buddha's features are wondrous in the Ōtsu-style painting
The Master's inscription, a single profound and subtle verse
Praise or censure—to him it's all the same
This life he regards as the whirling foam in a cup of bitter tea

sun.⁹⁶ One could sense that this was someone who had accumulated merit over many previous lives. Such a worthy monk is indeed rare to encounter in this degenerate age. Venerating the way of the recluses, his whole life long he never traded upon his teacher's transmission, never sought important clerical office or accepted an invitation to the imperial palace, but spread the Dharma in his plain black robes,⁹⁷ and for this Lord Hosokawa held him in particular reverence. When his lordship was in Edo, in order to hear the Dharma he erected a residence within [the grounds of] his mansion and invited Unpo to stay there, listening to him discuss the teaching morning and night. Unpo, too, had been ordained by Master Igan and was one of Tōsui's Dharma brothers.

Once, when Lord Hosokawa was on his way to Edo for his period of alternate attendance, Unpo passed through Ōtsu in a *kago*, accompanied by four or five monks. He had his servants set down the *kago* in front of a tea shop, and while he let them rest, a white-haired old man of over sixty passed by, carrying on his back a large quantity of straw horseshoes.

The pack-horse drivers called to him, "Hey, grandpa, two pair over here!" "Three pair here!"

"Coming, coming," the old man replied, as he bustled about selling his wares.

When Unpo looked out of the *kago* to see what was happening, there was Tōsui.

Having previously heard that the Master was begging in the vicinity of Kyoto, Unpo was still on the lookout for him,⁹⁸ and was overjoyed. Fearing that the Master might run off, without a word to his attendants Unpo suddenly emerged from the *kago*, and going right up to the old man, seized his hand and said, "Tōsui, is it not? Surely you remember me. What are you doing dressed like this?"

The Master replied, "Of course I know you. Where are you going?"

Tears streaming down his cheeks, Unpo said, "In recent years, I have received the patronage of Lord Hosokawa, and am now accompanying him to Edo. What luck to cross paths with you and see you again!"

Tōsui told him, "As I've become a beggar, this is how I look, but I've nothing at all to be ashamed of. We shall probably not meet again. Live long and take care of yourself. Since you are virtually a retainer, duty to your lord is all-important."

With this the Master hurried off, flapping his sleeves.

The crowds of passersby who observed this, including the people of

At the Post-Horse Station, Meeting an Old Acquaintance
The boundless ocean of the priesthood is an incalculable treasure
The giant oyster spits out a pearl, illumining the universe
Abandoning his position in the world, one friend has assumed a
    lowly state, concealing himself in a pauper's robes
Idling away his time, the other has become revered, the prized
    jewel of a lord of the realm
Their paths have diverged for many years like the arch-rivals
    Ch'u and Yüeh[l]
Then one seizes the other's hand and the two exchange smiles
    like the bosom companions Lei and Ch'en[m]
It matters not which is older brother, which younger brother,
    which is superior or inferior in rank
But the Master returns to the life of one endowed with the eye
    that discerns and illumines

Ōtsu who had watched what occurred, exclaimed, "So all along that old man was no ordinary person!"

As a result, from that evening on, rich merchants and others of the sort came to visit the Master, so that after a day or two, he fled Ōtsu, leaving no clue as to his whereabouts.

Later, describing these events to the assembly of monks at Tenpukuji, Unpo remarked, "Tōsui's words, 'Duty is all-important,' could be applied either to religious or worldly affairs, and left me utterly bathed in sweat!"

• • •

In the castle town of Shimabara in Hizen lived the Master's nun disciple Chihō.[99] The mother of a wealthy merchant, Chihō attempted to discover the Master's whereabouts, praying to the gods and buddhas that she might meet him again, and even going so far as to consult an oracle. Chihō had a dream in which she met the Master in Kyoto, and, under the pretext of making a pilgrimage to the Ise shrine,[100] provided herself with funds. She also had new night clothes and bedding made, intending these as presents for when she saw the Master. At the shrine, the first thing Chihō did was to pray that she might meet him.

On her way back, Chihō stayed at the home of a relative in Kyoto. She told her host, "I hate to trouble you, but I'm anxiously searching for someone. The problem is, I don't know his whereabouts, or even whom I could ask to see if there's anybody who knows him. What's more, apart from me, there's no one, not even any of the servants I've brought, who is familiar with what he looks like, so unless I search for him myself my hopes will never be realized."

Day after day, accompanied by a maid and a manservant, Chihō searched all over the city. Some twenty days had passed in this manner, when, returning from Kiyomizu,[101] she came upon a large group of beggars gathered in the dry riverbed under the Gojō Bridge.[102] But though she scrutinized them carefully, Chihō could find no one she recognized. Thinking to herself, "Perhaps I ought to try asking," Chihō descended to the area under the bridge and distributed coins among the beggars, in the course of which she questioned them, saying, "For the past several years, the person I'm looking for has been living in concealment among the beggars. I've searched everywhere, but failed to find him. Since my business with this person is urgent, I've come all the way from Hizen just to look for him, having had a dream which revealed that I would find him in Kyoto. I've gone out searching for him every day for the last twenty days or so, but since there's no one apart from myself who knows him, there's no way anyone can help me. Is there no one among you who knows someone resembling the person I've described? And if not in Kyoto, have you perhaps come across a person like this anywhere else?"

None of them, however, could recall such a person.

Meanwhile, off to one side, lying on a mat he had spread, there was a leper who sat up and declared, "Why, that sounds like the fellow who was nursing me recently! He isn't the sort of person you normally see around here, so I questioned him all about himself, but he wouldn't tell me a thing. He did say that today he was going to buy some medicine and bring it to me. I haven't seen him since last night, but early this afternoon he's sure to be bringing the medicine. I was thinking over your Reverence's words, and somehow this person seemed to match your description. If you have business elsewhere, you could attend to that first and then try coming back here in the early afternoon and see if he's about."

"Surely that must be he!" Chihō rejoiced.

Chihō walked around the area, and when early afternoon arrived, concealed herself in the vicinity of the bridge. Sure enough, who should appear but Tōsui himself. On his back, he carried a straw mat; his legs were bare below the knees. His white hair had grown shaggy and unkempt; his whiskers were grizzled and long. In his hand he clutched a staff and a bundle wrapped in paper. He approached the leper with rapid steps and knelt at his side.

As Chihō looked on, she found the care and solicitude with which the Master nursed the leper beyond imagination or description.

The nun disciple then went directly up to the Master, and, weeping, declared, "I am the nun from Shimabara. While on pilgrimage to the Ise Shrine I learned of your Reverence's whereabouts and came all the way here to look for you. To have met you miraculously now like this is the realization of all my prayers!" So saying, she dissolved into tears.

The Master told her, "A woman's heaviest burden is sentimental attachment. While this may be all right in the secular world with one's children and grandchildren, what use can there be in seeing again someone like me who's free from the ties of affection? Just have faith in the power of the Three Treasures and don't lose your original aspiration in becoming a nun; then it's the same as being with me all the time. Now, go home at once!"

In spite of the Master's thoroughly indifferent reception, the nun disciple earnestly implored, "I have but one request. I fervently beg your Reverence to grant it."

The Master demanded, "What sort of request?"

The nun said, "From today on, I humbly entreat your Reverence to find a hut for yourself somewhere in Higashiyama[103] and settle there. Out of my own means, I can easily manage to supply you with food for as long as you live, and will see to it that you are regularly provisioned by relatives of mine here in Kyoto. I have brought with me now various kinds of bedding and so forth that I've just had made up and will deliver to your new lodgings. And I've also brought along sufficient money to purchase the hut. I beg your Reverence to grant my wish and to let me see you settled there before I return home.

"I earnestly beseech you," she tearfully implored, "grant this wish!"

The Master told her, "If you really understood me, you wouldn't suggest such a stupid idea! If what I really wanted was to live in a hut, I could do it tomorrow, without having *you* tell me to do so. It's precisely because that's repugnant to me that I'm living as I am. I won't do what you ask!" The Master, shaking his head, was adamant in his refusal.

The nun, seeing nothing could be done, declared, "Since I brought this money and these bed things here with such high hopes, I'm not going to take them back with me, so let me offer them directly to you. Please do with them as you wish, even if you throw them away or toss them into the river. The very fact that I was able to see you and speak with you again shows that our destinies are linked for eternity. So [even if you will no longer receive me in this present life], allow me at least to become your disciple in every one of my future births so that I may continue to receive your spiritual guidance."

Then, weeping, Chihō sent someone to fetch the bed things and money from her lodgings and presented them to the Master.

The Master told her, "Your attitude that it's all right even if I throw these things away or toss them into the river is the highest expression of charity. Very well, then!"

And so saying, the Master abruptly took the bed things, and told the leper, "Your luck has changed! Get rid of that old mat and spread out this futon. Throw away that straw wrap and put on these bedclothes."

The Nun and the Master Meet Again

Dharma indebtedness is known to oneself alone

With many gifts of fine silk, the nun searches for her teacher, a devotion truly deserving of sympathy

She makes vows to the buddhas, prays to the gods, and divines a chance meeting

Performing her duty, she realizes her wish, fulfilling her karmic destiny

Her tears stream down to mingle with the waters under the Gojō Bridge

Steam gathers and cooking smoke rises from a thousand homes

A millionaire may boast all the money in the world

But in the land of the dead he won't be worth even half a cent

As Chihō watched, overcome with emotion, the Master handed the bed things directly to the leper. The Master then had the money changed. The smaller coins he immediately distributed among the beggars who were then present under the bridge. The larger coins he directed the chiefs of the beggars to distribute [later to those who were absent], instructing them, "One *bu*[104] to be divided among each group of several persons."

The Master then told Chihō, "You've performed an excellent act of charity! There's nothing better than this for planting merit in the future. Now I must be off."

As he left the nun, the Master placed a small quantity of the money in his sleeve, saying, "Near Tōji,[105] there's a pauper who's ill."

Thereupon he vanished without a trace. It is said that after this, the Master never again returned to the area under the bridge.

> Master Rōin Chōgen of Zenjōji in Kumamoto heard this account from the nun herself when Rōin was in residence at Kōtōji in Shimabara.[106] I, in turn, heard Rōin relate it in casual conversation when I was in residence at Zenjōji.

● ● ●

In a certain year, on his way back from Edo, the Zen master Unpo visited the therapeutic hot springs at Arima in Settsu,[107] remaining there for almost a month. One day, after leaving the baths, he was strolling about the area when he noticed an old man approaching from the opposite direction. He carried a bamboo pole from which hung a jug of soy sauce[108] and some ten bundles of leeks.

The old man looked him over and said, "Unpo, taking the cure at the hot springs?"

At the sound of the old man's voice, Unpo realized to his amazement that it was Tōsui.

"My, my!" Unpo exclaimed, delighted. "Where are you staying?"

The Master said, "Since spring my back has been hurting me, and in order to cure myself at the hot springs, I came here and went to work as a servant. But I've been kept far busier than I'd expected, and even though the hot springs are here at hand, I've had no time to use them. How about letting me take the baths at *your* place?"

"Nothing could be simpler!" Unpo replied, delighted. "Come straight over!"

The Master thereupon simply abandoned his load at the corner of a house and prepared to accompany Unpo to his lodgings.

Unpo said, "I'd better have a servant deliver those things you were carrying. Where [should I have them brought]?"

"You needn't bother," the Master replied. "If I leave them right where they are, I can just come get them any time."

And, quite unconcerned, he left the parcels and accompanied Unpo to his lodgings.

Looking extremely pleased, the Master exclaimed, "My, it's a good thing I ran into you! Now I can heal the pains in my back."

The Master spent more than ten days bathing in the hot springs. Then one day, while enjoying the waters with him, Unpo asked, "What name are you going by now? I imagine you must change your name fairly often to suit your changing circumstances."

The Master replied, "Nowadays I call myself Yūan [Possessed of Peace]." Laughing, the Master explained, "I came up with that from *sangai muan* [In the three worlds there is no peace]."[109]

Unpo then asked, "When did you come to Arima? And before that, where were you living?"

The Master said, "From last year on, I was staying in Higashiyama in Kyoto, but hoping to bathe in the hot springs, I came here at the end of the first month. When I go back, I can resume living in my hut there again."

That evening, Unpo asked the Master, "Do you still like literature?" He then handed him a poem.

What a treat was at hand! The poem must have recalled to the Master the time of his youth,[110] for, lying down, he recited a companion verse:

> In those days long ago when I traveled on pilgrimage
> I was troubled by the [desires for] fortune and fame
> Now I'm an old man but I'm still not completely free of those
>   things
> I've been lucky enough to find myself a quiet retreat in
>   Higashiyama
> Come there and keep company with the wind and moonlight
>   of the imperial city[111]

To which the Master added, laughing, "Of course, if you come to visit, I can't guarantee I'll actually be there!"

That evening, the Master bathed twice in the hot springs. When dawn arrived, however, he had disappeared. Thinking he must be in the bathhouse, Unpo went there with his monk attendant, but the Master was nowhere to be found.

Unpo, it is said, never met the Master again.

● ● ●

Probably because of the infirmities of old age, from around the time of his visit to Arima, the Master experienced frequent illness and discomfort. As a result, it seems to have become difficult for him to make long journeys and perform arduous work. He still had his hut in Kyoto, but so many people had discovered his existence and come to pay him homage that he once again abandoned the capital and settled in Ikeda in Settsu.[112]

Although the Ōbaku monks Chinshū and Chiden lived apart from the Master, they were aware that he had been in Kyoto. Now, however, not knowing where he had gone, they were unable to visit him.[113]

The Zen teacher Gūhaku of Jōgōji in Izumi[114] had been a fellow practitioner of the Master's and learned of his whereabouts. Though the weather at the end of the first month remained bitterly cold, Gūhaku made ready a new paper robe[115] and set out to visit the Master with [his disciple] Chijun.[116]

The Master was living in a deserted hut in the town. The door was shut, and when Gūhaku inquired in the neighborhood, he was told that the Master had probably gone out begging and would likely be back around noon.

They entered the house and waited. At about the eighth hour,[117] the Master returned, wearing a threadbare robe thrown over a lined cotton undergarment. His hair and whiskers had grown long, so that it was impossible even to tell he was a monk.[118] When he saw Gūhaku, all he said was, "You seem to resemble Gūhaku, but we've both become so old and decrepit we can no longer recognize one another. It's really quite pointless your coming to visit."

The Master then made a fire and, warming in some hot water the small amount of cold leftover rice he had on hand, proceeded to eat his meal.

Bowing, Gūhaku presented the Master with five hundred *mon* and the paper robe, adding, "In honor of this visit."

Taking the Hot-Spring Cure at Arima

By chance the Master can forget his beggary and avail himself of
   the hot springs
What a pleasure to find a friend in the Dharma already at the
   baths!
They share the same quilt, their conversation wandering over a
   thousand miles of rivers and mountains
Talking the whole night away, they traverse a hundred years of
   wind and moonlight
Having destroyed the dream of "the three worlds without peace"
The Master penetrates the powerful Zen of buddhas throughout
   the ten directions
"If after I've gone, anyone asks about me, say:
'The new moon hangs in the middle of the sky'"[n]

The Master told him, "Nowadays I don't take any pleasure in receiving alms. They're only a nuisance, since I just have to give them to someone else. Take your things and go home."

Nevertheless, Gūhaku, it is said, left the items before he returned.

• • •

The Master remained only a year or so in Ikeda, and then returned to his hut in Kyoto. Those who during his previous stay had come to revere him now banded together and, determined not to let him get away again, secretly conspired to keep him in Kyoto permanently.

Chijun, the monk who had accompanied Gūhaku, later became abbot of a leading Sōtō temple, and under the name Master Daizui, served as abbot of Hōun'in[119] in Higo.

• • •

There was a certain Suminokura[120] who belonged to a wealthy Kyoto merchant family and had been a follower of the Ōbaku teacher Kōsen. Having heard of the Master, Suminokura invited him to stay in his home.

It once happened that he asked the Master, "How does one go about doing Zen meditation?"

The Master just looked up at the ceiling and observed, "Soy sauce should be made in midsummer; miso should be made in winter."

That was all he would say.

Suminokura was greatly impressed by this.

In Suminokura's household was the follower of a Master So-and-So of Kurodani.[121] He was continuously reciting the nenbutsu, like someone unreeling the silk thread of a cocoon. "I can't rest unless I do at least so many tens of thousands of recitations a day," he would insist, repeating the nenbutsu even while chatting casually.

Bowing before the Master, the man told him that he recited the nenbutsu constantly and asked if the Master could offer any religious instruction beyond this.

While out Begging, Visitors Arrive

Drifting with the waves, he floats like duckweed from north to south

At Ikeda by a rice paddy he has situated his thatch hut

In the shadow of a graceful cassia tree he relaxes under a clear sky

The wind soughs in the pines, scattering the evening mist from the hills

An empty begging bowl has always been the true practice of the Buddhist mendicant

A broken window of itself signifies the active dwelling of a monk

What a delight! Learning of his whereabouts, an old friend in the Way comes to visit

A paper robe, some coins—the Master turns the wheel of Dharma three times°

Finding an inkstone at hand, the Master took a brush and wrote a comic verse, which he gave to the man:

> It's useless forcing yourself
> To repeat the nenbutsu
> What if you overshoot the Pure Land?[122]

While the Master was in Kyoto, Suminokura became his devoted follower. With the Master growing increasingly old and frail, Suminokura was concerned that if he continued traveling back and forth on long journeys, he might expire along the road somewhere. He therefore hit on a way to have the Master settle permanently in the neighborhood, and determined to get the Master to agree to his plan.

One day, when the Master had come to stay at his home, Suminokura remarked during an informal chat, "Throughout the world, in both the past and the present, monks have always lived on people's alms. Yet I suspect that your Reverence, somehow or other, finds this to be objectionable. Your Reverence's mind is beyond the understanding of a mere layman, and I have no intention of forcing myself on you as a donor offering support. But seeing that your Reverence finds charity objectionable, I have devised a way by which I can support you for the rest of your life without your having to be burdened in any way by my patronage. May I explain?"

The Master replied, "How can there be any such thing? It hardly seems likely!"

Suminokura said, "We laypeople practice what's known as keeping accounts. My own family business supports a large number of people, both high and low. But since everyone is good at keeping accounts, we can continue from generation to generation without diminishing the family's wealth. As a result, I've become expert at managing household finances. If you're agreeable, I could explain."

The Master said, "All right, explain to me then: What sort of way is there for you to support me without my accepting your patronage?"

Suminokura said, "As you see, my family supports a large number of people, both high and low. Consequently, the amount of rice we cook in the morning and evening is huge.[123] It's impossible to prepare exactly the right amount for the number of people we have to feed. And when we are even a little bit short, it causes problems for those who come to

Expounding Zen to a Patron
In the capital there lives a good patron
Cherishing virtue he constantly reveres the Master
Specially burning rare aloes wood incense, he seeks the Master's precious words
Instead the Master stares at the ceiling and muddies the waters
The poison dragon dashes forward impetuously—who can touch it?
The drunken elephant charges fiercely about and no one can restrain it
So the Master's wisdom penetrates the ten directions
And Mara[p] and Buddha alike are revealed as no more than illusions clouding our eyes

eat. The result is that we usually end up making a great deal more rice than we actually need. Even if we distribute what remains to the poor, very often we still have some left. We can't just throw the precious three grains[124] into the river or canal.[125] And even the dogs, horses, mice, and cats all leave food over, so there's a lot to throw away.

"It occurred to me that if you were to make vinegar with all the rice we throw out, in the course of a year you could produce several caskfuls, and with the proceeds from selling the vinegar, you could regularly provide for yourself. Even if certain details may seem to suggest otherwise, essentially you would have no patron, so it couldn't be considered patronage. And since this [rice] is something that I'd just be dumping into the river or canal, how can you consider it to be charity?

"If this meets with your Reverence's approval, by good fortune an old employee of mine, the vinegar maker Mosuke,[126] is living in Takagamine in Kitayama.[127] The house next door to him is mine, as well, so please make it your home, use my old servant, and have him sell the vinegar. That way, it seems to me, you'll be providing for yourself regularly and there won't be any question of charity at all. This servant is an old family retainer, someone I'm committed to support for as long as he lives, so you needn't fear you'll be burdening yourself [with any charity from me]."

Suminokura having thus described his plan in detail, the Master declared: "That really is an interesting idea! I'm growing older and older, and it's hard for me to get around, so it's probably time to settle down. If that's what you suggest, I'll do it."

From then on, the Master lived in Takagamine, employing the old servant and selling vinegar. Sometimes he called himself Vinegar Maker Tsūnen (Wish Fulfilled) and sometimes Vinegar Maker Dōzen (Perfecting the Way).[128]

[In this manner,] the Master lived on for seven or eight years without any illness whatever. On the nineteenth day of the ninth month of the third year of Tenna (1683), he passed away peacefully seated in meditation. By his side, he left a final verse inscribed in his own hand:

> More than seventy years, how happy I've been!
> What are they good for, these piss-reeking bones?
> What about the place where one truly returns?
> On Takagamine the moon shines bright, the breeze is fresh

Passing Away Seated in Meditation
Throughout his life the practice of meditation has been the
    realm of cosmic play
Now that the end has come, why should he be any different
    from usual?
The blades of grass draw in the night air, turning it gradually to
    dew
The rocks reflect the light of the rising sun, speeding the
    departing frost
Like the tortoise dragging its tail to erase its tracks, the clouds
    drift past, quiet and solitary
The stream with its burbling waters hurries along
After entering nirvana the Master reveals the excellent physical
    signs of a buddha
Never has he bothered trying to leave his mark upon the empty
    sky

The old servant rushed to report the Master's passing to Suminokura, who promptly dispatched a messenger to inform Chiden and Chinshū. Arriving together from Bukkokuji, they received the Master's remains. Kōsen offered incense and conducted the funeral.

The Master's grave[129] still remains on the grounds of Bukkokuji. I myself visited it and paid my respects. The inscription reads, "Stupa of the Venerable Monk Unkei [Tō]sui."

● ● ●

At age twenty-one, I had the opportunity to meet Zen Master Shingaku Echū of the Edo Saizen'an[130] and to hear his Dharma instruction.

Master Echū was at that time about seventy years of age.

Echū happened to mention Master Tōsui, remarking, "His final verse says 'over seventy years,' but it's surely more like over eighty! At the time I was a novice, it seemed to me he was already well advanced in years. That's why I feel he must have been over eighty."

Master Echū was a disciple of Igan and a Dharma brother of Tōsui's.

● ● ●

The Master, in the manner of a free-spirited sage, appeared and vanished without constraint for over thirty years. So for this period, there is no way anyone can know the details of where he was at any particular time. I have therefore limited myself to setting down in random fashion such facts as I have garnered from others with respect to particular times and places.

● ● ●

Reverently recorded on the nineteenth day of the ninth month of the second year of Kan'en (1749).

● ● ●

Woodblocks in the possession of the Koyudani Unryūzan Shōtan Zen Temple. Winter of the fifth year of Meiwa (1768).

The Pagoda at Bukkokuji
Grand indeed is the precious stupa at Bukkokuji
Its like not to be found south of the Hsiang or north of the T'an[q]
The patterns of moss are freshly spread over the earth
The melody of the wind in the pines rises as of old to the heavens
The mourners prostrate themselves, their heads striking the ground till blood soaks the stone
They recite dharani and light incense, their tears mingling with the rising smoke
Seen for the first time in Japan, a true freewheeling sage
One who can readily stand side by side with the likes of Han-shan and Shih-te![r]

Preface to the Life of Master Tōsui
(*Tōsui oshō densan jō*)

In the Buddha's time, monks simply begged, and thus passed their days. That is why there was no cooking in the monasteries. In later ages, however, monks' capacities declined and the Dharma decayed. Yet there were still Hyakujō's no eating,[131] Jōshū's no cooking,[132] Fuyō's rice broth,[133] and the [founder of] Eiheiji's tradition of austerity.[134] There is nothing odd in such things. These masters did not waste their time, but sincerely revered the ways of the past, wholly devoted to mastering the three studies.[135]

In our own corrupt period, this is hardly the case. Monks covet rich storehouses of rice and millet, devouring the nation's wealth, merely scheming to live at ease with servants to carry them in litters and wearing robes of embroidered brocade. Examine such people and you will find they neither uphold the precepts, practice meditation, nor cultivate wisdom. Instead they shorten the summer days by playing chess and keep the winter nights from stretching on endlessly by guzzling wine. If eight or nine in ten are like this, how can they conduct themselves like followers of Buddha? It is precisely to prevent such behavior that the Buddha warned about molten copper and red-hot iron balls.[136]

Let us turn to the case of a venerable monk who lived some seventy years ago. His formal name was Unkei, his common name, Tōsui. He was a nineteenth-generation Dharma descendant of [the founder of] Eiheiji. As a youth he was a prodigy. He spent a long time searching for a teacher, and later, by imperial decree, assumed high office at Sōjiji in Noto. In addition, at the request of Lord Kōriki, he served as abbot of Zenrinji in Shimabara in Hizen, where, raising the Dharma banner,[137] he instructed his disciples. Once, at the end of the summer retreat,[138] he suddenly vanished and mingled with the dust of the world. Thereafter, he appeared and disappeared for more than thirty years, testing himself through difficult practices, hard to endure. All this was an expression of his samadhi of play. Later, at Takagamine, on the northern outskirts of the imperial city, he passed away seated in meditation. He ordained two individuals of outstanding ability, who became disciples of the Zen master Kōsen of Bukkokuji and succeeded to Kōsen's Dharma.[139]

Recent histories of monks have included only abbreviated accounts of the Master's biography. Such mendacity is intolerable, slandering as it does the worthies of the past. How can one bear to witness it? Because I had a Dharma relationship with the Master, from childhood I heard of his curious history in my own teacher's daily conversation. I have therefore taken up my brush to record this in Japanese,[140] providing illustrations to which I added my own appreciatory verses, in order to make the account accessible to the public at large. Among those who read this biography and reflect sincerely on themselves so that perspiration beads their brows, if even one in a thousand finds the inspiration to attain enlightenment in the future, my labors will have been amply rewarded.

● ● ●

Fifteenth day of the sixth month of the third year of Kan'en (1750). The monk Menzan Zuihō of the Dharma family personally recorded this preface at the temple guest quarters in Higashiyama in Kyoto.[141]

How I Came to Recount the Life of Master Tōsui

(Tōsui oshō den shojutsu innen)

By Menzan Zuihō

Zen Master Igan Sōtetsu, the late abbot of Sōjiji, was the second-generation abbot of Kōtokuzan Ryūchōin,[142] located in Tsuboi in Kumamoto, Higo Province. This venerable monk was an eighteenth-generation descendant of [the founder of] Eiheiji, and his Dharma lineage is traced from the temple's sixth-generation abbot, Tsūgen Jakurei,[143] as follows: Sekioku Shinryō, Chikuko Shōyu, Kishi Iban, Daian Shueki, Zengan Tōjun, Sokuō Eiman, Tenpo Zonsa, Kihaku Zuihō, Daiyū Sōshun, Ichiō Hōkei, Bun'ō Zengei, Denshi Rinteki, Igan Sōtetsu.[144]

This Igan was a venerable monk of mysterious powers. Once when he was returning from a visit to Kyoto, he stopped to have lunch at the foot of Mount Kokonoe in Bungo.[145] The following day, when he paused for lunch at the Futae Pass in Higo,[146] a wolf, holding something white in its mouth, approached from the opposite direction. As he watched the wolf come closer and closer, right up to his knees, Igan realized it was holding a paper handkerchief and toothbrush he had dropped at Mount Kokonoe the day before. Thinking it miraculous indeed, he gave the wolf the Three Refuges,[147] whereupon it bowed its head and departed. This is why the portrait of the master that was originally at Ryūchōin shows a wolf standing at his side, holding a handkerchief in its mouth. It is said that later, in Sengan's time, the portrait was presented to En'ōji[148] in Hizen at that temple's request.

During his lifetime, the Zen master [Igan] ordained ten disciples: Sengan, Zaiten, Shōun, Tōsui, Nenshitsu, Keichū, Hikizan, Unpo, Echū, and Daiyū.[149] Whenever the Zen Master would ordain a disciple, he would recite each day the entire Lotus Sutra with the words, "So that my disciple so-and-so may enjoy long life, thereby augmenting his study of Dharma." In this way, he chanted the sutra countless thousands of times, transferring the merit to the Three Treasures [and] the nagas and devas.[150] As a result, after the master's death, there was not one of the ten disciples who did not live past the age of seventy. Seven received abbacy at an eminent temple, three did not. Yet these three spread their teachings even more widely than their Dharma brothers who were awarded such abbacies.

As a novice, I had the honor of meeting the two worthies Unpo and Echū. Now I realize that these were both venerable monks of rare wisdom. Sengan held the rank of head monk. He served as Igan's assistant and became the third-generation abbot of Ryūchōin. My own ordination teacher, the late abbot of Eiheiji Master Kohō Ryōun, received ordination from Sengan and served as the fifth-generation abbot of Ryūchōin. At age sixteen I received ordination on the fifth day of the second month, and for the six years until my teacher departed for the east, in the sixteenth year of Genroku (1703) in the second month of my twenty-first year, I served him as personal attendant. In this year, my teacher left Ryūchōin intending to live in obscurity beneath the province's Mount Kinbō.[151] In early spring, he therefore instructed me to carry a message to this effect to Master Gizetsu of Daineiji in Chōshū.[152]

After my return, I reported to my teacher and asked him if I might leave for the east.[153] He told me, "I will shortly be retiring, but if you put off leaving till then it will be too late. Don't wait even one more day! Let me give you a gatha on my retirement:

> Throwing down the great burden, I rest my shoulders
> From here on, the world and I naturally part ways

> I'll grab a hoe and farm the spring mountains
> Looking forward to my old age

He then said with a smile, "In a year or two when I pass away, I'll use this poem again, as my death verse."

I told him, "I can't see any signs of illness. Your Reverence is not even sixty-one.[154] How can you be so sure that you'll pass away in a year or two?"

My teacher only replied, "Think of the founder of Eiheiji,"[155] suggesting that this might be our last meeting. Tearfully, I bid him farewell.

On the evening of New Year's Day of the second year of Kyōhō (1717), I was in the meditation hall of Taishin'in in Sendai in Mutsu[156] when in a dream I saw, in the direction of the western sea, a dragon rise from the ocean to the heavens. On waking, I had an uncanny feeling. At the end of the second month I traveled to Edo, where I received a message from home informing me that my master had passed away on the eighteenth day of the first month. His death verse read:

> Over fifty years discerning dreams in a dream
> Now the dreams are smashed, the phantoms gone
> Reality manifests itself, clear and serene

My teacher was a native of Yanagawa in Chikugo, a nephew of Master Tōsui. At age eleven, Tōsui personally brought him from Yanagawa to Ryūchōin and had him become a disciple of Master Sengan. When he grew older, he traveled on *angya* in the Kantō, and on Master Tōsui's instructions went, like his brother monk Tengan,[157] to [Mount] Ōbaku, where he served for more than ten years as attendant to Master Mokuan. Tengan later became Dharma heir to Dokutan[158] and served as abbot of Jusen'in.[159] My teacher returned to Sengan, dividing his time between Sengan's temple and Zenshōji in Suō.[160] He afterward served as abbot of Ryūchōin.

In my teacher's daily conversation, he would always speak of how from childhood on he owed a great spiritual debt to Master Tōsui. I would often hear him say that he wished to compose a record of Tōsui's life and to make it available to people everywhere, instructing future generations as well about Tōsui's remarkable character. And so, having heard my teacher speak of this from my early years, I have long had it in mind to set down Tōsui's biography as a small repayment—a mote of dust or a droplet of water—of my debt to my teacher, a debt high as a mountain and deep as the ocean. Having been preoccupied with the compilation of more mundane texts, I have had to put off the task till now. But fearing that my worthless life cannot be prolonged till the fiftieth anniversary of my teacher's passing,[161] I have taken up my brush and composed this biography, to express, in place of my late teacher, our spiritual indebtedness to Master Tōsui.

Biographical Addendum
Tōsui's Story

From what we learn of him in the *Tribute*, Tōsui, during his colorful later years, was very much of a loner, someone who went to great lengths to live in anonymity, to leave no traces, his activities and whereabouts often a mystery even to his closest disciples and colleagues. It is the sort of life that readily attracts anecdote and legend but defies biography, at least in the usual sense of a detailed and coherent chronological record. The *Tribute*, as its author Menzan freely admits, reflects many of these problems, and while its contents are presented according to a kind of rough chronology, the text itself consists largely of miscellaneous episodes whose sequential relationship often remains vague. When the *Tribute* does supply figures for the lengths of time Tōsui spent at one place or another, they are frequently imprecise ("seven or eight years," "more than ten years") or, when considered together, simply fail to add up. Even at their most conservative, the periods Menzan assigns for Tōsui's various activities from his transmission in summer 1657 to his death in fall 1683, when combined, leave only two years for his entire life as a beggar and itinerant laborer—including his year at Ikeda and the time in his hut in Kyoto. This is a picture clearly at variance with the overall tenor of Menzan's account—with the nun Chihō's remark that Tōsui spent several years simply living in concealment among the beggars; with the *Tribute*'s description of Tōsui's extensive comings and goings centering on the Kyoto area; and above all with Menzan's own statement in the preface that Tōsui "appeared and disappeared for more than thirty years" after abandoning his temple, Zenrinji, about 1667 or 1668.[1] Even when the *Tribute* indicates specific time spans, then, they are often best viewed in more general terms, as "a number of years" rather than the seven, or eight, or thirty years indicated in the text.

For all its shortcomings as a biography, Menzan's *Tribute*, completed in 1749, remains our principal source for Tōsui's life, supplemented only by the two brief biographical sketches referred to previously: the short biography included in the 1717 *Jūzoku Nichi-iki tōjō shosoden* (shortened title, *Tōjō shosoden*) by the Sōtō priest Zōsan Ryōki and the nearly identical sketch in the 1727 *Nihon Tōjō rentō roku* by the Sōtō priest Ryōnan Shūjo.[2] (As a rule, where Ryōnan's biography of Tōsui simply reproduces Zōsan's, only the latter, earlier work is referred to below.) These three texts are essentially all that remain to testify to Tōsui's distinctive career, and it is only through them that Tōsui's story, such as it is, survives to us. For this reason, these works, and above all the *Tribute*, necessarily form the basis for any discussion of Tōsui's life.

Tōsui was born in Yanagawa,[3] a picturesque castle town on the Chikugo River, in what is today Saga Prefecture and in the Edo period formed part of the province of Chikugo, in Kyushu, the southernmost of Japan's five main islands. Situated not far from the ocean, Yanagawa lay in an agricultural area of rice paddies and canals, the seat of the powerful Tachibana clan, whose leader, Muneshige (1567–1642), had received Chikugo in 1587 as a fief from Toytomi Hideyoshi. Muneshige had fought against the Tokugawa at Sekigahara and, having backed the losing side, saw his domain confiscated and included temporarily in the holdings of a Tokugawa ally, Tanaka Yoshimasa (d. 1609). By 1620, however, Muneshige was back in favor and the Tachibana reinstated at Yanagawa.

The *Tribute* tells us that Tōsui was born into a Yanagawa merchant family and that his parents were devoted followers of the Pure Land sect (Jōdōshū). There is no mention of any brothers or sisters[4] or of Tōsui's lay name as a child. Like much else about Tōsui's early life, uncertainty surrounds even the date of his birth. Menzan provides a precise date for Tōsui's death (the nineteenth day of the ninth month of the third year of Ten'nen [1683]), and in the death verse recorded in the *Tribute*, Tōsui speaks of his "more than seventy years." Menzan adds that Tōsui's younger Dharma brother Shingaku Echū personally assured him that, Tōsui's poem notwithstanding, the Master when he passed away must have been over eighty. Perhaps the most that can be said is that, at his death in 1683, Tōsui was in his seventies or eighties, and hence was born sometime during the Keichō era (1596–1614). This lack of clarity regarding the year of Tōsui's birth, however, makes it impossible to know precisely how old the Master was at any given date.

According to the early biographies, as a child Tōsui appeared to be simple and dull-witted, an impression that, the biographies claim, concealed an underlying mental acuity.[5] Tōsui's ostensible slowness and doltishness may well have contributed to his parents' conviction that their son was unsuited to business; and this, combined with the family's reported piety, probably helped to shape their decision to have the seven-year-old Tōsui become a temple novice. Whether Tōsui at this tender age had shown any inclination to pursue a religious calling is unknown. The *Tribute*'s stories about Tōsui's early childhood all stress his affinity with Buddhism—specifically, his spontaneous attraction to Buddhist images, demonstrated by seizing the Amida statuette from the family shrine and refusing to surrender it in exchange for coins. But these materials have a suspiciously cliched character that contrasts with the vividness of the episodes describing Tōsui's later years, episodes for which Menzan could often draw on eyewitness accounts. Like the "strange" dream of Tōsui's mother that heralds the Master's birth, these childhood stories invoke elements common to Buddhist hagiography and may well have been appended at some point to Tōsui's legend to fill in the blank picture of his early years.

Tōsui entered En'ōji, a Sōtō temple in neighboring Hizen Province whose abbot, Igan Sōtetsu (n.d.), was heir to a teaching line centered in the headquarters temple Sōjiji. It is unclear why, if Tōsui's family were devout Pure Land school followers, they consigned their son to a Sōtō temple, although Igan's spiritual accomplishments and distinguished Zen lineage, both attested to in the *Tribute*'s *Innen* section, conceivably played a role in their choice. Unfortunately, nothing is known of Igan or his teaching apart from what little is recorded in the *Tribute*, and it is therefore impossible to judge the extent of his influence on Tōsui. Nevertheless, Igan's instruction to his disciples on the difficulty of overcoming the twin desires for fame and wealth pointedly anticipates the mature Tōsui's own insistence on a life of extreme obscurity and austerity.

By the time Tōsui reached adolescence, Menzan tells us, his innate intelligence and adroitness had begun to reveal themselves, and he was easily able to best a layman who sought to match wits with him. This scene, too, however, like the descriptions of Tōsui's infancy, betrays a distinct formulaic quality, recalling the often comic tales of the Zen monk Ikkyū's verbal agility, popularized in Tokugawa Japan by the collections known as *Ikkyūbanashi* (Ikkyū tales).[6]

Tōsui's Zen training seems to have begun in earnest from about age fifteen or sixteen. It apparently involved a variety of practices, including intensive periods of chanting, fasting, and seated meditation, and was largely self-directed. Tōsui's sustained, independent efforts elicited admiring attention and earned from Igan the epithet "madman" (*fūtenkan*), a classic backhanded expression of praise for Zen monks and perhaps also Igan's teasing commentary on the extremes to which this diligent novice carried his personal quest for enlightenment.

Tōsui's *angya*, or Zen pilgrimage, begun at age twenty, seems to have been an extension of his fervent pursuit of realization. It is traditional for Zen monks who have advanced in their training to leave their home temple for a period of study with other Zen masters to refine their understanding and practice. During his own years of pilgrimage, Tōsui seems to have encountered many of the leading Zen teachers of the day, although we have no details of his experience with these famous masters or of the impression they made on the zealous young monk.[7] Of the teachers Tōsui met at this time, Menzan cites the Myōshinji masters Daigu, Gudō, and Ungo, the Sōtō priest Shōsan, and the Daitokuji master Takuan, all of whom have been discussed previously. Some notion of the period during which Tōsui traveled on *angya* may be gleaned from the *Tribute*'s statement that he visited Takuan in Edo, where the Daitokuji master lived on and off from 1632 to his death in 1645. As to the content of Tōsui's studies during his pilgrimage years, it is probably safe to assume that they included, along with regular periods of *zazen*, some form of koan practice. When, for example, Tōsui's Sōtō colleague Unzan Gūhaku (d.1702) was traveling on *angya* as a young monk, he studied under Gudō at the master's temple in Edo and was assigned the *mu* koan, which he reportedly worked at faithfully for many years.[8]

While on pilgrimage, Tōsui also spent time at Kichijōji, a well-known Sōtō temple in Edo, and during his stay at another Sōtō temple in the capital rescued a group of memorial tablets being used to fence in the monastery and its vegetable garden. Tōsui, we are told, repaired this sacrilege by erecting a new fence himself, purchasing lumber with alms he solicited daily on the city's streets—the *Tribute*'s first mention of the Master's freelance urban begging activities.

Menzan offers no indication of precisely how long Tōsui's pilgrimage continued. At some point in his travels, however, Tōsui learned that his teacher, Igan, had become abbot of Ryūchōin, a Sōtō temple in what is now Kumamoto City (Kumamoto Prefecture), and which in the Tokugawa period lay in the Kyushu province of Higo, just south of Tōsui's native Chikugo. According to the *Tribute*, Tōsui returned to see Igan and remained with him as attendant for more than ten years.

Although Tōsui's return to Igan presumably marks the close of his years of pilgrimage as such, he does not seem to have abandoned his readiness to search out new and promising Zen teachers, and it was apparently during this period that Tōsui traveled to meet the Ōbaku master Yin-yüan Lung-chih. Tōsui's meeting with Yin-yüan, which the *Tribute* places in Nagasaki, can be dated to some point between the Chinese master's 1654 landing in the port city and his departure for Settsu the following year.[9] Tōsui would have been among the multitude of Japanese Rinzai and Sōtō monks who flocked to Nagasaki to meet Yin-yüan and to observe the regular practice in his assembly. Although no record remains of Tōsui's initial response to Yin-yüan and his Chinese followers, the close relations with the Ōbaku school that Tōsui maintained through much of the remainder of his life suggest that Yin-yüan must have impressed him favorably.

Tōsui was now middle-aged, having spent the years since childhood as a Zen monk and Igan's disciple. He had an extensive experience of temple life and, as a result of his years on *angya*, a broad acquaintance with Japanese Zen, both Sōtō and Rinzai. Returning to Igan after his travels, Tōsui naturally assumed his place as one of his teacher's senior disciples and was appointed head monk (*banjū*) at Daineiji, a Sōtō temple in Chōshū (present-day Yamaguchi Prefecture), a province lying just across the straits from Kyushu, on the southern tip of Japan's main island. Such an appointment, which involved supervision of the monks' hall, was often preliminary to receiving advanced rank within the sect.

On the eleventh day of the seventh month of the third year of Meireki (1657), Tōsui became Igan's Dharma heir in a ceremony that formally marked the culmination of his Zen studies. By proclaiming Tōsui an heir to his Dharma, Igan both sanctioned Tōsui's realization of Zen and acknowledged him as a successor in his teaching line, a line that traced itself back through the generations of teachers to the Sōtō school's founder, Dōgen, and thence to Shakyamuni Buddha.[10] Tōsui was now to become a Sōtō Zen master in his own right, able to assume the abbacies of his line's temples, to take on disciples, and to designate new Dharma heirs as he saw fit. The 1657 transmission from Igan is the earliest fixed date for Tōsui provided by the *Tribute*. While there is no mention of Tōsui's actual age at the time, with what we are told of Tōsui's age at death, it can be safely assumed that by 1657 the Master was well into middle age.[11]

The following year (1658) Tōsui traveled to Sōjiji where, as Igan had done before him,[12] he underwent the ceremony of imperial abbacy. In premodern Japan, certain eminent temples enjoyed the privilege of having their abbacies conferred by imperial decree. In the Zen school these institutions included Daitokuji, Myōshinji, Eiheiji, and Sōjiji, the last having received the honor in 1589. Menzan clearly regarded Tōsui's abbacy at Sōjiji as important: he mentions the event not only in the *Tribute*'s main text but in the work's Preface and *Innen*. It is doubtful, however, that Tōsui remained long at Sōjiji or assumed any administrative or technical duties at the temple. During the Tokugawa period, abbacies at Zen headquarters temples were often perfunctory, largely symbolic affairs. Essentially, recipients like Tōsui received the imprimatur of the main temple of their line, officially confirming their status as authenticated Zen masters. The headquarters temples, for their part, derived enhanced authority and prestige from the arrangement, which not only encouraged organizational cohesion but also provided the temples tangible economic benefits. As part of their investiture, candidates for abbacy might be expected to make a special donation to the temple's upkeep, the necessary funds presumably supplied by their home institution or by wealthy lay patrons.[13] Investiture did not necessarily involve any actual responsibilities at the main temple, and following completion of the ceremony many of the new "abbots" departed promptly. Takuan, for example, left Daitokuji three days after becoming abbot in 1609;[14] and Bankei, when he became Myōshinji abbot in 1672, left immediately after the ceremony to return to his native Harima.[15] In the same way, the *Tribute* indicates that Tōsui did not linger at Sōjiji, but returned directly to Higo to take up his first active position as a master in Igan's line, assuming the abbacy of Jōsuiji (a.r., Seisuiji), a temple in the town of Hisakino (Kumamoto Prefecture). Unfortunately, however, we have no details concerning Tōsui's stay at Jōsuiji and no record of how much time elapsed before Tōsui assumed the next abbacy described in the *Tribute*, that of Hōganji, a Sōtō temple in the city of Osaka.[16]

Osaka in Tōsui's day was a thriving commercial center and port, a teeming metropolis of some 280,000.[17] For reasons the *Tribute* leaves unexplained, Hōganji itself had fallen on hard times and was experiencing difficulty in finding an abbot. One of the patrons knew Tōsui and prevailed upon him to accept the position. Tōsui's attitude toward his new post seems to have been casual in the extreme, and he exasperated the temple's supporters by regularly absenting himself for long periods. Still worse was in store for the Master's long-suffering patrons, and the *Tribute* offers a hilarious account of the crisis Tōsui provokes when an unemployed samurai acquaintance from Higo turns up and is invited by Tōsui to stay at the temple along with his womenfolk and armed retainers. The shogunate was leery of unauthorized groups of heavily armed men being quartered in the towns, and such parties had to be registered promptly with the authorities. When a Buddhist temple was host to such groups, the sect's local representative was personally responsible for alerting the government to the fact. Tōsui, however, with his customary insouciance, fails to notify the temple official. As a result, he soon involves himself and the entire Osaka Sōtō hierarchy in an investigation by the city's outraged samurai magistrate—an imbroglio from which Tōsui extricates himself and his terrified colleagues only by charming the magistrate with his frankness and naiveté.

Tōsui's childlike openness and directness, his complete lack of cunning or pretense, also seem to be the theme of the two episodes in the *Tribute* that directly precede Tōsui's encounter with the Osaka magistrate. These are the accounts of Tōsui's comic attempt to feed his famished guests, Kōrin and Daiyū, from the contents of his meager larder and of Tōsui's blithely strewing manure over the Ryūchōin vegetable plot during the visiting Zen teacher Tetsugen's lecture. As noted previously, Tetsugen is known to have delivered lectures in northern Kyushu during the early 1660s,[18] but precisely what period of Tōsui's career the first of these anecdotes describes is left vague, and Menzan's purpose in including it here seems to be thematic rather than chronological, namely, as further evidence of the Master's simple and straightforward character.

The *Tribute* notes that while abbot at Hōganji, Tōsui would go out with his attendants to solicit alms, personally distributing whatever he received to the city's beggars and their children. Even the local merchants were said to be impressed and would donate generously to Tōsui on his rounds. Formal group begging (known as *takuhatsu*, literally, "carrying a [begging] bowl") was a standard practice in Tokugawa Zen temples, and even today lines of begging Zen monks, eyes carefully lowered, can be seen snaking through the streets of Japanese cities and towns. Generally, the alms that monks receive in this way contribute to the support of their temple and its occupants. By contrast, Tōsui's begging is here intended exclusively to assist the city's poor and their families, and expresses for Menzan the compassion that naturally springs from Tōsui's utter lack of selfish attachment. This sense of selflessness is also the basis of a poem from Tōsui's Hōganji period, composed by the Master at the request of a visiting Sōtō priest named Ejō. The poem emphasizes the importance of complete "letting go," and like the account of feeding the Osaka beggars, which directly follows, contributes to Menzan's picture of Tōsui as wholly free and unencumbered, someone who gives away even the alms he receives—a theme that, like Tōsui's association with the beggars, reappears later in the text.

Tōsui left Hōganji after serving as abbot for more than two years, and at some point thereafter returned to his native Yanagawa. Evidently word of the Master's virtue had filtered back to his home district, and the Yanagawa Buddhist community asked Tōsui to stay and address them. In memory of his parents, now deceased, Tōsui lectured on the Final Teachings Sutra, a brief, popular text that purports to be the Buddha's final instructions to his disciples.[19] The crowds who came to listen made large donations, but we are told that Tōsui refused to accept any of the offerings for himself and merely passed them on to the host temple. Tōsui was urged to settle permanently in Yanagawa, but declined, and instead took up temporary residence at Seiunji, a temple in the castle town of Shimabara in neighboring Hizen Province. Here he attracted the attention of the domain's daimyo, Kōriki Takanaga (1605–1676), who offered Tōsui abbacy of another Shimabara Sōtō temple, Zenrinji.[20]

Lord Kōriki, the temple's leading supporter, had a fairly sinister reputation. He inherited the Shimabara fief in 1655 on the death of his father, Tadafusa (1583–1655), who had received the domain following the shogunate's suppression of the Shimabara rebellion, a 1637 insurgency by aggrieved samurai, peasants, and Christian adherents. One of the causes of the insurrection had been the oppressive administration of the ruling daimyo, Matsukura Shigeharu (d. 1638), who was subsequently deprived of his domains by the shogunate, banished, and forced to commit seppuku. Unfortunately, Takanaga's own administration in Shimabara was characterized by a similar pattern of abuse, affecting both samurai and commoners. A 1662 memorial of protest by Takanaga's own chief retainer charged that rapacious taxes had reduced the farmers to destitution and noted that any complaints met with severe punishment. In 1667 the local people appealed to a government circuit inspector, and the following year an official investigation led to Takanaga's removal from office and exile to Sendai (Miyagi Prefecture), in northern Japan, where he remained under house arrest until his death in 1676.[21]

Although nothing is mentioned of it in the *Tribute*, the story of Takanaga's tyranny and eventual downfall must have been well known in Menzan's day; it is chronicled in *Hankanbu*, a history of daimyo of the early Tokugawa period by the Confucian scholar-official Arai Hakuseki (1657–1725).[22] There is no suggestion in the *Tribute* of any friction in Tōsui's own relations with the notorious daimyo. Indeed, Takanaga expresses admiration on learning that Tōsui's first act as abbot is to uproot his predecessor's prize peonies and replace them with humble local tea plants. Only the *Tōjō shosoden* hints at difficulties with Takanaga, recording that "the Master remonstrated with the temple's patron [i.e., Lord Kōriki], but without success. He then left and settled in Kawajiri in Higo."[23] The *Nihon Tōjō rentō roku* remarks merely that Tōsui left because the temple "did not suit him." It is possible that the *Shosoden*'s claim that Tōsui "remonstrated" with the daimyo is simply the repetition of a legend elaborated retrospectively to enhance the Master's hagiography, since Takanaga was known as an oppressive ruler and was just the sort of shameless figure an eminent priest would be expected to upbraid.

The *Tribute* states that Tōsui remained at Zenrinji approximately five years and describes a winter meditation retreat the Master held at the temple. Two such retreats (*kessei* or *ango*), each lasting ninety days, are traditionally observed in Zen monasteries, the first (*geango*) during the spring and summer months, the second (*tōango*) stretching from fall to midwinter and customarily concluding on the morning of the sixteenth day of the new year. It is common for the teacher leading the retreat to lecture on a selected Zen text, and Tōsui, we are told, chose *Tribute to the Authentic School of the Five Houses*,[24] a Yuan-dynasty collection of Ch'an monk biographies that was popular in Tokugawa-period Zen temples.

Tōsui's growing fame as a teacher is attested by the large number of monks attending the winter retreat, 120 according to the *Tribute*, and by the presence of several distinguished Zen masters, including Gyōgan Unpo, Tōsui's Dharma brother under Igan, and Tōsui's colleagues Kengan and Unzan Gūhaku.[25] Kengan is almost certainly the Rinzai Zen master Kengan Zen'etsu (1623–1701),[26] abbot of Tafukuji, a Myōshinji-line temple in the town of Usuki (Ōita Prefecture), on Kyushu's northwest coast. A well-known Zen teacher in his day, Kengan had studied under the Myōshinji's Gudō Tōshoku as well as with the Ming master Tao-che Chao-yüan. Unzan, who has been referred to previously, was an heir of the Sōtō master Gesshū Sokō. A Kyushu native, from Higo, Unzan, like Tōsui, had trained under a variety of Rinzai masters before succeeding to his Sōtō teacher's Dharma. These included Tōsui's own erstwhile teachers Gudō, Daigu, and Ungo, as well as Kengan and Tao-che, the last of whom Unzan served in Nagasaki for a time as attendant.[27]

At the close of the winter retreat, the departing monks arrived at the abbot's quarters to bid farewell to Tōsui. But the Master had vanished, taking with him his traveling gear and leaving behind only a poem announcing that he had decamped for parts unknown stuck to the wall.[28] The distraught assembly immediately attempted to overtake Tōsui, but without success. Takanaga, too, was greatly disturbed by the news of Tōsui's disappearance and ordered all ferry crossings suspended, no doubt anticipating that Tōsui might avail himself of the various water routes that connected Shimabara with the rest of Kyushu, including Tōsui's home province of Chikugo. However, Takanaga, too, failed to find the Master, who had indeed returned to his native Yanagawa, visiting his parents' graves before setting off for the main Japanese island, Honshu. Here he traveled overland through the southwestern provinces known as Chūgoku, probably arriving at one of the busy port cities on the Inland Sea. From there he boarded a boat to Osaka, only some forty miles from the Kyoto area, which seems to have been his final destination.

The *Tribute* offers no explanation for Tōsui's sudden departure from Zenrinji other than to note that it marked the "beginning of his life among the ordinary people of the world," a period, the preface says, during which the Master "appeared and disappeared for more than thirty years"—a reference to Tōsui's later experiences as a beggar and itinerant laborer. All this, the preface adds, was Tōsui's manifestation of the "samadhi of play" (*yūgyōzammai;* Skt. *lila*), a Buddhist term for the realized individual's joyous oneness with the free-flowing activity of the universe. Menzan thus indicates that Tōsui's abandoning of his position as a Sōtō abbot, at the very height of his professional success, had a direct spiritual connection with his subsequent life as a nameless urban drifter. By leaving Zenrinji, the *Tribute*'s account suggests, Tōsui signaled his break with the life of a career priest in the Sōtō school, summarily divesting himself of his prestige as a Zen master, his temple, his powerful patron, and his adoring disciples—a dramatic letting go that recalls the repeated injunction in Tōsui's poem to Ejō at the Osaka Hōganji ("Let your wisdom and meditation be clearly illuminating/ And then and there you'll let things go/ Let go! Let go even of letting go/ Then what will be left to let go of?"[29]).

The *Tribute* next describes how, immediately after Tōsui's disappearance from Zenrinji, he is followed to Kyoto by his close disciples Chinshū (d. 1706) and Chiden (d. 1709), who had apparently surmised their teacher's destination. Each day, in search of the Master, the two novices split up to scour the city. Summer passes, and finally in mid-autumn Chinshū discovers Tōsui, ragged and unkempt, living among a band of beggars. After Chinshū repeatedly asks to be allowed to accompany him, the Master reluctantly agrees. But the sensitive young monk, as Tōsui predicts, soon recoils before the demands of the beggar's life and, along with his brother disciple, is sent packing by Tōsui to the Ōbaku teacher Kao-ch'üan Hsing-tung at Kao-ch'üan's temple, Bukkokuji, in Kyoto's Fushimi district.

Menzan notes that he heard this story from his teacher Ryōun, who, in turn, had been told it by Chinshū himself. As Tanaka Shigeru has observed, however, the account errs in placing the disciples' search immediately after Tōsui's departure from Zenrinji, a sequence of events that, while dramatically effective, is historically inconsistent with other details Menzan provides.[30] Given the facts as set forth in the *Tribute*, Tōsui's exit from Takanaga's domain must have occurred at some time before the daimyo's exile to Sendai in early 1668; yet Bukkokuji, the temple to which Tōsui dispatches his two heartbroken disciples after they follow him to Kyoto, was not founded till some ten years later, in 1678. Such errors, according to Tanaka, are part of a larger problem with this section of the text, which jumps from Tōsui's departure from Zenrinji to his life as a beggar and hired laborer, ignoring a critical period that separates these phases of the Master's career. Tanaka argues convincingly that this gap in Menzan's chronology represents the years Tōsui spent at Manpukuji, the Ōbaku temple at Uji, near Kyoto, which from 1661 served as the headquarters of Yin-yüan and his followers.

Tōsui, it will be recalled, had met Yin-yüan, Manpukuji's founder, in Nagasaki, and the *Tribute* adds that Tōsui later spent "seven or eight years" at the temple, making the acquaintance of the immigrant Chinese teachers Mu-an Hsing-t'ao and Kao-ch'üan.[31] It is not unreasonable to infer that Tōsui's earlier visit to Yin-yüan must have made a lasting impression and that like other priests dissatisfied with the current state of Japanese Zen, Tōsui took up residence at Manpukuji to study the recently imported teaching of the Ming masters at first hand.

The *Tribute* provides no details of Tōsui's experience at Ōbakusan (a.r., Ōbakuzan), "Mount Ōbaku," as Manpukuji was generally known. Tōsui may have renewed his studies with Yin-yüan, though the Chinese teacher was now elderly and had retired as abbot in 1664, succeeded by his heir Mu-an. But perhaps the most important ties Tōsui forged during his years at the temple were with the Ōbaku master Kao-ch'üan. Kao-ch'üan, who would become Manpukuji's fifth abbot, was among the leading figures in the Ōbaku school.[32] Born in Fukien, he entered the monastery as a child and served as Yin-yüan's attendant at Wan-fu ssu, ultimately becoming heir to Yin-yüan's successor Hui-men Ju-p'ei (1615–1664). In 1661, at Hui-men's urging, Kao-ch'üan traveled to Japan to visit Yin-yüan, landing in Nagasaki with four brother monks. Yin-yüan persuaded the younger teacher to remain in Japan, where Kao-ch'üan assisted him and was instrumental in revising *Ōbaku shingi*, Manpukuji's influential monastic code. In 1678, Kao-ch'üan was invited to become founder of Bukkokuji, a restored temple in Fushimi, a short distance north of Manpukuji, in present-day Kyoto.[33] Like other eminent Zen teachers of the period, Kao-ch'üan was patronized by the retired emperor Gomizuno'o, with whom he carried on an extensive correspondence and for whom he is said to have composed his work *Fuso Sōhōden*, a collection of Japanese monk biographies. Kao-ch'üan also attracted various daimyo followers, and in 1695 he traveled to Kyoto, where he had an audience with the shogun Tsunayoshi (1646–1709) and delivered a Dharma talk in the shogun's castle. Kao-ch'üan died in the tenth month of that year, and was posthumously awarded the title of National Teacher (*kokushi*).[34]

It is unclear whether during Tōsui's sojourn at Manpukuji he actually studied Zen under Kao-ch'üan, Mu-an, or other Ming priests in the assembly or whether their relationship was primarily collegial. In any event, Tōsui's stay at the Ōbaku temple seems to mark the end of his ties with the Sōtō establishment. It is true that, despite his extended residence at Manpukuji, Tōsui never changed schools, never became an Ōbaku priest or a formal disciple of Yin-yüan, Mu-an, or Kao-ch'üan. Yet henceforth an unspoken shift in the Master's allegiance becomes apparent. Even after he abandons Manpukuji, Tōsui's preference for Ōbaku Zen is unmistakable, and when offering guidance to young Sōtō monks in the *Tribute*, he invariably directs them to Ōbaku rather than Sōtō monasteries. Tōsui orders his faithful disciples Chinshū and Chiden to leave him and follow Kao-ch'üan, whose heirs in the Ōbaku school both ultimately become. And Tōsui sends his own nephew, the Sōtō priest Kōhō, to Manpukuji, where Kōhō serves ten years as Mu-an's attendant before returning to the Sōtō school and his original teacher, Tōsui's Dharma brother Sengan.[35] As noted previously, Tōsui was even buried at Kao-ch'üan's temple, Bukkokuji, with the Chinese master presiding at his funeral service. Unfortunately, the *Tribute* offers no hint of the specific forces that drew Tōsui to Manpukuji and the Ōbaku teachers and away from his roots in the Sōtō school. Again, one can only speculate that Tōsui shared the malaise that led others of his brethren in the Rinzai and Sōtō temples to forsake their own institutions for Mount Ōbaku and what they saw as the promise of a fresh start for Japanese Zen.

It is not known how long Tōsui remained at Manpukuji, and the *Tribute*'s figure of seven to eight years is, as usual, imprecise at best. What seems clear is that, in the end, Ōbaku Zen, too, was unable to fully satisfy him. As he had previously left behind the Sōtō school and the privileged position of a Buddhist abbot, Tōsui now abandoned temple life altogether, exchanging his priest's robes for a beggar's ragged cloak and straw sleeping mat. Letting his hair and whiskers grow and concealing his identity as a Zen master, Tōsui virtually disappeared into the landscape, drifting for years among Japan's urban poor, his whereabouts a mystery even to his closest colleagues and disciples. Rarely staying for long in any one place and pushing on as soon as he was recognized, Tōsui was often on the move, changing his name as readily as he changed his appearance and means of support. He lived for the most part hand to mouth, begging his way or simply taking up whatever menial jobs offered themselves.

The Master by this time was already an old man, in his mid-sixties or seventies. But he seems to have been amply repaid for the physical hardships of his new existence by an exhilarating sense of freedom, of liberation from institutions, patrons, and nettlesome followers, from the insidious desires for fame and fortune of which his teacher had long ago warned. This feeling of exultation and release is conveyed by the poem Chinshū overhears Tōsui reciting to himself after the Master spreads his mat for the night at a lonely forest shrine:

> This is what my life is like
> This is what it's like, broad and free
> A worn-out robe, a broken bowl
>   —how peaceful and calm!
> When hungry, I eat, when thirsty, I drink
> That's all I know
> I've got nothing to do with the world's "right and wrong"[36]

By contrast, the *Tōjō shosoden* records an anecdote suggesting that Tōsui's life of privation and toil represented a practice of deliberate self-mortification.

> There was yet another person who knew the Master. He happened to meet Tōsui and puzzled by his appearance, asked him, "Your Reverence, why have you turned into a slave?"
> The Master said, "These days, monks only talk with their mouths about the body being like a worn-out broom. But they don't know what this really means. So I'm getting rid of that body myself and trying to find out!"[37]

However, this dialogue has about it a certain artificiality, and it may simply be the priest-anthologist's attempt to supply a seemly rationale for the elderly Tōsui's unorthodox behavior.

The episodes from this period recorded in the *Tribute* appear to have been chosen deliberately to dramatize Tōsui's reputation as a stubborn, if charming, loner and maverick. Many of the vignettes share a similar format, with various figures from Tōsui's past as a Zen abbot shocked to discover the Master, gray and disheveled, eking out a bare existence at the fringes of society and Tōsui, in turn, rejecting offers of assistance and strenuously avoiding anything more than fleeting contact with former friends and followers.

As with other phases of Tōsui's career, it is not known precisely when his life of begging and odd jobs began or ended, or even roughly how long it continued. The figure of thirty years for this period in Menzan's preface is plainly an exaggeration; the actual account in the *Tribute*'s text mentions altogether some five-plus years,[38] and one modern biographer speculates that the entire period lasted not more than ten years.[39] Despite such uncertainties, the *Tribute* records Tōsui's activities during this time in what purports to be a kind of chronological record, although the erratic nature of Tōsui's comings and goings and the random, anecdotal character of much of Menzan's material make such an approach precarious at best.

With his novice disciple Chinshū in tow, Tōsui is described as begging and traveling east of Kyoto in the province of Ōmi (Shiga Prefecture), following an itinerary that takes him from the vicinity of Lake Biwa to the castle town of Ōtsu, the province's capital. After sending away Chinshū, Tōsui continues west to Ise (Mie Prefecture), where he joins the beggars congregated at the famous Shinto shrine. A popular pilgrimage site, Ise in Tōsui's period was a natural magnet for beggars, fortunetellers, and others who lived off the crowds of visitors who thronged the shrine precincts. Tōsui's wanderings also took him as far as Nagoya (Aichi Prefecture), capital of Owari Province and, like Ise, a distance of some seventy miles from Kyoto. Generally speaking, however, the cities and towns mentioned in this portion of the *Tribute* indicate that Tōsui rarely ventured beyond a twenty-five-mile radius from Kyoto,[40] which seems to have served him as a kind of base.

In the course of his travels, in addition to begging, Tōsui reportedly took on a variety of menial jobs. At Nara, the *Tribute* records, Tōsui worked as a sweeper at the Great Buddha statue (*daibutsu*); at Kusatsu, a post town in what is now Shiga Prefecture, he was employed as a servant. For a time he was involved in transport, working as a palanquin (*kago*) carrier and associating with pack-horse drivers in Kyoto's Awadaguchi, a neighborhood where the Tōkaidō, the highway linking Kyoto and Edo, entered the city. (Although from the Heian period wheeled oxcarts had been employed to carry courtiers, wheeled vehicles were not generally used in Tōsui's Japan. Goods were moved overland by pack horse, while travelers of means rode on horseback or were carried in palanquins, whose appointments, or lack thereof, varied with the passenger's station and ability to pay.)

Tōsui's connections with the lower rungs of the transportation industry may have led to his next line of work described in the *Tribute*, manufacturing straw horseshoes in the town of Ōtsu. Like *zōri*, the traditional Japanese sandals, horseshoes in premodern Japan were woven from straw. Tōsui probably produced both horseshoes and sandals,[41] servicing *kago* carriers along with grooms, pack-horse drivers, and their animals. As a major station on the Tōkaidō and thus the site of considerable horse traffic, Ōtsu must have provided ample business opportunities for Tōsui. The town even housed a shrine dedicated to protecting horses from epidemics and popular for talismans that, it was claimed, exorcised sickness-producing demons that afflicted the animals.[42]

Tōsui, we are told, began by carrying large loads of his horseshoes to hawk on the streets; but in the course of his two years at Ōtsu, he developed such a reputation for his wares that he was able to set up shop in a small lean-to where he could eat and sleep and receive customers' orders. It is apparently during this earlier stage of production that Tōsui crosses paths with the palanquin of his Dharma brother Unpo, en route to Edo with his patron, the daimyo of Kumamoto. Stopping before a tea stall, Unpo is astonished to recognize Tōsui peddling straw horseshoes to the pack-horse drivers, who boisterously shout out their orders. Overjoyed to behold his brother disciple again, Unpo leaps from his palanquin and hails the Master, asking the reason for his bedraggled appearance. Tōsui explains brusquely that he is now a beggar and therefore dresses like one (this despite his ostensibly brisk trade). He then strides off, after pointedly reminding Unpo of the vast differences in status and responsibility that now separate them. The encounter between the ragged horseshoe maker and the distinguished abbot in the daimyo's train does not, however, go unnoticed. Tōsui is soon besieged by rich merchants and others who suspect his true identity, and to escape their unwanted attentions, he vanishes from Ōtsu in a matter of days.[43]

We next encounter Tōsui in Kyoto, where he is the object of a fervent search by his disciple the nun Chihō, who has traveled all the way from her home in Shimabara in hope of finding the Master. The *Tōjō shosoden* states that while in Kyoto, Tōsui worked as a hired laborer, hauling firewood on his back and begging for food in the streets, and the only clue Chihō has to guide her in her search is the information that the Master has spent the past few years living anonymously among the city's beggars. Armed with this intelligence and accompanied by a pair of servants, Chihō hunts for Tōsui over some three months and eventually manages to surprise the Master as he nurses an ailing leper under the Gojō Bridge. Chihō, the mother of a wealthy merchant, is pained to find her old teacher living as a homeless beggar and implores Tōsui to let her purchase and provision a retreat for him in the city's Higashiyama district. True to form, Tōsui abruptly dismisses Chihō and rejects outright her offer to improve his living conditions. The Master only agrees to accept the money and new bed things Chihō has brought for him when she promises to allow him to dispose of her offerings in any way he sees fit. Tōsui promptly bestows the bed things on the leper and has the money distributed among the other beggars under the bridge, putting aside a few coins to carry to another ailing vagrant before setting off on his way.

This story, whose colorful details Menzan received from the Shimabara priest Rōin Chōgen, who had heard them recounted by Chihō herself, reveals something of Tōsui's peculiar attitude toward charity. Tōsui's response to Chihō's generosity shows he was not opposed to alms or charity as such—he did, after all, resort periodically to begging. But he would only accept assistance that was wholly unconditional, without strings, that left him beholden to no one, free to live where and how he wished. Moreover, what offerings Tōsui did receive in this manner he as often as not passed on to others in need. In this, Tōsui contrasts with his Dharma brother Unpo, whose position and material support are virtually guaranteed by a powerful patron, a patron for whom, Tōsui ironically reminds him, Unpo is "virtually a retainer."

As if to emphasize this contrast, Tōsui's encounter with the nun Chihō is bracketed in the *Tribute* by accounts of the Master's meetings with Unpo. Unpo's second, and final, meeting with Tōsui occurs in Arima, where Unpo has stopped on his way back from Edo to enjoy the famed therapeutic hot springs. Once again, Unpo runs into Tōsui on the street. This time, however, the Master is not bearing horseshoes but a shoulder pole from which are suspended a jug of soy sauce and several bunches of leeks. Tōsui explains that he has been suffering from back pain (a condition the load on his aged shoulders is hardly likely to improve) and, hoping to find relief at the hot springs, came to Arima, where he hired on as a servant. Thus far, Tōsui admits, his work has left him no time for the baths, and he promptly invites himself to share Unpo's accommodations, a suggestion with which Unpo happily falls in. Without a moment's hesitation, Tōsui drops his goods and sets off with Unpo, asserting with characteristic simplicity that his things will be there waiting for him whenever he returns.

After ten days relaxing together at the hot springs, Unpo elicits from the normally reticent Tōsui some interesting details concerning the Master's life of late. His current alias, Tōsui reveals, is Yūan, "Possessed of Peace," a play on the famous phrase from the Lotus Sutra, *"sangai muan,"* "In the three worlds there is no peace." According to Buddhism, the three worlds of desire, form, and formlessness constitute collectively the realm of delusion, of sentient existence, the locus of human suffering and ignorance, which the sutra compares to a burning house. In a comic reversal, Tōsui's assumed name suggests that he has discovered genuine serenity and joy in fleeing the regulated safety of the temple to live amid the flames of the secular world.

Tōsui also informs Unpo that he had spent the previous year in Kyoto, staying in a hut in Higashiyama to which he expects to return after effecting his cure. (Tōsui, it will be recalled, had declined to allow the nun Chihō to purchase for him precisely such a retreat in Higashiyama.) He even composes an impromptu poem inviting Unpo to visit him at his home in the imperial capital. However, the next day, when Unpo looks for Tōsui at the baths, the Master is nowhere to be found, presumably having left Arima for Kyoto without even a word to his indulgent host.

From roughly the period of his stay at the hot springs, the *Tribute* reports, Tōsui began to succumb to the frailties of old age. Often ill and in pain, he found it increasingly difficult to travel or to perform manual labor. Nor could Tōsui allow himself simply to stay put. Even at his retreat in Higashiyama he was dogged by the frequent and importunate visitors who invariably found him out wherever he settled. Once more, Tōsui fled Kyoto, this time for the town of Ikeda, some twenty-five miles to the west, in Settsu, today the Osaka municipal district.

Ikeda is the setting for the last of Tōsui's chance encounters in the *Tribute*, the meeting with his Sōtō colleague Unzan Gūhaku. Unzan, abbot of a temple in Izumi Province, just south of Settsu, hears that Tōsui is in Ikeda and sets out to visit him, accompanied by a disciple and taking as gifts a new robe and some cash. When Unzan arrives at Tōsui's shack, he finds the Master gone, and a neighbor advises him that Tōsui is probably out begging and should return by noon. The winter day is severely cold, and Unzan and his disciple decide to wait indoors. Some hours later, Tōsui appears, clad in a tattered robe, his hair long, his face unshaven. Far from appreciating the time and trouble his old friend has taken to call on him, Tōsui only seems irritated, and, ignoring his guests, proceeds to prepare and consume his meager midday meal. He declines the money and robe Unzan has carried from Izumi, explaining testily that such alms only complicate his life, as he has to pass them on to other people. Before going, Unzan leaves the items, nonetheless. But Tōsui's message is plain. He has everything he needs in his new life and wants nothing more, not clothes, funds, friendship, or sympathy. However well-meaning their efforts, the most his old acquaintances can do for him is to leave him alone and undisturbed.

An alternate version of Unzan's visit appears in the *Tōjō shosoden*. In this version, set in Kyoto rather than Ikeda, Unzan spots Tōsui at the Gōjō Bridge peddling vegetables from a straw basket. Surreptitiously, Unzan follows Tōsui to his house, where he observes him at a table, sharing his meal with an old woman. Tōsui warmly welcomes Unzan, and together they talk over old times. The mention of the old woman is intriguing, but the text offers no further information, and nothing about such a female companion appears in the *Tribute*. The *Tōjō shosoden*'s editor probably errs, however, in placing the story in Kyoto, as Tōsui's farewell poem to Unzan invites the latter to visit him in his Kyoto retreat.[44]

After spending a year or two in Ikeda, the *Tribute* relates, Tōsui returns to Kyoto and his hut in Higashiyama. During his earlier sojourn in the city, Tōsui had attracted a circle of admirers, and the members of this group now confer on a strategy to have the Master remain permanently in the old capital. Tōsui, meanwhile, comes to the attention of a wealthy local merchant surnamed Suminokura, a lay follower of the Ōbaku priest Kao-ch'üan. Suminokura invites Tōsui to stay at his home and is won over by the Master's straightforward if quizzical responses to questions about Zen and other aspects of Buddhism, thus joining the ranks of those anxious to keep Tōsui in Kyoto.

Now greatly weakened by age, Tōsui is finding it harder to fend for himself, and Suminokura fears what might happen if the Master once again takes to the road. Knowing, however, that Tōsui will never accept assistance that smacks of regular charity or patronage, the merchant formulates a plan to ensure the Master's well-being, a plan carefully tailored to his particular character and needs. In discussion with Tōsui, Suminokura proposes that the Master go into the business of manufacturing and selling rice vinegar, using as his raw material the leftover cooked rice from Suminokura's large household. Since the rice in question will otherwise just be discarded, Suminokura explains, the Master will in no way be beholden to him and by supporting himself can remain independent. In addition, the pious merchant offers Tōsui a house he owns in Takagamine, just north of Kyoto, and with it the services of the old vinegar maker living next door, a pensioned former employee named Mosuke who will handle the actual sale of the vinegar.

Acknowledging that he has grown too frail to continue a life of wandering, begging, and physical labor, Tōsui at last agrees to Suminokura's offer. At heart, of course, the offer is little more than a well-meaning deception. Despite Suminokura's elaborate disclaimers, readers of the *Tribute* can safely infer that the wealthy merchant stands ready in private to make up any shortfalls in Tōsui's supply of leftover rice.

Tōsui's final years, the *Tribute* records, were spent in Takagamine selling vinegar under the adopted Buddhist names Vinegar Maker Tsūnen (Wish Fulfilled) and Vinegar Maker Dōsen (Perfecting the Way). The *Tribute* claims that this phase of Tōsui's career lasted altogether some seven or eight years, but given the work's admitted vagueness about chronology, there is no way to confirm its figure for this period, which may have occupied no more than the last year or two of Tōsui's life.[45]

Tōsui's death is said to have occurred on the nineteenth day of the ninth month in year three of the Tenna era (1683), a date first recorded by the *Nihon Tōjō rentō roku*, and the same day and month for which Menzan has inscribed the text of the *Tribute*, his memorial to Tōsui. The Master died quietly, the *Tribute* reports, seated in meditation posture, leaving by his side a final poem:

> More than seventy years, how happy I've been!
> What are they good for, these piss-reeking bones?

What about the place where one truly returns?
On Takagamine the moon shines bright, the breeze is fresh.[46]

The old vinegar maker Mosuke hastened to inform Suminokura of Tōsui's death, and the merchant immediately sent word to Tōsui's former disciples Chinshū and Chiden at Bukkokuji. The two priests then conveyed the Master's remains to the temple, where Kao-ch'üan held a funeral service. Tōsui's ashes were interred in an ovoid stone pagoda, or *nuhōtō*, bearing the inscription "Stupa of the Venerable Monk Unkei [Tō]sui."[47]

The *Tribute*'s description of his funeral and grave inscription make plain that Tōsui was buried and memorialized as a Zen monk. For all his unconventional ways and obvious loathing for the constraints of monastic institutions, Tōsui never formally renounced the priesthood. Nevertheless, once having embarked on his life outside the temples, he seems to have strenuously avoided all but the most temporary contact with other Buddhist priests, and particularly with his own former colleagues and disciples. Judging from the account in the *Tribute*, Tōsui's later years were spent almost exclusively among commoners, from beggars, sweepers, and pack-horse drivers to tradespeople and merchants such as Suminokura.

Tōsui did not forsake the temple and his duties as teacher and abbot for the serenity of a remote rural retreat, but for the bustle and clamor of the new urban Japan. The *Tribute* tells us that he lived and worked side by side with the humblest city dwellers, ostensibly indistinguishable from his secular neighbors. Yet in the towns, as in the temples, Tōsui seems to have remained a loner and outsider, shunning any enduring friendships or ties, very much his own person, a monk in the word's original sense of one who is single and solitary.

Even while in the secular world, Tōsui was apparently indifferent as ever to his own material comfort, giving away whatever surplus he accrued and always prepared to pull up stakes and be off the moment he was recognized. The *Tribute*'s portrait makes the case that Tōsui sought freedom from the "desires for fame and wealth" as avidly outside the monastery as he had within it. In an age with an intense and at times almost obsessive interest in affluence, status, and group affiliation, Tōsui, having risen to the position of a Sōtō abbot, chose to obliterate his past and to live on his own at the margins of Tokugawa society. The Zen master who hired out as a servant, hawked vegetables, and begged in the streets, who ended his days laboring at a vinegar stand, truly seems to have been, as the expression has it, in the world but not of it.

Apart from a handful of informal comments he directs to various students and colleagues, the *Tribute* only hints at Tōsui's own approach to Zen. The work indicates that during his years as a Sōtō master Tōsui lectured on sutras and Zen texts, but it records nothing of the contents of his talks or of the day-to-day instruction he offered his male and female disciples and lay followers. Tōsui's written legacy, meanwhile, consists only of the eight short poems in the *Tribute* and early biographies, two of the poems being comic verse. Menzan himself, as observed before, is presenting Tōsui's Zen not through writings or lectures, but through the Master's life, the stubborn quest for freedom and authenticity whose details are the principal focus of the *Tribute*. Tōsui, as Menzan depicts him, is not so much teaching Zen as living it; and in this sense his life *is* his teaching.

As a Zen master, given what is often meant by that term, some might well consider Tōsui a failure. Traditionally, in Japan, Zen masters have been expected not only to teach and exemplify Zen but also to train enlightened Dharma heirs who can carry on their lineages and become Zen masters themselves. As previously noted, in the Sōtō school during the Tokugawa period, Dharma transmission was to assume particular importance through the efforts of the reformer Manzan Dōhaku, who regarded preservation of Dharma succession in an unbroken line from teacher to disciple as crucial to the survival of Dōgen's Zen. Manzan even went so far as urging Sōtō masters to bestow transmission on unenlightened disciples, if necessary, in order to ensure the continuity of their teaching line.[48]

Tōsui, it is obvious, would not have shared Manzan's convictions. Although he himself received transmission from his teacher Igan, nothing in the *Tribute* indicates that during his years as a Sōtō abbot Tōsui ever bestowed Zen transmission on any of his own disciples or made any effort to continue his teaching line. Instead, he methodically divested himself of his students and of his ties to the Sōtō organization, ordering his young followers Chinshū and Chiden to continue their training under a Chinese teacher of the recently established Ōbaku school. Handing on his Zen by sanctioning favored disciples who could then carry his lineage into future generations in the traditional manner hardly seems in keeping with the solitary and cantankerous personality portrayed by Menzan in the *Tribute*. Once having quit the temple for the city streets, Tōsui may well have lumped such concerns together with the other rejected elements of his former life as obstructions on his chosen path, figments of the world of "fame and wealth."

It is worth recalling that there were other Japanese masters of the day who, like Tōsui, did not produce successors to their teachings. A prime example, noted before, is the Daitokuji master Takuan—the temple's most famous Tokugawa period priest—who, like his medieval predecessor Ikkyū, openly declared that he would not appoint a Dharma heir.[49] Another Zen teacher without a successor was the Ōbaku master Tetsugen Dōkō (1630–1682),[50] who makes a brief appearance in the *Tribute* and is regarded as the most illustrious of the Japanese Ōbaku priests.

While assuredly unique in particular respects, then, Tōsui's story is by no means wholly without parallels in Zen tradition. Similarities between Tōsui and the various celebrated teachers with whom he studied have been described earlier. But one of Tōsui's most obvious counterparts derives not from Japanese but from Chinese Buddhism, the medieval Ch'an monk Pu-tai (J. Hotei, d. 916[?]). One of the quintessential figures of Ch'an legend, Pu-tai, like Tōsui in his later years, is described in his early biographies[51] not as an eminent abbot presiding over a busy monastery, but as a ragged eccentric, a lone vagrant who frequents the streets of villages and towns. Familiar in the West as the "laughing Buddha" depicted in countless imported curios, Pu-tai was a semilegendary Ch'an monk thought to have lived during the late ninth and early tenth centuries. A native of what is now eastern Chekiang, he wandered the country begging for alms and sleeping wherever darkness overtook him. Recognizable by his deeply wrinkled brow and exposed bulging stomach, he is said to have always carried his belongings in a huge cloth sack (*pu-tai*) that hung from a staff resting on his shoulder. This trademark accouterment led people to dub him Pu-tai shih, "Master Cloth Sack," though the name he assigned himself was the more elliptical Ch'i-tz'u, "Realizing This." He would eat whatever offerings of food came his way, including meat and fish, forbidden to priests, stowing any leftovers in his sack. Besides serving as a carry-all and portable larder, Pu-tai's bag was also an indispensable prop in Ch'an encounters: when questioned by curious monks or other Ch'an masters,

Pu-tai would suddenly drop the sack and stand before his questioner, arms folded. He is said to have been regarded as an incarnation of the Bodhisattva Maitreya, the Buddha of the future, who meditates in the Tushita heaven waiting to appear at the end of the present eon and occasionally manifesting himself in human form. Pu-tai reportedly died in the second year of the Chen-ming era of the Later Liang dynasty (916), seated in meditation posture on a flat rock and reciting a final verse:

> "A Maitreya! A true Maitreya!
> He transforms himself into a million bodies
> He shows himself once in a great while
> To the people of the age
> But they never know who he is."[52]

Pu-tai was among the Ch'an subjects popular with Sung dynasty brush painters, who often favored weird, madcap figures and wizened sages drawn from the Ch'an pantheon. As such, he was depicted not only by Ch'an priest-painters of the time but by secular artists like Liang K'ai and Li Ch'üeh (both n.d., active thirteenth century). Of particular interest, however, is Pu-tai's appearance as the aged vagabond who embodies the final stage of the *Ten Ox-Herding Pictures* in the celebrated version of the work by the Southern Sung Lin-chi master K'uo-an Shih-yüan (active ca. 1150). First popularized during the early Sung dynasty, the ox-herding pictures are a series of ten images describing the Ch'an student's search for and ultimate realization of his original nature, represented allegorically as a contest between a young oxherd and an untamed water buffalo, the "ox" of the title. K'uo-an's version, which survives only in Japanese copies, consists of ten small round paintings, one for each stage of the student's quest, with a title, comment, and poem composed by K'uo-an to accompany each image.[53]

K'uo-an's tenth and concluding stage, "Entering the City, Hands Dangling at Ease,"[54] shows a bedraggled, beaming Pu-tai, often depicted standing under a gnarled pine and being venerated by the young herdsman, over whom he towers incongruously. The sage's chest and belly are bared, and his bulging patchwork sack, which threatens to burst its seams, has been tied, along with a gourd, to the end of a long wooden staff that leans comfortably against one shoulder. Pu-tai's absurdly casual, deliberately uncouth image is a kind of poetic shorthand by which Kuo-an expresses the essence of the parable's tenth and final stage, the dynamic physical manifestation of Ch'an enlightenment in the midst of the everyday world, a theme further articulated in the final comment and poem:

> His thatched cottage gate is closed, and even the wisest know him not. No glimpses of his inner life are to be caught; for he goes on his own way without following the steps of the ancient sages. Carrying a gourd he goes out into the market, leaning against a staff he comes home. He is found in company with wine-bibbers and butchers, [and] he and they are all converted into Buddhas.
>
> > Bare-chested and bare-footed, he comes out into the market-place;
> > Daubed with mud and ashes, how broadly he smiles!
> > There is no need for the miraculous power of the gods,
> > For he touches, and lo! the dead trees are in full bloom.[55]

Kuo-an's picture of the awakened sage mingling anonymously with the humblest of his neighbors, to all appearances the lowliest as well as the most free and contented of men, is in some respects an apt portrait of Tōsui in the Master's final years. This is not to suggest that Tōsui consciously followed such models in evolving his distinctive way of life, though Pu-tai's image and legend remained popular in Tokugawa Japan,[56] and Kuo-an's ox herding pictures were certainly familiar to numbers of Tokugawa-period Zen priests.[57] Yet in composing the *Tribute*, Menzan, as a scholar and historian of Zen, would have been implicitly aware, as would the more knowledgeable of his readers, of the congruences and spiritual affinities linking Tōsui with fabled figures of Ch'an's past such as Pu-tai. Exceptional as Tōsui's tale was, Menzan surely recognized that in the end what made the details of this obscure life worth collecting and chronicling for posterity was that they conveyed not merely Tōsui's own remarkable story, but a living part of the ongoing story of Zen.

APPENDIX
Biography of Master Tōsui
(Tōsui oshō den)

By Zōsan Ryōki

(*The earliest surviving record of Tōsui's life, Tōsui oshō den appears in* Jūzoku Nichi-iki tōjō shosoden *[1717], a compendium of biographies of ninety-four Chinese and Japanese Sōtō teachers, composed in 1717 by the priest Zōsan Ryōki [n.d.], a disciple of the noted Sōtō Zen master Tokuō Ryōkō [1649–1709].)*

The Master's formal name was Unkei, his common name Tōsui.[1] His birthplace is not definitely known. He entered the monastery as a child. By nature he was sharp-witted, but outwardly he seemed stupid. When he was mature, he resolved to find a teacher under whom he could thoroughly investigate Zen. Unless a person were fully realized, he would not study with him.

The celebrated monks Kengan [Zen'etsu] and [Unzan] Gūhaku simultaneously declared their firm friendship with the Master, and early on were instrumental in his move to Kōtōji in Shimabara. There the Master remonstrated with the temple's patron,[2] but without success. He then left and settled in Kawajiri in Higo for eight years.

Later the Master served as abbot of Hōganji in Settsu. Monks gathered around the Master, delighting in the elegant simplicity [of his teaching]. One day he secretly fled, and for several years no one knew his whereabouts.

When the Master's disciple Mitsuzen was traveling through a post town in Ise Province, there was a bald man weaving sandals in a thatched shop. As Mitsuzen gazed at him, he realized it was the Master. Astonished, Mitsuzen prostrated himself and declared, "Having lost my teacher I am like an infant separated from the breast. Day and night I yearn bitterly [for your return]. What are you doing here?"

Smiling, the Master spoke with him. He then presented the gatha that contains the final verse, "I'm not concerned with the world's right and wrong," and Mitsuzen tearfully bid him farewell.

There was yet another person who knew the Master. He happened to meet the Master and, puzzled by his appearance, asked him, "Your Reverence, why have you turned into a slave?"

The Master said, "These days, monks only talk with their mouths about the body being like a worn-out broom. But they don't know what this really means. So I'm getting rid of that body myself and trying to find out!"

Later, the Master went to Kyoto, where he worked at times as a hired laborer, carrying firewood on his back hither and thither. At other times he lived as a beggar, begging his food on the street.

One day, Unzan Gūhaku was crossing the Gojō Bridge when he saw the Master carrying a straw basket on his shoulder and peddling vegetables. Gūhaku followed the Master to his house. There he found him sharing a dish of rice with an old woman. The Master was overjoyed to see Gūhaku and invited him to join them at the table. They reminisced about the past. After a while Gūhaku had to depart. The Master sent him off with a gatha:

> In those days long ago when I traveled on pilgrimage
> I was troubled by the [desires for] fortune and fame
> Now I'm an old man but I'm still not completely free of those
>   things
> I've been lucky enough to find myself a quiet retreat in
>   Higashiyama
> Come there and keep company with the wind and moonlight
>   of the imperial city

Shortly thereafter, the Master moved, settling at the foot of Takagamine. He wore a paper robe and rope belt and made his living by selling vinegar, so that at that time people called him "Vinegar Maker Mosuke."

One evening, the Master inscribed a gatha over the hearth:

> The green hills go wandering
> The bright moon winks

> Leaving this world I utter a shout
> Deafening as the fall of an iron hammer

With that, the Master laid down his brush, closed his eyes, and calmly passed away.

The local people, it is said, assembled to cremate his remains, and gathered the relics.

Notes to Text

Abbreviations

DNBZ   Suzuki Gakujutsu Zaidan, ed. *Dai Nihon Bukkyō zensho*. Tokyo, 1970–1973.

SSZ   Sōtōshū zensho kankōkai, ed. *Sōtōshū zensho*. Tokyo, 1929–1936.

T   Takakusu Junjirō et al., eds. *Taishō shinshū daizōkyō*. Tokyo: 1914–1922.

Preface

1. Full title: *Tribute to the Life of Master Tōsui of Takagamine on the Northern Outskirts of the Imperial City* (*Hokuraku Takagamine Tōsui oshō densan*); shortened title: *Tōsui oshō densan*, or simply *Densan*. In *SSZ*, 17:327–364.

2. Tanaka Tadao, *Kōjiki Tōsui*, 98.

3. Miyazaki Yasuemon, *Yasei Tōsui oshō*, 199.

4. Tanaka Tadao, *Kōjiki Tōsui*, 2.

5. *Densan*, 328–329.

6. The term "Dharma brother" (*hōtei*) refers here to one's brother disciples under a particular Buddhist teacher, in this instance Tōsui's transmission teacher, the Sōtō master Igan Sōtetsu (n.d.).

7. *Tōsui oshō den* (*Biography of Master Tōsui*), in *Jūzoku nichi iki tōjō shosoden* (1717), by Zōsan Ryōki (n.d.). In *DNBZ*, 70:282c; and *Sesshū Hōganji Tōsui Unkei zenji* (*Zen Master Tōsui Unkei of Hōganji in Settsu Province*), in *Nihon Tōjō rentō roku* (1727), by Ryōnan Shūjo (1645–1752), *DNBZ*, 71:93a–93b. A translation of *Tōsui oshō den* appears in the appendix, p. 121–123.

8. The *Tribute* records only four fixed dates for Tōsui's biography: Tōsui's transmission from his teacher in 1657; his abbacy at Sōjiji the following year; his conferring of the bodhisattva precepts on his disciple Zekan in 1662; and his death in Kyoto in 1683.

9. See below, p. 146, n. 1.

Introduction

1. The issue of precisely what is meant by the terms medieval or Middle Ages (J. *chūsei*) in the context of Japanese history and Japanese Buddhism remains a subject of scholarly debate. For convenience' sake, I have adopted the traditional meaning of the

terms, as referring to the years spanning the Kamakura (1192–1333) and Muromachi (1333–1600) periods. For an overview of the different formulations, see Kokushi daijiten henshū iinkai, ed., *Kokushi daijiten* (Tokyo, 1988), 9:502c–d.

2. See Yampolsky, *Zen Master Hakuin*, 11–16, 27; Isshū and Sasaki, *Zen Dust*, 25, 28–30; and Dumoulin, *Zen Buddhism*, 2:367, 381–385, 393.

3. Background information on the Sōtō revival of the early Tokugawa period is drawn from Furuta Shōkin, "Dokuan Genkō no shisō"; Kagamishima Genryū, "Nihon zenshūshi: Sōtōshū," 114–121; idem, *Dōgen zenji to sono monryū*, 67–49; idem, *Manzan/Menzan*, 18:15–42, 60–69; Kurebayashi Kōdō, "Shishōron ni okeru Tenkei no shisōteki genryū"; and Bodiford, "Dharma Transmission in Sōtō Zen."

4. Manzan uses the term *"chūko"* (recent antiquity), which he subsequently specifies to mean "over the last two hundred years." *Shūtō fukkoshi*, in Sōtōshū zensho kanokōkai, ed., *Zoku Sōtōshū zensho*, 1:538a and 539a, respectively. The work, composed in 1741 by Manzan's disciple Sanshū Hakuryū (1669–1760), opens with Manzan's point-by-point assessment of the problems confronting the Sōtō transmission.

5. Ibid.

6. The movement identified with the views of Manzan and his colleagues became known as *shūtō fukko*, "restoration of the [Sōtō] sect's authentic transmission." Manzan's views on the transmission are also presented in his work *Tōmon ejoshū*, SSZ, 15:119–131.

7. *Shūtō fukkoshi*, in *Zoku Sōtōshū zensho*, 1:539a–539b.

8. *Dokuan kō*, SSZ, 5:728. Dokuan's reference to "paper transmission" appears in the following sentence: "A paper transmission is not a transmission of mind. And a secret oral transmission is not the special transmission outside the scriptures." Ibid.

9. Ibid., 587.

10. Yün-mēn Wēn-yen (862/4–949).

11. *Wu-mēn kuan*, case 21, T.48:295c.

12. Chao-chou Ts'ung-shēn (778–897).

13. That is, what is the truth that Bodhidharma (d. 532), the first patriarch and semilegendary founder of Ch'an, brought from India to China.

14. *Wu-mēn kuan*, case 37, T.48:297c.

15. Background material for the following general outline of Zen in the Kamakura period and the Muromachi Gozan is based on Akamatsu and Yampolsky, "Muromachi Zen and the Gozan System"; Bielefeldt, "Recarving the Dragon"; Collcutt, *Five Mountains*, 25–89; Faure, "The Daruma shū, Dōgen and Sōtō Zen"; Fujioka Daisetsu, "Gozan kyōdan no hatten ni kansuru itchi kosatsu"; Hirano Sōjō, *Daitō*, 9–44; Imaeda Aishin, *Zenshū no rekishi*, 13–150; Ōkubo Dōshū, "Sōtōshū no seiritsu ni tsuite"; Tamamura Takeiji, *Engakuji shi*; idem, *Gozan bungaku*; idem, "Gozan sōrin no tatchū ni tsuite"; idem, "Kitayama jidai zenrin no shichō"; idem, "Nihon no shisō, shūkyō to Chūgoku: zen"; and Yanagida Seizan, *Rinzai no kafū*, 5–91.

16. See article 9 of Hōjō Sadatoki's 1294 regulations for the Kamakura temple Engakuji: "Monks are forbidden to wear Japanese clothes." Kamakura shi hensan iinkai, ed., *Kamakura shi, shiryō hen*, 2, no. 24, pp. 25–26. The poetry examination at Kenchōji is described in *Musō kokushi nenpu*, a biography of the Zen master Musō Sōseki (1275–1351) by his disciple Shun'oku Myōha (1311–1388). Musō was required to take the examination in 1299 when he went to the temple seeking to study under

the Yuan master I-shan I-ning (1247–1317). According to the *Nenpu*'s account, "I-shan selected the most able students for admission to the temple by examining them in the composition of *geju* [Chinese Buddhist verse], personally conducting the examination in the abbot's quarters.... The teacher [i.e., Musō] was one of two monks to place in the highest rank." Zoku gunsho ruiju kansekai, ed., *Zoku gunsho ruiju*, vol. 9 pt. 2, p. 499.

17. The Gozan system was solidified in 1410 and generally followed for a long period thereafter, with the Kyoto Gozan consisting of (in order of precedence) Nanzenji, Tenryūji, Shōkokuji, Kenninji, Tōfukuji, and Nanjuji; and the Kamakura Gozan of Kenchōji, Engakuji, Jufukuji, Jōchiji, and Jōmyōji.

18. The use of the term *"rinka,"* and of the corresponding term *"sōrin"* to designate the Gozan temples, seems to have been introduced to modern scholarship by Tamamura Takeji, who states that the terms were employed during the late-medieval period. See Tamamura's essay "Nihon chūsei zenrin ni okeru Rinzai," 982–983, n. 3; and idem, *Gozan bungaku*, 250. An example of the contrasting use of the terms *"sōrin"* and *"rinka"* appears in a mid-sixteenth-century Myōshiji-line manuscript in the collection of the Matsugaoka Library. The text, a commentary on the Sung koan collection *Blue Cliff Record* (*Pi-yen lu*; J. *Hekigan roku*), asserts that the superficial, discursive treatment of the record's koans practiced in the *sōrin* is rejected by the *rinka*, which, it suggests, opts for a more direct, intuitive approach. The relevant portion of the text is quoted in Andō Yoshinori, "Chūsei zenshū ni okeru goroku shō no shokeitai," 166. The following discussion of the formation and characteristics of the medieval *rinka* schools draws on Tamamura, "Nihon chūsei zenrin ni okeru Rinzai," idem, "Zenshū no hatten," 1:992 ff.; idem *Engakuji shi*, 275 ff.; and Suzuki Taizan, *Zenshū no chihō hatten*, 124–212.

19. Instances of the latter practices appear in Keizan's monastic code, *Keizan oshō shingi*. See, for example, *SSZ*, 2:446–447. See also Hirose Ryōkō, "Sōtō zensō ni okeru shinjin dedo, akuryō chin'atsu."

20. Various terms are applied to such manuals, but in the Rinzai school they are commonly referred to as *missanchō* and in the Sōtō school as *monsan*.

21. Sources for the phrases are, respectively, *Blue Cliff Record*, T.48:153c; Shibayama Zenkei, ed., *Zenrin kushū*, 13; and *Blue Cliff Record*, T.48:148b. In particular, the *Blue Cliff Record* seems to have played a central role in the development of the *rinka* schools' transmission of *agyo*. See Andō, "*Chūsei zenshu ni okeru* goroku shō no shokeitai," 161–166; Ogisu Jundō, *Nihon chūsei zenshūshi*, 242–331; Hirano Sōjō, *Daitō zen no tankyū*, 95–97; and Suzuki Daisetsu, *Zenshisōshi kenkyū*, 1:243, and 4:11–17.

22. To my knowledge, Suzuki Daisetsu was the first modern scholar to investigate the *missan* system, which he described in *Bankei no fushō Zen*, and in *Zen shishoshi kenkyū*. In the postwar period, Tamamura Takeji, an authority on medieval Japanese Zen, examined aspects of *missan* history and practice in *Engakuji shi* and in a number of essays and articles contained in his *Nihon zenshūshi ronshū*, the most famous probably being "Nihon chūsei zenrin ni okeru Rinzai," referred to above. In a strictly Sōtō context, important research has been done by, among others, the late scholar Ishikawa Rikizan (see, for example, the articles on *kirikami* referred to below, n. 25). The study of *missan* Zen is still in its infancy, however, and many details of its content and history remain to be clarified.

23. Our earliest identified example of such a *missanchō*-type koan manual dates from this period. The work, *Ensō monsan*, by the Sōtō Tsūgen–line teacher Mugoku Etetsu (1350–1420), was inscribed 1423 and apparently transcribed during the late Muromachi period. It is an unpublished manuscript in the Matsugaoka Archive. See Kaneda Hiroshi et al., *Tōmon shōmono to kokugo kenkyū* 156, 279–280. While *Ensō monsan* is the earliest dated document of its type to survive, it remains unclear when Sōtō *monsan* were first produced. See Ishikawa Rikizan, "Mino koku Ryūtaiji shozō no monsan shiryō ni tsuite (II)," 195.

24. Critical comments about secret koan memoranda at the Kamakura temples are recorded by the Lin-chi master Wu-hsüeh Tsu-yüan (1226–1286), Engakuji's founder. Wu-hsüeh remarks caustically on the Japanese Zen priests' long-standing habit of using ponies for koan study, a practice that strikes him as both laughable and pernicious. *Bukkō Enman Jōshō kokushi goroku*, T.80:229b–229c. The passage occurs in the course of a lecture by Wu-hsüeh on koan practice.

25. For example, *kuketsu, hiketsu, himitsusho, kirikami*, etc. The last, *kirikami*, or *kirigami*, enjoyed great popularity in the Sōtō school. A form of secret oral transmission originally associated with Esoteric Buddhism, Shintō, and Shūgendō, the practice apparently entered Zen in the medieval period as a direct result of the sect's provincial expansion and seems to have become particularly popular in Sōtō temples during the sixteenth and early seventeenth centuries. In the late-medieval Sōtō school, certain important koans were transmitted as *kirikami*, as were various rites and procedures, including those pertaining to funerals. Originally confined to a single sheet of paper, *kirikami* eventually constituted whole manuals or notebooks. At times based on a *mondō* (question-and answer) format and embodying elaborate and arcane interpretations of Zen doctrine, many of the Sōtō *kirikami* fall clearly within the spectrum of *missan* Zen. While few of the medieval *kirikami* have survived, many are preserved from the Tokugawa period, when they appear in every branch of Sōtō Zen. See Sahashi Hōryū, *Chōkoku no kanwa*, 134–135; Ishikawa Rikizan, "Chūsei Sōtō shū kirikami no bunrui seiron," part 1, and part 2, 123; and idem, "Mino no kuni Ryūtaiji shozō no monsan shiryō ni tsuite (1)," 254.

26. Case five of the thirteenth-century *kung-an* collection *Wu-mēn kuan* (J. *Mumonkan*). Ch'an Master Hsiang-yen Chih-hsien (d. 898) describes the predicament of a man in a tree, hanging from a high branch by his teeth, his hands and feet dangling helplessly. At this moment, another man asks him the purpose of Bodhidharma's coming from the West. If he doesn't answer, he fails in his duty. If he does answer, he falls to his death. T.48:239c.

27. Quoted in Suzuki Daisetsu, *Zenshū*, 1:291. A (J. a) and *hūm* (J. un) are, respectively, the first and last syllables of the Sanskrit alphabet and thus considered to be the source of all sounds. In Shingon, they are said to embody the beginning and end of all existence, the realm from which all things emerge and the realm to which all return, the mind that seeks enlightenment and the realm of enlightenment itself.

28. *Chūteki himitsusho* (1660), *SSZ*, 14:357. Referring to the first case of *Wumēn kuan*: "A monk asked Chao-chou [778–897], 'Does a dog have Buddha Nature?' Chao-chou said, '*Wu* (J. *Mu*)!' " T.48:292c–293a. The character *wu* can mean "none" or "nothing," but Japanese Zen teachers today often emphasize concentration on the sound of the character rather than its literal meaning.

29. Ibid., 345–346. The four streams (*shika*) are four great Indian rivers that flow from Lake Anavatapta: the Ganges, Indus, Vaksu, and Sītā.

30. The *manji*, a swastika, is a sacred symbol originally derived from Hindu mythology and regarded as one of the auspicious signs appearing on the body of a buddha.

31. Kūgō. One of the four kalpas, or aeons. The empty kalpa is the period of time elapsing between the destruction of one world and the creation of the next.

32. *Shichi butsu daiji no sanwa, SSZ,* 20:488.

33. The earliest dated or roughly datable examples of such syncretic *missan*-type materials derive from the seventeenth century, but seem likely to reflect the period immediately preceding, i.e., the late sixteenth century. See, for example, *Ganzatsuroku* by Kohan Shūshin (n.d.), an early-seventeenth-century Engakuji master in the Genjū line, a Rinzai *missan* lineage that was prominent in the sixteenth century; and the 1660 Sōtō *Chūteki himitsusho*, referred to above. *Ganzatsuroku* is an undated manuscript in the Matsugaoka Library. Portions are quoted by Suzuki Daisetsu, *Zenshū*, 1:248, 295.

34. See Menzan's *Denbō shitsunai mitsuji monki, SSZ,* 15:176–177.

35. *Jikaishū*, in Yanagida Seizan, ed., *Shinsen Nihon Kōten bunko*, 5:358. Ikkyū here uses the term *tokuhō* to refer to the *missan*-style transmission of a particular koan or series of koans.

36. *Kanrin koroshū*, in Kamimura Kankō, ed., *Gozan bungaku zenshū*, 4:439.

37. *Missan* Zen entered the Kyoto and, later, Kamakura Gozan in the sixteenth century through the introduction of the Genjū-ha teaching line, referred to previously. The importance of the Genjū line's role in the expansion of *missan* Zen has been documented by Tamamura Takeji in *Engakuji shi*, 278–279, 350–355; idem, "Hōkei no kenkyū hōhō ni kansuru itchi kenkai"; and idem, "Rinzaishū Genjū-ha."

38. Tamamura, "Kenchōji no rekishi," 2:787.

39. See Bodiford, *Sōtō Zen in Medieval Japan*, 161, 135.

40. The following general discussion of the situation of Buddhism in the early Tokugawa period is based largely on Ienaga Saburō et al., *Nihon Bukkyōshi*, 28–56, 101–111, 184–210; Nakamura Hajime et al., *Ajia Bukkyōshi*, 5–60; Tamamuro Fumio, *Edo Bakufu no shūkyō seido shi no kenkyū*, 127–149, 209–210; idem, *Nihon Bukkyōshi*, 1–104; and Toyoda Michinosuke, *Nihon shūkyō seido shi no kenkyū*, 27–68, 111–127.

41. See Lehmann, *The Roots of Modern Japan*, 64–80. Lehmann prefers the term "estate" to "class," which he feels has misleading connotations in the context of Tokugawa Japan.

42. The Shingon, or "mantra" school, is the school of Esoteric Buddhism founded by Kūkai, noted previously. The Tendai school, founded by Kūkai's contemporary Saichō (767–822), advocates the teachings of the Lotus Sutra, but was also deeply influenced by Esoteric Buddhism. The Nichiren school, like Tendai, assigns prime importance to the Lotus Sutra, but combines this with a militant belief in the messianic role of its founder, Nichiren (1222–1282). The True Pure Land (Ikkō, or Jōdo shin) school is the school of Pure Land Buddhism founded by Shinran (1173–1262).

43. See Monbushō shūkyō kyoku, ed., *Shūkyō seido chōsa shiryō*, 6:170.

44. Quoted in Nakamura, *Ajia Bukkyōshi*, 40–41.

45. For an extended treatment of the anti-Buddhist debate during the early Tokugawa period, see Tsuji Zennosuke, *Nihon Bukkyōshi*, 10:1–403.

46. *Usa mondō*, in Atsuo Masamune, ed., *Banzan zenshū*, 5:293–294 (pages for all works in the series are numbered internally).

47. Ibid., 314.

48. Ibid., 293, 310. Again, alluding to India as Buddhism's homeland.

49. See, for example, ibid., 294; and *Shūgi gaisho*, in Atsuo, *Banzan zenshū*, 2:235–236, 238.

50. *Shūgi gaisho*, 237.

51. *Usa mondō*, 320.

52. *Usa mondō*, 314.

53. *Usa mondō*, 321.

54. *Shūgi gaisho*, 39–40.

55. *Shūgi gaisho*, 161, 152, 293.

56. *Sokushinki*, in Koda Rentarō, ed., *Shidō Mu'nan zenji shū*, 34.

57. The *Jiin honmatsuchō*, published in Jiin honmatsuchō kenkyū, ed., *Edo Bakufu honmatsuchō shūsei*, 3 vols.

58. See chart and comments in the essay by Tamamuro Fumio, ibid., 3:16–18. The True Pure Land (Ikkō) school was not counted in the survey. It was the principal group omitted, and clearly included a large number of temples. Ibid, pp.15–16.

59. Following the listing of sect affiliations for the Tokugawa daimyo in Hashimoto Hiroshi, ed., *Dai bukan*, 2:683–701. An'ei 2 (1773) is the earliest year for which the *Dai bukan* lists the affiliations. However, the relationship between particular clans and sects appears to have remained fairly constant, and the listing for Bunkyū 1 (1861), toward the close of the Tokugawa period, shows roughly the same number of Zen temples and similar distribution by sect. See ibid., 2:981–1020.

60. In both sects the seventeenth century seems to have been a particularly active period in the production of *missan* documents. The popularity of Sōtō *kirikami* transmission in the seventeenth century has been alluded to previously, and Kaneda Hiroshi states that the bulk of dated Sōtō *monsan* materials fall within the late sixteenth and seventeenth centuries. See chart facing p. 338 in Kaneda, *Tōmon shomono to kokugo kenkyū*. Similarly, in Kaneda's listings for Rinzai *missanchō* in the Matsugaoka Library, the overwhelming number of dated *missan* materials are seventeenth century (ibid., 138–141). These include *missan* documents by a number of seventeenth-century Daitokuji abbots. Persistence of *missan* practice at Engakuji is attested by another work in the Matsugaoka Library, the 1625 *Hekigan roku Kohan missan*, a transmission of the *Blue Cliff Record* by the Engakuji teacher Kohan Shūshin (see above, n. 33). The earliest dated Rinzai *missan*, the document is a manuscript copy dated 1714 and prepared by a descendant in Kohan's Engakuji line, indicating that *missan* study continued at Engakuji through the seventeenth and into the eighteenth century. See also Tamamura, "Genjū-ha," 925, and idem, *Engakuji shi*, 250–252.

61. See the introduction to Mangen's *Honchō kōsōden*, a 1703 collection of Japanese Buddhist biographies. *DNBZ*, 63:273. The date for Ungo Kiyō's birth is generally given as 1583 in standard modern reference works, but I have followed the

1582 (Tenshō 10) date in his biography *Ungo oshō kinen roku*, in Hirano Sōjō, ed., *Ungo oshō nenpu*. "Two hundred" years is the period typically cited by early Tokugawa monks to mark the decline, or expiration, of the Zen teaching, though the Myōshinji master Bankei Yōtaku (1622–1693) gives a figure of three hundred rather than two hundred years (*Bankei zenji seppō*, in Akao Ryūji, ed., *Bankei zenji zenshū*, 88); and the 1711 imperial decree awarding Yin-yüan Lung-chih the title of National Master (*kokushi*) praises Yin-yüan for reviving Japanese Zen after the teaching's three-hundred-year decline. (The document is reprinted in Hirakubo Akira, ed., *Shinsen kōtei Ingen zenshū*, 236. Yin-yüan is discussed below.) The basis for these calculations is unclear. It is conceivable that two hundred years refers to the era of Ikkyū Sōjun, and inferentially to the notion that Ikkyū was the last authentic Japanese master. In *Jikaishū*, Ikkyū portrays himself as a witness to the destruction of true Zen, and possibly Ikkyū's accusations against his contemporaries and his own heroic stance in the work influenced the historical perspective of some seventeenth-century Zen monks. In his 1672 *Mukai nanshin* (A compass in the foggy sea), for example, the Ōbaku master Chōon Dōkai (1628–1695) alludes to Ikkyū's criticisms in *Jikaishū* to support his own bitter attacks against the *missan* style of koan transmission, which he alleges has continued to afflict Japanese Zen since Ikkyū's period. Yamada Kōdō, ed., *Zenmon hōgoshū*, 3:163–164.

62. For Shōsan, see below, pp. 29–30. The teachers whom Menzan says Tōsui visited during his pilgrimage years are Gudō, Ungo, Shōsan, Takuan, and the Ōbaku master Yin-yüan. *Densan*, 335.

63. Conspicuous examples of Sōtō priests of Tōsui's period who studied with Rinzai masters (names in brackets) are Tōsui's colleague Unzan Gūhaku (d. 1702) [Gudō, Ungo, Tao-che Chao-yuan]; Gesshū Sōko (1618–1696) [Tao-che]; Manzan Dōhaku [Tao-che and Yin-yüan]; Dokuan Genkō [Tao-che]; Tesshin Dōin (1593–1680) [Tao-che]; Yuie Dōjō (1634–1713) [Tao-che and Yin-yüan); and Tenkei Denson (1648–1735) [Bankei Yōtaku]. Tao-che (d. 1662) was a Ming master belonging to the same teaching line as Yin-yüan Lung-ch'i (1592–1673), the founder of the Ōbaku school (see below, pp. 34 ff.). Tao-che arrived in Nagasaki in 1651 and instructed many Japanese students before returning to China in 1658.

64. See, for example, the Ōbaku master Chōon Dōkai's complaint that "for two hundred years the lamp of Zen has been extinguished" (Yamada, *Zenmon hōgoshū*, 3:163), and nearly identical statements by Ungo Kiyō and Suzuki Shōsan (*Ungo oshō kinen roku*, in Hirano, *Ungo oshō nenpu*, 179; and *Roankyō*, in Fujiyoshi Jikai, ed., *Shōsan*, 159.)

65. *Zokudan*, SSZ, 5:634.

66. The importance of this phenomenon in early Tokugawa Zen is discussed by Kimura Seiyū in "Tokugawa shoki ni okeru Rinzai zen no teimei to sono dakai," 437–447. Kimura suggests that belief in the necessity of relying wholly on oneself in the quest for enlightenment may be one reason for the emergence of so many individual teaching styles in early Tokugawa Zen, contributing to a kind of "Zen renaissance."

67. The cases of Daigu and Ungo are discussed below. Although Isshi Bunshu had trained at Daitokuji under Takuan Sōhō, he is said to have pursued his mature Zen studies largely on his own, and, after realizing enlightenment in 1634, despaired of finding any masters in Japan capable of confirming his realization. Finally, at the request of the retired Emperor Gomizuno'o (1596–1680), the Myōshinji master Gudō

Tōshoku sanctioned Isshi's independent enlightenment, praising Isshi as "one who immediately awakened himself without having to depend on others in his search" (*Butchō kokushi nenpu*, T.81:187c; and Mujaku Dōchū, *Shōbōzanshi*, 35). It should be noted that Daigu, Ungo, Isshi, and other "self-enlightened" teachers all remained within the lineage of their particular temples—here Myōshinji—holding the *inka* of established masters of their line and fulfilling their roles as members of the temple organization. Such arrangements ensured their standing within the sect and satisfied the formal requirements for succession and temple office.

68. Evidence for Shōsan's independent enlightenment comes from *Sōan zakki*, an anonymous work published in 1669, fourteen years after Shōsan's death, with the aim of dispelling misconceptions about his Zen. In the course of a dialogue, a questioner asks whether Shōsan was heretical since, although he attained enlightenment, he did not succeed to any particular school of Zen, and was "*mushi jishō*," "without a teacher and self-certified." The author answers that the transmission of mind to mind is a matter of "knowing for oneself and attaining for oneself" (*jichi jitoku*), and that this is what is meant by completing the teaching. "To transmit some written statement or a robe," he argues, "is not the true Way." The *Zakki* is an unpublished manuscript in the possession of Komazawa University. The portion cited here is quoted in Kashiwabara Yūsen, *Kinsei shomin Bukkyō* (Kyoto, 1971), 219, n. 7.

69. The *Daigu oshō gyōjitsu*, an undated, anonymous biography of Daigu. Previously existing only in manuscript, it has been published by Zen bunka kenkyūjo in Katō Shōshun, ed., *Daigu ihō* (Kyoto, 1970). As this volume is unavailable in American libraries, I have relied on Kimura Seiyū's paraphrasing of the *Gyōjitsu* in his articles "Ungo Kiyō," 115, and "Tokugawa shoki," 438. Mangen Shiban's biography of Daigu in *Honchō kosōden* includes the story of Daigu's abandoning his temple and his subsequent enlightenment, but omits his turning to the "buddhas and patriarchs" for sanction. *DNBZ*, 63:276. Additional biographical information on Daigu has been drawn from Mujaku, *Shōbōzanshi*, 147–149; Matsukura Zentei, "Daigu Sōchiku zenji no gyōjō"; and Furuta Shōkin, *Zensō no yuige*, 115–122.

70. *Ungo oshō kinen roku*, referred to above, in Hirano, *Ungo nenpu*. Biographical information on Ungo in the following pages is based on the *Kinen roku*. For Ungo's enlightenment, see 178–179, 218.

71. The Mahayana bodhisattva Avalokiteshvara, embodiment of compassionate wisdom.

72. Literally, *tennen no gedō*, a heretic who denies the law of cause and effect and holds that things occur spontaneously. In Zen, the term is often used in discussing those who are self-enlightened and self-certified.

73. *Kinen roku*, 179.

74. Ibid.

75. The province of Settsu included portions of what are now the Osaka municipal district and Hyōgo Prefecture.

76. Matsushima is a picturesque archipelago lying in Matsushima Bay, in the northeast of the Sendai domain, now Miyagi Prefecture. It is celebrated as one of Japan's three famous beauty spots (*sankei*). Among Matsushima's own traditional "eight attractions" (*hakkai*) is the ringing of the evening gong at Zuiganji.

77. The hermitage was known as Keisentei. Ungo had first settled there in 1650.

78. *Ungo oshō kinen roku*, 258.

79. *Tōkai oshō kinenroku*, in Takuan oshō zenshū kankōkai, ed., *Takuan oshō zenshū*, 6:75–76.

80. *Rōsō yuikai no jōjō*, *Banshō goroku*, in *Takuan zenshū*, 2:185.

81. Ikkyū's remarks appear at the close of *Jikaishū*: "I have never given *inka* to anyone. . . . So if after I'm gone, someone comes claiming to have my *inka*, you should report him to the authorities and prosecute for criminal misconduct. That's why I'm telling everyone the facts by way of a written testament." *Jikaishū*, in Yanagida, *Shinsen Nihon kōten bunko*, 5:378.

82. *Tōkai yawa* (2), in *Takuan zenshū*, 5:75.

83. See the capsule biography in Komazawa Daigaku, *Zengaku daijiten*, 1:634.

84. *Gesshū yawa*, in Yamada, *Zenmon hōgoshū*, 1:403.

85. Two other such Zen priests are the medieval Daitokuji master Ikkyū ("Ikkyū san") and the Sōtō priest-poet Ryōkan ("Ryōkan san").

86. *Takuan zenshū*, 5:1–174. (There is no overall numbering of pages within the volume; pages are numbered within each work.)

87. Ibid., 1–79.

88. Ibid., 1–27.

89. *Fudōchi shinmyō roku*, ibid., 19–20.

90. See, respectively, *Fudōchi shinmyō roku*, ibid., 2, 4–7, 12, 19–20; *Ketsujōshū*, ibid., 26; and *Ketsujōshū*, ibid., 27.

91. Shōsan's biography appears in *Sekihei dōnin gyōgōki*, compiled by Shōsan's disciple Echū (1628–?), *Shōsan zenshū*, 1–11. For Shōsan's career and thought, see also Royall Tyler, *"Suzuki Shōsan,"* 1–136; Yanagida Seizan et al., "Suzuki Shōsan o kataru," 62–63; Fujiyoshi Jikai and Mizukami Tsutomu, *Ryōkan, Shōsan, Hakuin*, 77–144; Fujiyoshi Jikai, "Suzuki Shōsan no nenbutsu zen"; and Herman Ooms, *Tokugawa Ideology*, 122–151. For a translation of selections from *Roankyō*, a posthumous collection of Shōsan's teachings, see Arthur Braverman, *Warrior of Zen*.

92. *Shōsan zenshū*, 49–60, 61–72, and 93–105.

93. *Ninin bikuni*, in *Shōsan zenshū*, 101–102.

94. *Roankyō*, in *Shōsan zenshū*, 251.

95. Ibid., 187; and *Mōanjō*, in *Shōsan zenshū*, 49–50.

96. *Roankyō*, in *Shōsan zenshū*, 171.

97. Ibid., 138–139, 187.

98. Ibid., 171.

99. *Butchō kokushi nenpu*, T.81:188c.

100. See, for example, the statements concerning the recent degeneration of Chinese Zen and the greater authenticity of Japanese practices in *Zenrin shūheishū*, a 1700 anti-Ōbaku work attributed to the Myōshinji teacher Keirin Sūchin (1653–1728). The work exists only in manuscript. The statements referred to are cited in Tsuji, *Nihon Bukkyōshi*, 10:362–369; and Takenuki Genshō, "Nihon zenshūshi" (8), 41. In his sermons, Tōsui's contemporary Bankei Yōtaku offers a more "even-handed" indictment, asserting that the true teaching had long ceased to exist in *both* Japan and China. See *Bankei zenji seppō* (1), in Akao, *Bankei zenji zenshū*, 18.

101. Background information on the early Ōbaku school is based on Akamatsu Shinmyō, *Ōbakushū kōyō*, 5–10, 17–35; Hirakubō, *Ingen*, 133–136, 191–234; Imaeda, *Zenshū no rekishi*, 217–222; Kawakami Kōzan, *Myōshinji shi*, 2:119–129, 195–200; Makita Tairyō, *Minmatsu Chūgoku Bukkyō no kenkyū*, 66–75, 96–112, 418; Morimoto Sangai, "Ōbaku no nenbutsu zen"; Ogisu Jundō, "Ingen zenji to Ōbakusan"; idem, *Zenshūshi nyūmon*, 220–224; Oishi Morio, "Ōbaku shingi no kenkyū"; 142–149; Rinoie Masafumi, ed., *Ōbaku sanketsu Egoku zenji den*, 49–53, 144–145; Tamamura, *Engakuji shi*, 378–380; and Tsuji, *Nihon Bukkyōshi*, 9:297–298, 318–374. For late Ming Buddhism, see Leon Hurvitz, "Chu-hung's One Mind of Pure Land and Ch'an Buddhism"; and Yu Chung-fang, *The Renewal of Buddhism in China*, esp. 29–36, 47–100.

102. Jacques Gernet, *A History of Chinese Civilization*, 465–469.

103. The Chinese Ch'an teachers who traveled to Japan during the Kamakura period had also emigrated in the wake of an invasion by foreign forces, the Mongol armies that destroyed the remains of the Sung dynasty and established their own dynastic rule, the Yuan (1260–1368).

104. Following the 1686 *Nansan Dōsha zenji goroku*, cited in Rinoie, *Egoku zenji den*, 144. Even *mondō*, or Zen exchanges, with Tao-che's Japanese students were conducted in writing. Such a *mondō* between Tao-che and Bankei Yōtaku is described in Bankei's biography *Shōgen kokushi gyōgō myakki* (Akao, *Bankei zenji zenshū*, 232); and fragments of what appear to be a written *mondō* between Bankei and Tao-che are preserved on a scroll at Bankei's temple Ryōmonji, in Aboshi (Hyōgo Prefecture). The text of the scroll is transcribed by Akao ibid., 719.

105. Rinoie, *Egoku zenji den*, 49.

106. *Zenrin kaju*, published in 1662. There is no modern edition of the text. Portions referred to are cited in Hirakubō, *Ingen*, 196. Manpukuji's founding is discussed below, p. 37. Mantra and dharani are the formulas, and mudra the hand gestures, employed in Esoteric Buddhist traditions.

107. See the section "Nien-fo Kung an" in Yu, *Renewal of Chinese Buddhism*, 53–57. Yu quotes statements by various Ming Ch'an monks urging students to treat the *nien-fo* as a koan by examining the question "Who is this person reciting the *nien-fo?*" Helen Baroni observes, however, that there is no evidence that Yin-yüan assigned the *nien-fo* koan to any of his Zen students. See Helen J. Baroni, *Obaku Zen*, 116.

108. See, for example, *Ōbaku shingi*, T.82:771c, 772a, and 779b.

109. For Ungo's syncretism of Zen and Pure Land, see Ogisu Jundō, ed., *Myōshinji*, 72–73; Watanabe Yoshikatsu, "Ungo nenbutsu"; and Kimura, "Ungo Kiyo." For Isshi's advocacy of the precepts, see Amakuki Setsusan, ed., *Myōshinji roppyakunen shi*, 371; and Isshi's work *Daibaizan yawa*, in Yamada, *Zenmon hōgoshū*, 2:603, 606.

110. Yin-yüan's biography is included in *Honchō kosōden*, DNBZ, 63:277–278. His collected works have been published in a twelve-volume modern edition, *Shinsen kōtei Ingen zenshū*, edited by Hirakubō Akira.

111. *Usa mondō*, *Banzan zenshū*, 5:308. The Mongol expeditions, directed against Japan's southern island of Kyushu, occurred in 1274 and 1281. Banzan suggests that just as the Ōbaku priests arrived in Japan in the aftermath of the Manchu conquest of

Ming China, the early Ch'an masters who settled in Kamakura in the thirteenth century had arrived following the Mongol invasion of Sung China.

112. I have focused on the struggle over Yin-yüan at Myōshinji because the episode offers important details about Yin-yüan's teaching and its reception in Japan (the majority of Yin-yüan's early Japanese students were reputedly drawn from Myōshinji) and because Tōsui was acquainted with three of the principal masters who figured in the drama: Daigu, Gudō, and Yin-yüan himself.

113. *Zenrin shūheishū*, cited in Takenuki, "Nihon zenshūshi (7)," 41; and Tsuji, *Nihon Bukkyōshi*, 9:362–369. Sitting meditation in Zen temples is commonly broken with periods of walking meditation (J. *kinhin*).

114. *Ōbaku geki*, cited in Minamoto Ryōen, *Tetsugen*, 85; and Takenuki, "Nihon zenshūshi (7)," 41. An anti-Ōbaku text dated 1720, *Ōbaku geki* is the principal record of Myōshinji opposition to Yin-yüan. Although authorship of parts of the text remains uncertain, in the main it is generally acknowledged to be the work of the Myōshinji scholar-priest Mujaku Dōchū (1653–1744), the heir of Jikuin Somon (1610–1677), an early follower of Yin-yüan who subsequently broke with the Chinese master. *Ōbaku geki* is is not readily available in a modern printed edition. An English translation is included in Baroni, *Obaku Zen*, 205–217.

115. Minamoto Ryōen, *Tetsugen*, 102, 104; and Tsuji, *Nihon Bukkyōshi*, 9:357. The episode concerning Tao-che's *inka*, or written sanction, from his teacher, Hsüanhsing Hsin-mi (1603–1659), is cited in *Genshiken ganmokukan*, a collection of sermons by the Myōshinji-line master Bankei Yōtaku, one of Tao-che's Japanese disciples. The problems between the two Chinese teachers are attributed by the account to Yin-yüan's jealousy of Tao-che's greater success and superior character. See Fujimoto Tsuchishige, ed., *Bankei zenji hōgoshū*, 173. There seems to have been considerable friction between Tao-che and Yin-yüan, who apparently regarded the former as something of an interloper, and Tao-che's return to China may have been prompted in part by the resulting tensions. Minamoto concludes that the *inka* incident, or similar incidents, may well have occurred. Minamoto, *Tetsugen*, 105.

116. Minamoto claims that nearly all Yin-yüan's early Japanese monk students were drawn from Myōshinji. Minamoto, *Tetsugen*, p.62.

117. The text of the letter is published in Amakuki, *Myōshinji roppyakunen shi*, 356–358.

118. In this regard, Minamoto points out that Kirei's letter was written before Yinyüan's leading Chinese students had arrived to join him in Japan. These students, masters in their own right, included the celebrated teachers Mu-an Hsing-t'ao (J. Mokuan Shōtō, 1611–1689), Chi-fei Ju-i (J. Sokuhi Nyoichi, 1616–1671), and Tōsui's colleague Kao-ch'üan Hsing-tung (J. Kōsen Shōton, 1632–1695). See Minamoto, *Tetsugen*, 62.

119. Mujaku, *Shōbōzanshi*, 161.

120. For the debate and relevant documents, see Kawakami, *Myōshinji shi*, 2:195–200; and Minamoto, *Tetsugen*, 88–90.

121. Chinese abbots remained the rule at Manpukuji till the mid-eighteenth century. After 1740, Japanese Ōbaku priests were permitted to assume Manpukuji's abbacy, and since 1786 all the temple's abbots have been Japanese.

122. The practice is presented in *Tōzui hen*, a 1705 work compiled by Ōbaku monks for the Japanese imperial family. Before his departure from China, Yin-yüan

claimed to have received a spirit-writing oracle from Chen Tuan in which the deity foretold the birth of the Japanese emperor Reigen (1654–1732). Terence C. Russell, "Chen Tuan's Veneration of the Dharma."

123. Tamamura, *Engakuji shi*, 379; Imaeda, *Zenshū no rekishi*, 227. Manzan's views on the precepts are presented in his works *Zenkai ketsu* (T.82:615b–618b) and *Taikaku kanwa* (SSZ, 3:5–20). See also Kagamishima, *Dōgen*, 151–171; and Ishizuki Shōryū, "Manzan zenji to zenkai shisō." Interest in the precepts was shared by certain early Tokugawa Rinzai teachers as well, the most noted example being Isshi Bunshu. See, for example, his *Daibaizan yawa*, in *Zenmon hōgoshū*, 3:603–606.

124. T.47:495a–506c. According to Yanagida Seizan, it was not until the Tokugawa period that the *Lin-chi lu* was studied in Japan in its own right, as opposed to the study of the so-called Rinzai koans derived from the text. The Ming founders of the Ōbaku school are said to have been instrumental in stimulating this broader study of the classic. See Yanagida Seizan, *Rinzai Nōto*, 79–83.

125. Statements to this effect appear, for example, in Tsuji, *Nihon Bukkyōshi*, 9:296; Tamamura, *Engakuji shi*, 380; Imaeda, *Zenshū no rekishi*, 215; Miura and Sasaki, *Zen Dust*, 27; and Ogisu, "Ingen," 12.

126. Although he received Tao-che's sanction, after the Chinese teacher's return to China Bankei had no contact with the Ōbaku teachers of Yin-yüan's line and received transmission in his original teacher's Myōshinji lineage. In later life, in his sermons, Bankei expressed his reservations about Tao-che and his low opinion of contemporary Chinese Ch'an as a whole. See *Bankei zenji seppō*, in Akao, *Bankei zenji zenshū*, 11–12, 72.

127. *Densan*, pp. 329, 335. Kao-ch'üan and Bukkokuji are discussed below, p. 140.

Translation

Notes to the poems begin on p.153.

1. Zen teachers in premodern Japan generally had two names, known as *imina* and *azana*, each consisting of two characters. As a rule, the *imina*, or formal name, was received when the teacher first entered the priesthood; the *azana*, or common name, was conferred when he was recognized as a Zen teacher. Monks generally referred to themselves, and to other priests, by the *azana*. Thus, in the present biography, Menzan refers to Tōsui for the most part as "the Master," but also at times simply as "Tōsui." The characters of Tōsui's *azana* have the literal meaning "peach water," suggesting an image of peach petals floating on a spring stream.

2. A castle town in what is now Saga Prefecture.

3. The Japanese school of Pure Land Buddhism based on the teachings of Hōnen (1133–1212).

4. The Sōtō Zen master Igan Sotetsu (n.d.).

5. In present-day Takeo, Saga Prefecture.

6. Sōtō temple in what is now Kumamoto City (Kumamoto Prefecture). The temple was founded in 1600 by Igan's teacher Denshi Rinteki (n.d.).

7. The rainy season, or *tsuyu*, generally corresponds to the month of June in the Western calendar.

8. *Fūtenkan*. Madman or lunatic. The term, used ironically as an expression of

praise for a Zen monk's attainment, appears several times in the *Lin-chi lu*. See, for example, T.47:503a.

9. An area consisting of eight provinces in eastern Japan, including Edo (present-day Tokyo). The provinces are Hitachi, Shimotsuke, Kōzuke, Musashi, Sagami, Shimōsa, Kazusa, and Awa.

10. An important Sōtō-school temple in Komagome. At the time of Tōsui's pilgrimage, the temple was in the capital's Kanda Dai area, but it was destroyed in the great fire of 1657 and moved to its present location. Here it became a sectarian academic temple, or *danrin*, and a celebrated center of Sōtō Zen scholarship during the Tokugawa period.

11. In present-day Tokyo's Taitō ku (ward).

12. *Ita no tōba*. Long, flat wooden funerary tablets inscribed with a sacred name or dharani and the posthumous name of the deceased. They are set up on tomb mounds or beside graves. Normally, after the requisite period of mourning has passed (usually forty-nine days), the tablets are ritually burned or placed in a river to pacify the spirit of the deceased. In Tōsui's period, however, it was common for temples to recycle them as fence planks, and the practice, while disrespectful to the dead, was frequently winked at because of the relative scarcity of lumber. In Japan, the term *"tōba"* (stupa) generally calls to mind the vertical stone grave markers (*gorintō*) of five differently shaped circles symbolizing the five elements of the universe—earth, water, fire, wind, and space—unified by the sixth element, consciousness. As seen in the woodblock illustration, the distinctive outline of the "five-circle" stupa is reproduced at the top of the wooden tablets, and for Tōsui the wood stupas are clearly as deserving of reverence as their more imposing stone counterparts.

13. A river that passes through the eastern part of Tokyo before entering Tokyo Bay.

14. The Myōshinji-line Rinzai Zen masters Daigu Sōchiku (1584–1669), Gudō Tōshoku (1579–1661), and Ungo Kiyō (1582–1659) and the Sōtō Zen teacher Suzuki Shōsan (1579–1655).

15. The Daitokuji-line Rinzai Zen master Takuan Sōho (1573–1645). Takuan was an intimate of the shogun Iemitsu, who erected a temple for him in Edo, Tōkaiji, in 1639.

16. The Ming Zen master Yin-y'üan Lung-ch'i (J. Ingen Ryūki, 1592–1673), founder of the Japanese Ōbaku school. Yin-y'üan arrived in Japan in 1654.

17. Ōbakusan, the mountain name of Yin-y'üan's headquarters temple, Manpukuji, in Uji (present-day Kyoto municipal district).

18. The Ming Zen masters Mu-an Hsing-t'ao (Mokuan Shōtō, 1611–1684) and Kao-ch'üan Hsing-tung (J. Kōsen Shōton, 1633–1695).

19. Daineiji is in the town of Fukagawa in present-day Yamaguchi Prefecture.

20. Jōsuiji is in the village of Hisakino in present-day Kumamoto Prefecture.

21. Nothing is known of Kōrin apart from the information provided in Menzan's intertextual note, below.

22. A Dharma brother of Tōsui's. His dates are not known.

23. A premodern unit used for measuring distance, a *ri* is approximately 2.4 miles. Hence, ten *ri* would be about twenty-four and a half miles.

24. Approximately ten to eleven P.M.

25. Referring here apparently to boiled barley. Before it can be cooked, raw barley must first be hulled, a laborious and time-consuming process. The humor of this episode lies in Tōsui's naive attempt to make the boiled barley literally from scratch, first hulling and then cooking it.

26. I have been unable to identify Hōonji or Chishōin.

27. Tōsui's Dharma brother Sengan Rintetsu (n.d.).

28. Menzan's ordination teacher, Kohō Ryōun (d. 1717).

29. The Ōbaku-school Zen master Tetsugen Dōkō (1630–1682). Tetsugen was a student of both Yin-y'üan and Mu-an and was noted for his sermons on various Buddhist texts. In 1663, in Higo, Tetsugen delivered lectures on the Sūrangama Sūtra at Zenjōji, a Sōtō temple in the vicinity of Kumamoto and Ryūchōin, and the following year (1664), in Chikuzen, he lectured on the Lotus Sutra in honor of his late father.

30. It was not uncommon in temples during Tōsui's period to recycle worn-out altar covers and the like as monk's robes.

31. Tōsui seems to have seized this moment to fertilize the garden in anticipation of a sudden shower. Presumably the rain would leach the manure's nutrients into the soil, and afterward, the manure would act as a mulch, helping to retain the moisture.

32. A monk-official who acted as liaison between the priesthood and the shogunal government.

33. *Machi bugyō.* During the Tokugawa period an official who served as a kind of combination municipal chief of police and presiding judge.

34. It would have been rare for the Osaka magistrate himself to be present at investigations, which normally would be conducted by subordinates (just as it would be exceptional today for the district attorney of New York or Los Angeles to personally conduct a criminal hearing). Even if the magistrate were present, it would have been highly unusual for him to carry out the questioning in person. For readers of Menzan's period, the magistrate's direct participation would have served to underline the gravity of the matter under investigation.

35. I.e., Tōsui, here referred to by the name of his temple, Hōganji.

36. Unidentified. The two Chinese characters of Ejō's name mean literally "wisdom and meditation," the source of a pun in Tōsui's poem below.

37. Gyōgan Unpo (n.d.) had been Tōsui's Dharma brother under Igan Sōtetsu.

38. J. *ge.* A Buddhist poem or hymn. In Japan, such poems would generally be composed in Chinese. Gatha composition was popular among Japanese Zen monks from the Kamakura through the Tokugawa periods.

39. *Yuikyōgyō.* A short scripture popular in the Zen school. It purports to be the Buddha's last instructions to his disciples. T.12:1110c–1112b.

40. *Tsuifuku.* According to popular Buddhist belief, the merit accrued from the performance of good deeds—including, as here, lectures on sacred texts—could be transferred to the spirits of the departed.

41. Seiunji is unidentified.

42. The former castle town of Shimabara lies in what is today the southeast portion of Nagasaki Prefecture.

43. The daimyo Kōriki Takanaga (1605–1676). Lord Kōriki, who inherited the Shimabara fief in 1655, was exiled for misrule in 1668.

44. Ninji is unidentified. Presumably it was a district of Shimabara. The *Jūzoku Nichiiki tōjō soshoden* and *Nihon Tōjō rentō roku* cite a temple called Kōtōji rather than Zenrinji as Tōsui's temple in Shimabara. Kōtōji is mentioned in Menzan's interlinear notes below.

45. There are several towns by this name in the old province of Hizen (now included in Nagasaki and Saga Prefectures), but it is unclear which is referred to here.

46. Two ninety-day intensive meditation retreats are normally observed in Zen temples, one in the spring and summer months, the other in fall and midwinter.

47. Probably referring to Kengan Zen'etsu (1623–1701), a well-known Rinzai monk of the period. Kengan, a master of the Myōshinji line, studied under the eminent Myōshinji master Gudō Tōshoku, as well as under the émigré Ming teacher Tao-che Chao-y'üan (J. Dōsha Chōgen, d.1662), and was a friend of Bankei Yōtaku, another celebrated student of Tao-che's.

48. Unzan Gūhaku (1619–1702), an heir of the influential Sōtō master Gesshū Sōko (1618–1696). Like Kengan Zen'etsu, Unzan studied under both Gudō and Tao-che, and also under the Ming master Mu-an Hsing-t'ao, Tōsui's colleague.

49. The Sōtō Zen Master Shingaku Echū (n.d.), Tōsui's Dharma brother under Igan.

50. Unidentified.

51. *Wu-chia cheng-tsung tsan* (J. *Goke shōshūsan*; Tribute to the authentic school of the five houses), a collection of biographies of seventy-four Ch'an monks with appreciatory verses, completed in 1254. It was a popular text in Japanese Zen temples during the Edo period. Maeda Eun, ed., *Dai Nihon zoku zōkyō*, 2B:8.5.452a–498c.

52. Customarily, at Zen temples, the winter retreat ends on the morning of the sixteenth day of the new year.

53. *Kesabukuro*. The satchel-like affair in which the monk keeps his *kesa*, the traditional stole worn over the Buddhist monk's robe, and other belongings.

54. Chūgoku is the old name for the southwest portion of the main Japanese island, Honshū. Tōsui apparently crossed the Straits of Shimonoseki, which separate Kyūshū and Honshū, landing in Chūgoku and traveling overland to one of the busy port cities on the Inland Sea, where he boarded a boat to Osaka.

55. Referring to Tōsui's monk disciples Zekan (n.d.), Chinshū (d. 1706), and Chiden (d. 1709).

56. In the Sōtō school, a title that frequently indicates the rank of a monk who has been ordained and entered a teacher's assembly.

57. *Kechimyaku*. A term often used to refer to documents testifying to secret transmissions in Japanese schools of Buddhism.

58. *Bosatsu kai*. The precepts for bodhisattvas, generally referring to the ten major and forty-eight minor precepts of the *sila*, the ethical precepts for both the Buddhist clergy and laity, in contrast to the *gusokukai*, or *vinaya*, the monastic rules for priests and nuns. Transmission of the bodhisattva precepts had become a popular practice in Sōtō Zen during the Middle Ages. See Bodiford, *Sōtō Zen in Medieval Japan*, 170.

59. "I," here and throughout the text, indicates the *Densan*'s author, Menzan Zuihō.

60. Kiyomizudera (also read Seisuiji) is a noted temple which is headquarters of the Hossō school of Japanese Buddhism. The temple was founded in 798. I have been unable to identify the Yasui imperial temple. Higashiyama, "eastern mountain," is a district in Kyoto, as well as the mountain that gives the district its name.

61. An old province in what is today Shiga Prefecture.

62. The castle town that was the capital of Ōmi and remains the capital of present-day Shiga Prefecture.

63. A town in present-day Shiga Prefecture.

64. A scenic town on the southwest shores of Lake Biwa (Shiga Prefecture).

65. A unit of measure equivalent to approximately five U.S. bushels. In the Edo period, wealth was frequently calculated in terms of *koku* of rice.

66. Literally, *wari no kayu*, (broken-rice gruel). This is a gruel often reserved in Japan for infants or the ill or infirm, in which the raw rice grains are pulverized into small pieces (*wari*) before boiling, making the final product sweeter and easier to swallow.

67. The Ōbaku Master Kao-ch'üan (Kōsen) has been referred to previously. His temple, Bukkokuji, founded in 1678, is in Fukakusa, in Kyoto's Fushimi district.

68. I.e., Tōsui.

69. I.e., Lake Biwa, a famous scenic area in present-day Shiga Prefecture. In Tōsui's time, the lake would have been about a half-day's journey by foot from Kyoto.

70. Menzan's ordination teacher, Kohō Ryōun, referred to previously.

71. Unidentified. The first character, *tō*, is the same as the first character of Tōsui's name, presumably Chinshū's way of honoring his former teacher.

72. Unidentified. The "Shōshū" of the temple's name may refer to *Shōshūsan*, the text on which Tōsui lectured at the Zenrinji winter retreat. See above, p. 00. Like Tōgen'an, Shōshūin was presumably an Ōbaku-line temple.

73. *Rantō*. An egg-shaped tombstone carved from a single piece of rock, frequently used to mark the graves of Zen priests. See the final woodblock illustration.

74. Town in present-day Mie Prefecture. It is the site of the Ise shrine, Japan's most celebrated Shinto shrine, dedicated to the Sun Goddess, Amaterasu.

75. *Naikū, gekū*. The two principal shrines at Ise. The inner shrine (*naikū*) is dedicated to Amaterasu, the outer (*gekū*) to her progenitor, the god Izanagi. As with famous Buddhist temples, Shinto shrines such as Ise that were popular pilgrimage sites in Tokugawa Japan were a magnet for beggars.

76. Nagoya was the capital of the province of Owari and is the capital of present-day Aichi Prefecture.

77. Nara, the imperial capital between 710 and 784, is in present-day Nara Prefecture.

78. The Daibutsu referred to here is a massive bronze statue of Dainichi Buddha erected in 749 at Tōdaiji, the Nara temple that is headquarters of the Japanese Kegon school.

79. A post station in what is now Shiga Prefecture. In Tōsui's day, Kusatsu was at the juncture of the Tōkaido and Nakasendō, important highways connecting Edo and Kyoto.

80. The *kago* was a sedan chair that was a popular means of conveyance in Edo-period Japan. Borne on the shoulders of trained carriers, the *kago* were used for both short- and long-distance travel; they varied from the basic, "no frills" platforms frequently pictured in Hiroshige's prints to lavish enclosed palanquins (such as that pictured in the illustration on p. 72) reserved for daimyo and other persons of means and importance.

81. Awadaguchi is an area in Kyoto's Higashiyama district where the Tōkaidō entered the city. Pack-horse drivers were important long-distance haulers during the Edo period and provided a crucial means of land transport for a variety of goods.

82. *Umagutsu zōri*. In the Edo period, horses were frequently fitted with horseshoes made from woven straw. The same technique is used to weave the familiar straw sandals, or *zōri*, that are a traditional Japanese footwear and would have been essential gear for both the *kago* carriers and the drivers of the pack horses. Although the text is somewhat ambiguous here, it seems likely that Tōsui produced both the sandals and horseshoes. The illustration on p. 70 shows Tōsui weaving sets of horseshoes from a bundle of straw that lies at his feet. The Master is pictured in conversation with a pack-horse driver, who holds a pair of the horseshoes in his right hand and his horse's bridle in his left.

83. A *shaku* here signifies approximately one square foot.

84. *Ōtsu-e*. Literally, "Ōtsu pictures." The term refers to a genre of folk art painting that was popular in the late seventeenth and early eighteenth centuries. The works probably derived their name from the fact that they were sold around the Oiwake and Mitsui temples in Ōtsu. The earliest examples were Buddhist images for ordinary use, but later Ōtsu-e came to include various comic subjects. Japanese writers on Ōtsu-e commonly cite this passage from the *Tribute* as among the earliest recorded references to the paintings in a seventeenth-century context. See, for example, Nihon mingei kyōkai, ed., *Ōtsu-e* (Tokyo, 1973), 12–13, 315–317; Asai Masahide, *Ōtsu-e* (Tokyo, 1957), 29–30; Ono Tadashige, *Ōtsu-e* (Tokyo, 1974), 10–11; and Suzuki Jun'ichi, *Ōtsu-e no bi* (Tokyo, 1975), 142–143.

85. Ashes and cinders from wood fires were a commodity in Tokugawa Japan. They were collected and sometimes rinsed in water for later use as a bedding for charcoal or wood fires or in food preparation, where they were thought to remove bitterness from certain fish and vegetables. The water in which the ashes were washed assumed a muddy, inklike color and served as a convenient writing medium for those too poor to afford ink sticks.

86. In Japan, once a main Buddha image (J. *honzon*) is installed in a home it becomes in a sense that Buddha's dwelling, and the Buddha thus becomes the "host." Hence Tōsui jocularly refers to Amida as if he is the landlord of the Master's tiny quarters. At the same time, Tōsui rejects as "cramped" any notion of relying on Amida's power to secure rebirth in the Buddha's Pure Land, expressing confidence in the strength of his own realization.

87. Tōsui's Dharma brother under Igan. Unpo's dates are unknown.

88. I have been unable to identify either Kakihara or Tenpukuji.

89. (1643–1714). Daimyo of the Kumamoto *han*, or fief, in present-day Kumamoto Prefecture.

90. An old province in what is today Ōita Prefecture.

91. *Jashū*. Apparently referring to Christianity. Bungo, like other areas of Kyushu, had been a hotbed of Christian missionary activity, and throughout the Tokugawa shogunate it remained a focus of the Bakufu's efforts to root out the forbidden faith.

92. *Sanbō*. Buddha, Dharma, and Sangha (the community of monks).

93. I have been unable to identify Nō'ninji.

94. The day on which the Buddha is said to have attained awakening. It is commonly commemorated in Zen temples by an intensive meditation retreat lasting from the first to the eighth day of the twelfth month.

95. *Byakugō* (Skt. *ūrna*). According to tradition, the *ūrna*, a white tuft of hair sprouting from the forehead, is one of the thirty-two physical marks that identify a buddha.

96. A *sun* is approximately 1.2 inches.

97. Monks' robes in Japan are commonly black. Distinguished and well-connected priests, however, might assume elaborate garments in various colors, such as the purple robes awarded at the behest of the emperor.

98. Ōtsu is just west of Kyoto, and Unpo was apparently concerned that he would leave the Kyoto area without catching sight of Tōsui.

99. Chihō's dates are unknown. As a Shimabara resident, she presumably became Tōsui's disciple during the Master's years as abbot at Zenrinji/Kōtōji.

100. Personal travel between provinces was restricted in Tokugawa Japan, and before setting out, Chihō would likely have required a permit from her temple and the seal of the local ward official in Shimabara, as well as a legitimate reason for her journey. During the Edo period, pilgrimage to the Ise shrine was popular among all classes of Japanese and was actively encouraged by the authorities as a form of patriotic observance. Here it serves as a convenient pretext for Chihō to travel in search of her former master. Although Ise was technically a Shinto shrine, Buddhist-Shinto syncretism constituted in many respects the common substratum of Japanese religion in the premodern period, and Buddhist monks not only figured prominently among the worshipers at Ise and other Shinto sites, but even served at times as Shinto priests, while the Shinto gods, or kami, including the Sun Goddess herself, were regarded as avatars of particular Buddhas and bodhisattvas.

101. Name given to the part of the Higashiyama district of Kyoto surrounding the famous Kiyomizu Temple, headquarters of the Hossō sect and a popular Kyoto sight. The temple was founded by Enchin in 780.

102. A well-known bridge across the Kamo River. Situated on the eastern outskirts of Kyoto, the bridge lay in a somewhat desolate section of the city, and perhaps for that reason attracted groups of beggars. The Kamo has a wide riverbed, which is often dry in the summer months, providing a natural camping ground of sorts. According to a popular Zen legend, Shūhō Myōchō (Daitō Kokushi, 1282–1338), founder of Daitokuji, spent twenty years after receiving his teacher's sanction living among beggars under the Gojō Bridge.

103. Higashiyama, referred to previously, was a scenic area of Kyoto, and many retired aristocrats erected retreats there for themselves. Chihō is thus proposing for Tōsui a very dramatic change of address. As seen later in the *Tribute*, Tōsui did ultimately settle in the area in a hut of some sort, though apparently on his own initiative.

104. A *bu* was a rectangular-shaped coin, worth approximately one-quarter *ryō*.

Ten *bu* were equivalent to one *mon*. In Tōsui's day, both gold and silver *bu* were in circulation.

105. A famous Kyoto Shingon temple. It was founded in 796 by Kūkai.

106. Both Rōin and Zenjōji are unidentified.

107. In present-day Hyōgo Prefecture. Arima has been known for its hot springs since the Heian period.

108. Japanese production of soy sauce (*shōyu*) increased significantly during Tōsui's period, largely because of the expanding urban market. The most popular story of *shōyu*'s origins claims that it was introduced from China by the Zen master Shinchi Kakushin (1207–1298) as *temari*, a flavoring made by fermenting soy beans, water, and salt. *Shōyu*, produced by adding wheat and extending the fermentation process, apparently evolved from *temari* during the sixteenth century.

109. That is, the three worlds of transmigration: the worlds of desire, form, and formlessness. Tōsui refers to a famous phrase in the Lotus Sutra: "Sangai muan yūnyo kataku" (In the three worlds there is no peace; it is just like a burning house). T.9:14c.

110. An alternative translation for this passage would be a direct response by Tōsui to his friend's poem: " 'What a rare pleasure!' the Master declared. 'It brings back to me the days of my youth!' And lying down, he recited a companion verse."

111. The poem also appears in the *Tōjō soshoden*. There, however, Tōsui presents it to Unzan Gūhaku, who discovers the Master peddling vegetables in Kyoto.

112. Ikeda is in present-day Osaka municipal district.

113. The meaning of these lines in the text is unclear. The translation is tentative.

114. The Sōtō Zen master Unzan Gūhaku, referred to previously. Jōgōji is a Sōtō temple founded by Unzan in the town of Kumatori. The province of Izumi, like Ikeda, the town where Tōsui had settled, is in present-day Osaka municipal district. Unzan was a teacher of the ruling Okabe clan of Izumi, and his material circumstances strongly contrast with those of his old friend.

115. *Kamiko*. A robe made of thick Japanese paper. The paper is spread with persimmon juice, which when dry makes it very soft to the touch; it is then exposed to the dew to remove the smell of the juice. Initially worn by monks of the Ritsu, or Precepts, sect, paper robes had by Tōsui's period become popular among the general population and even the demi-mondaines of the gay quarters.

116. Unidentified.

117. Approximately 2 P.M. by modern reckoning.

118. The *Tribute*'s illustration for this scene is clearly inconsistent with the text, portraying Tōsui with a priest's neatly shaven head and a black priest's robe showing no evident signs of wear. Although nothing in Menzan's account indicates a return to clerical garb, Tōsui is represented in the *Tribute*'s remaining illustrations formally dressed as a Zen master, perhaps an homage to the nature of Tōsui's final years rather than a realistic depiction of his actual grooming and attire.

119. Unidentified.

120. Suminokura is the merchant's surname. His personal name and dates are unknown.

121. Referring to the Kyoto Tendai-school temple Shōryūji, a noted center of Pure Land practice.

122. Amida's Pure Land is said to exist "ten thousand billion worlds" away. Tōsui's poem teasingly suggests that the man's fanatical devotions may actually cause him to miss his target.

123. In premodern Japan, there were two main meals, taken in the morning and evening, respectively. Except for senior managers, who might be given permission to marry and establish separate households, most family members and employees of large merchant clans lived and worked under the same roof. Hence the large amounts of food prepared at mealtimes by Suminokura's staff.

124. The three grains are rice, wheat, and beans.

125. In the merchant culture of Tōsui's day, thrift was enshrined as a cardinal virtue, and the presence of rice floating in the waterway or sewage canal behind a merchant's home was invariably construed as a sign of laxness in the management of the family business. Scuttlebutt of this sort was naturally to be avoided, as it could be injurious to a merchant house's carefully nurtured reputation for discipline and efficiency.

126. The *Tōjō soshoden* states that "Vinegar Maker Mosuke" was a name Tōsui himself assumed when he began to sell vinegar in Takagamine, though in light of the *Tribute*'s more detailed account, this would appear to be an error.

127. Kitayama (Northern Mountains) is the name of a hilly area of northern Kyoto, as well as the name for particular mountains in the area. Takagamine lies in what is now the northern part of Kyoto, but in Tōsui's day it was situated just north of the city. During the seventeenth century, Takagamine was home to several famous figures in religion and the arts. The painter Hon'ami Koetsu (1558–1637) lived in Takagamine from 1615 to 1635 on land provided him by the Tokugawa Bakufu, and the Sōtō reformer Manzan Dōhaku settled there in the early 1690s.

128. The tone of these sobriquets is humorous and somewhat self-derogatory. In seventeenth-century Japan it was not unknown for poor monks in cities and towns to resort to various trades if they were unable to command the support of patrons and donors, and their neighbors might refer to them caustically by their commercial titles. Here Tōsui playfully bestows the names on himself.

129. *Muhōtō*, literally, "seamless stupa." Identical with *rantō* (n. 72).

130. Saizen'an is unidentified.

131. Referring to the Tang dynasty Ch'an master Pai-chang Huai-hai (Hyakujō Ekai, 720–814). To keep the aged Pai-chang from overexerting himself, his attendants are said to have hidden his tools. Declaring that "a day of no work is a day of no eating," Pai-chang refused to accept any food, and the students were then forced to return the master's tools.

132. The celebrated late-Tang-dynasty Ch'an master Chao-chou Ts'ung-shēn (J. Jōshu Jūshin, 778–897). I have been unable to locate a reference to this episode in Chao-chou's record or in any of the standard biographies of the Master.

133. The Ts'ao-t'ung Ch'an master Fu-yung Tao-k'ai (J. Fuyō Dōkai, 1043–1118) was known for his frugality. It is said that when there was not enough rice to serve the monks, he would make rice gruel; and if there were not enough rice even to make gruel, he would make a very thin broth. The account appears in *Chia-t'ai p'u-teng lu*, a collection of Ch'an biographies and teachings compiled during the Chia-t'ai era (1201–1204). Maeda, *Zoku zōkyō*, 2B:10.2.174b.

134. At Eiheiji, the celebrated temple he established in Echizen, Dōgen Kigen, the Sōtō school's founder, stressed the importance of strict and austere monastic practice.

135. The three studies are precepts, meditation, and wisdom.

136. In the Buddhist hells, sinners are punished by being forced to swallow molten copper and red-hot iron balls.

137. A euphemism for delivering lectures or sermons. At Zen temples a banner is traditionally hoisted when the master is due to speak.

138. Menzan here contradicts his statement in the body of the *Densan* to the effect that Tōsui departed Zenrinji immediately following the winter retreat.

139. Referring to Tōsui's disciples Chiden and Chinshū, who became followers of the Ming Zen master Kao-ch'üan .

140. That is, as opposed to the classical Chinese (*kanbun*) in which most hagiographies by Japanese Buddhist monks were traditionally composed.

141. The particular temple to which Menzan refers is not identified.

142. Kōtokuzan (Mountain of Broad Virtue) was Ryūchōin's formal, or "mountain" name. Such names were commonly assigned to Japanese Zen temples, an allusion to the mountain locales of many of the Zen school's celebrated early Chinese monasteries.

143. Tsūgen (1322–1391) was founder of an important medieval Zen line that became the principal line of Japanese Sōtō Zen.

144. Dates are unavailable for Ichiō, Bun'ō and Denshi. Dates for the other teachers are as follows: Sekioku Shinryō (1345–1413), Chikuko Shōyu (1380–1461), Kishi Iban (1405–1468), Daian Shueki (1406–1473), Zengan Tōjun (d. 1495), Sokuō Eiman (1425–1505), Tenpo Zonsa (d. 1586), Kihaku Zuihō (1463–1547), and Daiyū Sōshun (d. 1552).

145. Present-day Ōita Prefecture.

146. Present-day Kumamoto Prefecture.

147. Refuge in the Buddha; the Dharma, or teaching; and the sangha, the community of monks—often referred to collectively as the Three Treasures. One customarily receives the Three Refuges on becoming a Buddhist.

148. Igan's temple in present-day Saga Prefecture, referred to above. It was at En'ōji that Tōsui was originally ordained.

149. Echū has been mentioned above. Of Igan's remaining nine disciples, dates and full names for all but Tōsui and Gyōgan Unpo (d. 1698) are unknown.

150. Divinities said to serve as protectors of Buddhism. Nagas are dragonlike creatures, frequently associated with water; devas are heavenly beings.

151. Kinbōzan (a.r., Kinbusen). There are a number of sacred mountains by this name in Japan. Menzan is apparently referring to one situated in Higo province (present-day Kumamoto Prefecture), in which Ryūchōin is situated.

152. Gizetsu is unidentified. Daineiji is a Sōtō temple in the town of Fukagawa, in present-day Yamaguchi Prefecture. Tōsui served there for a time as head monk.

153. The reason for Menzan's trip to the east and the urgency for his departure are unclear.

154. *Honke*. Sixty-one years represented the completion of a single "cycle" according to the traditional Chinese calendrical system.

155. Menzan's teacher seems to be alluding to the fact that Dōgen, Eiheiji's founder, died at a relatively young age, fifty-three.

156. Taishin'in is unidentified. Sendai was an important castle town in the old province of Mutsu; it is now the capital of Miyagi Prefecture.

157. Speculative dates for Sengan's disciple Tengan are 1666–1727.

158. The Ming Zen master Tu-chan Hsing-jung (J. Dokutan Shōkei, 1628–1706), Manpukuji's fourth-generation abbot.

159. Unidentified.

160. An old province in what is now Yamaguchi Prefecture. Zenshōji is unidentified.

161. I.e, 1767. The *Densan* was composed in 1749 and published in 1768, a year before Menzan's death.

Biographical Addendum

1. *Densan*, 327. Menzan repeats the statement about Tōsui's "thirty years" at the conclusion of the work (334). The dating of Tōsui's departure from Zenrinji is discussed below, p. 105. As noted earlier, the firm dates the *Tribute* supplies for Tōsui's career are those of Tōsui's Dharma transmission from his teacher Igan (1657), Tōsui's abbacy at Sōjiji (1658), Tōsui's bestowal of the bodhisattva precepts on his disciple Zekan (1662), and Tōsui's death in Kyoto (1683). In addition, Menzan offers specific time spans for periods in Tōsui's life. Briefly, he states that following Tōsui's 1657 transmission and 1658 abbacy ceremony at Sōjiji, he settled at Jōsuiji in Higo and later served two-plus years as abbot of Hōganji, in Osaka. Following a stay at Seiunji in Shimabara, Tōsui assumed abbacy of the Shimabara Zenrinji for approximately five years, leaving at some point before the 1668 exile of the temple's daimyo patron. He also spent seven to eight years at the Ōbaku headquarters temple Manpukuji, which had been completed in 1669. Subsequently, the *Tribute* records, Tōsui lived for some time as a beggar and an urban laborer, until, forced by old age to abandon his wanderings, he passed the final seven or eight years of his life as a vinegar seller in Kyoto. Totaling these figures of Menzan's, there remain at most two years and at the least no time whatever for Tōsui's "thirty years" as a beggar and itinerant worker.

2. Full citations for the two works have been given above (Preface, n. 7). As both are brief, single-page texts, references to them have not been specially footnoted.

3. Unless otherwise indicated, all biographical information is based on Menzan's account in the *Tribute*. The *Tōjō shosoden* states that Tōsui's birthplace was unknown; the *Nihon Tōjō rentō roku*, however, claims he was a native of Higo (present-day Kumamoto Prefecture), an error probably deriving from the fact that Ryūchōin, the temple of Tōsui's master Igan, was located in that province.

4. Tōsui apparently did have at least one sibling, as the *Tribute*'s Innen section states that he had a nephew from Yanagawa, Menzan's original teacher, Kohō Ryōun.

5. "By nature he was sharp-witted, but outwardly he seemed stupid" (*Tōjō shosoden*). "Outwardly, he seemed like a fool; but inwardly he was very clever" (*Nihon Tōjō rentō roku*).

6. Tōsui's punning reply to the layman about crosing the bridge "down the middle" matches closely an answer Ikkyū gives the True Pure Land priest Rennyo (1415–1499) in a tale cited by Yanagida Seizan. See Yanagida, "Shinshū bunka to Zen bukkyō," *Zen Bunka* 175 (January 2000): 8.

7. Tanaka Shigeru maintains that although Tōsui's *angya* took him to teachers and temples across Japan, he was uniformly disappointed by what he found (*Kōjiki Tōsui*, 55). However, Tanaka bases this conclusion not on the actual text of the *Tribute*, but on the poem by Menzan that accompanies the woodblock illustration of Tōsui on pilgrimage. Tōsui is pictured on the road, with the traveling monk's wide straw hat, satchel, and staff, while Mount Fuji rises in the background through a layer of cloud. The seventh line of Menzan's poem reads, "The Sōtō and Rinzai [temples] of Japan are filled with lazy fellows (*kankan*)." *Densan*, 333.

8. See Unzan's biography in *Zoku Nihon Kōsōden*, *DNBZ*, 64:55.

9. For Yin-yüan, see Introduction, p. 34 ff. In 1655, Yin-yüan was granted permission by the government to leave Nagasaki for Settsu and the temple of his student, the Myōshinji master Ryōkei Shōsen. Ryōkei's temple, Fumonji, was situated in Tomita, in present-day Osaka municipal district.

10. It is unclear how many Dharma heirs Igan designated in his lifetime, but the *Tribute*'s *Innen* section gives the names of ten disciples the master ordained and states that of the ten, seven became abbots of major temples (*shusse no oshō*)—here presumably indicating abbacy at Sōjiji, which would have required them to be their teacher's Dharma heirs. As the *Tribute* identifies three of the ten disciples—Tōsui, Sengan, and Unpo—as Igan's heirs and acknowledged Zen masters, it can probably be inferred that at least seven of the disciples, if not all ten, were appointed Dharma successors by Igan.

11. Following Tōsui's statement in his 1683 death verse that he was over seventy, the latest date for his birth would be 1612. (His brother monk Echū's insistence that Tōsui was over eighty when he died would push back the latest birth date by at least another decade.) By these calculations, in 1657 when he received Igan's Dharma transmission, Tōsui would have been at least forty-five and possibly as old as fifty-five or sixty.

12. Igan's Sōjiji abbacy is noted in the opening line of the *Tribute*'s preface.

13. Bankei, for example, in connection with his abbacy at Myōshinji in 1672, contributed funds for repair and refurbishing work at his line's subtemple, Shōtaku-in. See the documents cited in Fujimoto, *Bankei Kokushi no kenkyū*, 279. Such donations and the large number of abbacies they encouraged were apparently a prominent feature of late-medieval Sōtō temples, with as many as two abbots sometimes installed on the same day. See Bodiford, *Sōtō Zen in Medieval Japan*, 133, 212. Bodiford remarks that at Sōjiji alone, 231 new abbots were installed in the period 1510–1520 (137).

14. *Manshō soroku*, in *Takuan oshō zenshū*, 6:18.

15. Or, more precisely, to Ryōmonji, Bankei's temple in his hometown of Aboshi (Hyōgo Prefecture). See Fujimoto, *Bankei Kokushi no kenkyū*, 290–295.

16. The *Tōjō shosoden* and *Nihon Tōjō rentō roku* make no mention of Jōsuiji or of Tōsui's first position after completing the ceremony at Sōjiji. Both texts do take note of Tōsui's abbacy at Hōganji (the *Nihon Tōjō rentō roku* even incorporates the temple's name into the title of Tōsui's biography, *Sesshū Hōganji Tōsui Unkei zenji* [*Zen Master Tōsui Unkei of Hōganji in Settsu Province*]), but they place the event at a later period in Tōsui's career, following his abbacy at Zenrinji (see below). Tōsui's biography in *Zenrin kosōden* (1870), a Meiji-era compilation of biographies of eminent Japanese monks, also fails to mention Jōsuiji, but states that Tōsui assumed office at Hōganji a year after receiving Igan's transmission, that is, in 1658 (*DNBZ*, 69:57b).

This would imply that Hōganji, not Jōsuiji, was the first temple where Tōsui was installed as abbot following the 1658 ceremony at Sōjiji. Apart from this single fact, the biography, *Miyako Takagamine shamon Unkei den* (*Biography of the Monk Unkei of Takagamine, Kyoto, DNBZ,* 69:57a–c), simply repeats the information in the *Tribute*, on which it is obviously based, and it is unclear what source the work has relied on for this particular variant of the *Tribute*'s account. Tanaka Shigeru contends that the *Zoku kosōden*'s version here is correct, and argues that after leaving Sōjiji Tōsui took up his post as abbot of Hōganji, leaving some two years later to assume Jōsuiji's abbacy (*Kōjiki Tōsui*, 89–91, 271, 302). Tanaka seems to base his argument principally on the *Zoku kosōden* and on Menzan's interlinear note in the *Tribute*, stating that in fall 1662, Tōsui conferred the bodhisattva precepts on Zekan. Zekan, a native of Kumamoto, was originally ordained by Tōsui at Jōsuiji (see *Densan*, 342), and Tanaka believes that Tōsui must have been at Jōsuiji again when he gave Zekan the bodhisattva precepts (*Kōjiki Tōsui*, 295). Assuming this to be so, it would conflict with the *Tribute*'s subsequent time frame for Tōsui: i.e., his two-plus years at Hōganji; his trip to Yanagawa; his stay at the Shimabara Seiunji; and his five-year term at the Shimabara Zenrinji, ending at some point before the temple patron Lord Kōriki's exile in early 1668. Yet there is no evidence to warrant Tanaka's assumption that Tōsui was at Jōsuiji when he gave Zekan the precepts in 1662. While Menzan notes that Zekan spent a good part of his career in his native Higo (*Densan*, 342), he could certainly have joined Tōsui elsewhere, as well, traveling to receive the bodhisattva precepts at another of the Master's temples.

17. Osaka Fushi iinkai, ed., *Osaka Fushi,* 6:266. In 1669, Osaka is recorded as having a population of 279,610.

18. See Translation, n. 29.

19. See ibid. The text was also a favorite of the priest-poet Ryōkan, with whom Tōsui is sometimes compared. See Tōgō Toyoharu, *Shinshū Ryōkan,* 111.

20. The *Tōjō shosoden* mentions not Zenrinji, but yet another Shimabara Sōtō temple, Kōtōji. Kōtōji is also mentioned in the *Tribute*'s interlinear notes as the temple where Tōsui's nun disciple Chihō was later in residence (*Densan*, 355), and Tanaka Shigeru maintains that it, and not Zenrinji, was the Shimabara establishment whose abbacy Lord Kōriki offered Tōsui (*Kōjiki Tōsui*, 261). To add to the confusion, both temples are mentioned in Menzan's biography of Tōsui's colleague Unzan Gūhaku. The work, *Unzan Haku oshō tōmei narabi jō*, records that Unzan "stopped at the Shimabara Kōtōji, and took the opportunity to visit Tōsui at Zenrinji." *Zoku Sōtōshū zensho,* 3:206.

21. Tanaka Shigeru, *Kōjiki Tōsui*, 115, and *Sanbyakuhan hanshu jinmei jiten* (Tokyo, 1986), 4:459.

22. See *Hankanbu* (*kan* 11), in Yoshikawa Hanshichi, ed., *Arai Hakuseki zenshū*, 1:509.

23. As noted previously, the two early biographies refer to Kōtōji rather than Zenrinji as Tōsui's temple in Shimabara. Kawajiri is in present-day Kumamoto Prefecture. Neither Tōsui's departure for Kawajiri nor the eight years the early biographies claim he spent there are mentioned in the *Tribute*.

24. The work has been cited previously, p. 139, n. 51.

25. Unpo has been referred to previously. Kengan and Unpo are also mentioned in the *Tōjō shosoden* as famous teachers who were close associates of Tōsui's and were

instrumental in obtaining for him the abbacy of the Shimabara Kōtōji, although the source for this information is unclear.

26. Kengan's biography appears in Ogino Dokuon, *Kinsei zenrin sōhōden,* 3:49–59. Among Kengan's heirs was Kogetsu Zenzai (1667–1751), a leading figure in Myōshinji Zen during the mid-Tokugawa period.

27. For Unzan's biography, see *Zoku Nihon kōsōden*, 64:55; and Menzan's *Unzan Haku oshō tōmei narabi jō*, in *Zoku Sōtōshū zensho*, 3:206–209. Menzan's biography of Unzan makes no mention of Unzan's presence at Tōsui's winter retreat but records that he visited Tōsui at Zenrinji in spring of 1642, staying for the summer (ibid., 206). This, however, seems doubtful given even the rough chronology for Tōsui's career that Menzan lays out in the *Tribute*. Tōsui, for example, is not likely to have been appointed to the abbacy of a temple like Zenrinji until after receiving his teacher's transmission (1657); and Takanaga, who Menzan says invited Tōsui to assume the post, did not become Shimabara daimyo till 1655.

28. Menzan contradicts himself in the preface to the *Tribute*, where he says that Tōsui abandoned Zenrinji during the summer, rather than winter, retreat. Possibly this has some connection with the "summer" stay with Tōsui mentioned in Menzan's biography of Unzan (see preceding footnote). The *Tōjō shosoden* states that Tōsui's flight was not from Zenrinji, but from the Osaka Hōganji, where, it asserts, Tōsui served as abbot after leaving Shimabara—a reversal of the chronology in the *Tribute*.

29. *Densan*, p.342.

30. Tanaka Shigeru, *Kōjiki Tōsui*, 262–263.

31. Of the three early biographies, only the *Tribute* mentions Tōsui's connections with the Ōbaku school. Neither the *Tōjō shosoden* nor the *Nihon Tōjō rentō roku* record anything of Tōsui's residence at Manpukuji, his early encounter with Yin-yüan, or his subsequent relations with Kao-ch'üan.

32. Kao-ch'üan's premodern biographies exist only in manuscript. The information presented here is drawn primarily from Tsuji, *Nihon Bukkyōshi*, 9:379–383, and from the entry for Kao-ch'üan in Otsuki Mikio, ed., *Ōbaku bunka jinmei jiten*, 115–116.

33. In Tōsui's day, Bukkokuji, whose formal "mountain" name was Ten'ōzan Bukkokuji, was in the old province of Yamashiro, now the Kyoto municipal district. The temple is listed in Takenuki Genshō, *Kinsei Ōbakushū matsujichō shūsei*, 101.

34. In 1705, Kao-ch'üan received the title Daien Kōe Kokushi, and in 1727 was awarded the additional title Bucchi Jōshō Kokushi.

35. The concluding portion of the *Tribute*'s *Innen* section, where this information appears, notes that Kōhō's Dharma brother Tengan (n.d.) studied at Manpukuji as well, eventually becoming an heir to Yin-yüan's successor Tu-chan Hsing-jung (1628–1706). It is, however, unclear from the wording of the text at this point whether Tōsui was also responsible for sending Tengan to Manpukuji, though this is apparently Tanaka Shigeru's reading. See *Kōjiki Tōsui*, 139, n. 1.

36. *Densan*, 345. The *Tōjō shosoden* has Tōsui present this poem (of which it records only the final line) to an otherwise unknown disciple, Mitsuzen, who chances upon the Master making sandals at a post town in Ise Province (present-day Mie Prefecture). Eating when hungry, drinking when thirsty, and so on, are common Zen expressions for the enlightened mind's naturalness and freedom from constraint. See, for example, *Lin-chi lu*: "You have only to be ordinary with nothing to do—defecating,

urinating, putting on clothes, eating food, and lying down when tired" (R. F. Sasaki et al., *Record of Lin-chi*, Translation 12, Text, 6). Also compare the following poem by Ryōkan: "Since becoming a monk, I've passed the days letting things naturally take their course/ Yesterday I was in the green mountains/ Today I'm strolling around town/ My robe is a sorry patchwork/ My bowl a veteran of countless years ... /People may say, 'He's a no-account fellow.'/Well, this is how I am!" Tōgō Toyoharu, *Ryōkan zenshū* (Tokyo, 1959), poem no. 80, 1:101.

37. *DNBZ*, 70:282c.

38. I.e., two years at Ōtsu peddling straw horseshoes, "several years" (presumably two or more) among the beggars, and a year or so working as a servant in Ikeda before returning to his hut in Higashiyama—adding up to some five-plus years.

39. Tanaka Shigeru, *Kōjiki Tōsui*, 173–174. Tanaka contends that Tōsui's experiences as a beggar and a laborer represent two distinct periods of the Master's life. He argues that Tōsui lived as a beggar immediately after leaving the temple but ultimately rejected his dependence on alms to become entirely self-supporting, working at the variety of menial jobs described in the *Tribute*. Tōsui, Tanaka claims, only returned to begging reluctantly at the end of this period, when old age prevented him from continuing to work and pay his own way (hence the mention of Tōsui's begging at Ikeda, when Unzan Gūhaku comes to visit him in his hut). Tanaka views this alleged progression from priest to beggar to urban laborer as the central drama of Tōsui's search for spiritual freedom through self-reliance. But though it makes a charming notion, there is no evidence for this kind of sequence in the record. In fact, as Tanaka is forced to admit, all the sources mingle Tōsui's begging and work activities during this period (ibid., 173–176).

40. Another exception is the town of Arima (Hyōgo Prefecture), approximately thirty-seven miles from Kyoto, where Tōsui visits the famous hot springs.

41. See Tanaka Tadao, *Kōjiki Tōsui*, 220.

42. Inoue Yoritoshi, *Kyōtō minzokushi*, 196.

43. Attentive readers will note here a contradiction in the *Tribute*'s account. Menzan first states that Tōsui started in business by hawking his wares around Ōtsu but later set up production in a shack, where he lived and received customers. Subsequently, however, Menzan reports that Tōsui abandoned Ōtsu within days after Unpo found him peddling his horseshoes in the streets. The *Tōjō shosoden* says nothing of Tōsui's stay in Ōtsu but records that an otherwise unknown disciple, Mitsuzen, discovered Tōsui making sandals at a post town in Ise Province. This may well be a garbled version of the *Tribute*'s story of Tōsui's meeting with Unpo at Ōtsu, a story that Menzan could have heard from his teacher Ryōun, or from Unpo or one of Unpo's disciples.

44. As noted previously, this is the same verse Tōsui presents to Unpo in the *Tribute*.

45. See Tanaka Shigeru, *Kōjiki Tōsui*, 174, n. 2, and 264.

46. *Densan*, 334. The *Tōjō shosoden* records a different death verse, a gatha that it says Tōsui left above the hearth in his hut: "The green hills go wandering/ The bright moon winks/ Leaving this world I utter a shout/ Deafening as the fall of an iron hammer." Compared with the *Tribute*'s gatha, however, this verse betrays a certain stiffness and has a stereotyped quality absent in Tōsui's other poems. Given Menzan's

many connections to priests directly acquainted with Tōsui, and in particular his acquaintance with Tōsui's Dharma brother Echū with whom he discusses the poem recorded in the *Tribute* (*Densan*, 334), the *Tribute*'s gatha seems more likely to have been Tōsui's actual death verse.

47. Tōsui's grave can still be seen at Bukkokuji. A photograph of his tomb appears on the frontispiece of Miyazaki's previously cited *Yasei Tōsui oshō*.

48. *Tōmon ejoshū*, *SSZ*, 15:122. See also Ishizuki Shōryū, "Migo shihō no mondai."

49. See above, p. 26.

50. See the lineage chart in Otsuki, *Ōbaku bunka jinmei jiten*, 474.

51. The information on Pu-tai in the following pages is based on the entries in *Sung kao-seng chuan* (988), T.50:848b–848c, and *Ching-tē chuan-tēng lu* (1011), T.51:434a–434b.

52. T.51:434b. Translation by Sasaki Shigetsu (*Zen Notes*, 933 [Summer 1996]: 16).

53. Until recently the earliest painted copy of K'uo-an's *Ten Ox-Herding Pictures* (*Shih-niu t'u-sung*; J. *Jūgyū zuju*) was considered to be a Muromachi-period work, possibly fifteenth century, belonging to the Kyoto Zen temple Shōkokuji. It is reproduced in D.T. Suzuki's *Manual of Zen Buddhism*, together with Suzuki's translations of K'uo-an's headings, poems, and comments (127–134). In 1999 the Mary Griggs Burke Collection acquired a still earlier example, a colored Japanese handscroll of the *Ten Ox-Herding Pictures* with Kuo-an's text, inscribed Kōan 1 (1278) and, like the Shōkokuji version, believed to have been copied from a Chinese woodcut. See Miyeko Murase, *Bridge of Dreams*, 124–127. Kuo-an's Chinese character text appears in *Zoku zōkyō*, 2:18:5:459a–460b. The titles of K'uo-an's stages are (1) Looking for the Ox, (2) Finding [the Ox], (3) Seeing the Ox, (4) Catching the Ox, (5) Herding the Ox, (6) Returning Home Riding the Ox, (7) Forgetting the Ox, (8) Ox and Man Both Forgotten, (9) Returning to the Origin, Back to the Source, and (10) Entering the Marketplace, Hands Dangling at Ease. Other versions of the *Ten Ox-Herding Pictures* have different stages, illustrations, and text. Suzuki has published another such set, an anonymous, undated work, in *Manual*, 135–144.

54. *Ju ch'an ch'ui shou* (J. *nitten suishu*). There is some confusion over the correct translation and original meaning of *ch'ui shou* (literally, "letting fall, dropping, or hanging down the hands"), here rendered as "hands dangling at ease." Suzuki has translated the phrase "with bliss-bestowing hands" (*Manual*, 134), presumably based on *ch'ui shou*'s alternate meaning of "to show favor, to be kindly or gracious." Jan Fontein and Money L. Hickman prefer the more literal "with hands hanging down," a pose that, they contend, implies a casualness tinged with defiance (*Zen Painting and Calligraphy*, 117–118.) The expression *"ch'ui shou"* also conveys a sense of something easy and effortless, and in his book on the *Ten Ox-Herding Pictures*, Akizuki Ryomin quotes the Zen scholar Yanagida Seizan's opinion that the phrase, as originally used in China, meant "to aimlessly drop the hands, to be idle" in the Taoist sense of "doing nothing" (i.e., doing nothing contrived or artificial). Akizuki, however, maintains that the phrase, as used by Kuo-an, signifies "to extend one's hand to save sentient beings" (*Jūgyūzu, zazengi*, 129.) The tentative translation offered here, in line with Yangida's interpretation, emphasizes the element of relaxed informality.

55. Translation by Suzuki, *Manual*, 134.

56. Pu-tai was a popular subject for Tokugawa-period brush painters, both secular artists and Zen priests. The swordsman and painter Miyamoto Musashi (artist's name Niten, 1582–1645) produced several famous renditions of Pu-tai, as did two other of Tōsui's contemporaries, the reclusive Sōtō priest-painter Fūgai Ekun (1568–1654) and the Myōshinji master Isshi Bunshu. Later in the Tokugawa period, Pu-tai was frequently painted by the Zen masters Hakuin Ekaku and Sengai Gibbon (1751–1837). As he had in China, in Japan Pu-tai became a popular figure in folk religion, worshiped as one of the Seven Gods of Good Fortune (shichifukujin). For Hakuin's varied portraits of Pu-tai, see Ono Kyōsei, "Hakuin Ekaku zenji to kinsei kayō." For Sengai's depictions of Pu-tai, see D. T. Suzuki, *Sengai the Zen Master* (Greenwich, 1971), 52–53, 55, 180–181, 187.

57. While in China other variations of the *Ten Ox-Herding Pictures* exceeded Kuo-an's in popularity, in Japan Kuo-an's remained the standard version of the work, and various copies, mostly in printed woodblock editions, appeared during the Muromachi period. See Fontein and Hickman, *Zen Painting*, 116. Copies of Kuo-an's ox-herding pictures continued to be produced throughout the Tokugawa period, as well. See, for example, the listings in Komazawa Daiguaku, *Shinsan zenseki mokuroku*, 181.

Appendix

1. For Tōsui's name, the author mistakenly employs the character tō, as in Sōtō, instead of the correct character tō, "peach."

2. The Shimabara daimyo Kōriki Takanaga.

Notes to Poems

a. The artist has imagined the young Tōsui scattering a "string" of coins, clutched in his left hand. Coins in premodern Japan were pierced with holes (hence their name "bird's eye" [*chōmoku*]) and strung onto standardized lengths of twine that were knotted at both ends.

b. The five wisdoms (*gochi*) are (1) the wisdom that perceives the essential nature of the world of Dharma, (2) mirrorlike wisdom, (3) the wisdom of equality, (4) the wisdom of marvelous observation, and (5) the wisdom of action. These correspond, in turn, to the five elements symbolized in the stupa, which is regarded as a manifestation of the five wisdoms.

c. The dragon king (*ryūō*), revered as a protector of the Dharma, is said to rule over all ocean-dwelling beings.

d. In chapter 9 of the Vimalakirti Sutra, the enlightened layman Vimalakirti sets forth his teaching of the nondual nature of reality.

e. According to Buddhist cosmology, Sumeru is the highest mountain in the universe. Menzan appears to compare the merit of the farmers who labor to produce the rice offered to Buddhist priests to that of heavenly beings who, as they accumulate merit, are said to ascend to Sumeru's summit.

f. The seven evil acts (*shichishi*) are killing, stealing, lewd behavior, lying, idle chatter, harsh speech, and malicious gossip.

g. The king of the first, and lowest, of the four *dhyana* heavens. Beings there are said to be without sexual desire.

h. An area to the east of Kyoto.

i. Also known as Onjōji. A famous Tendai temple on the shore of Lake Biwa, in Shiga Prefecture.

j. *Dokuyaku daigo.* The term "poison" (*dokuyaku*) is often used in Buddhism to indicate false teachings. Ghee (*daigo*) is the most refined of milk products and is a common metaphor for the Buddha's supreme teaching, for Buddha nature, and for nirvana.

k. Devotees of Maitreya prayed for rebirth in his Tusita Heaven, the cult of which corresponded in certain respects to that of Amitabha's Pure Land.

l. Rival states in ancient China. Ch'u occupied what is now Hupeh and Hunan provinces, Yüeh, present-day Chekiang province. Yüeh was conquered by Ch'u in 334–333 B.C.E.

m. Lei I and Ch'en Ch'ung, two inseparable friends said to have lived in the Later Han dynasty (25–220 C.E.).

n. The new moon is sometimes conceived to represent the power to generate the process of enlightenment in people's minds. Menzan's verse suggests that Tōsui has the bodhisattva's power to spread enlightened wisdom.

o. Apparently referring to the "three turnings" (*santen*): teaching (*shi*), practice (*kan*), and realization (*shō*)—the three stages of the Buddha's four noble truths (the truths of suffering, the arising of suffering, the extinction of suffering, and the Way leading to the extinction of suffering). Menzan implies that in refusing the alms offered by Gūhaku, Tōsui expounds the Buddha's essential teaching of nonattachment.

p. In Buddhism, Mara is the demon king personifying the forces of ignorance, doubt, and sloth that obstruct the Dharma.

q. Two rivers in Hunan that roughly bounded, to the north and south, an area of the province where Ch'an flourished in the mid-Tang dynasty. The expression appears in case eighteen of the *Pi-yen lu* (T.48:157c), where it is used to mean "everywhere," "anywhere," or as one translator suggests, "south of the north pole, north of the south pole" (Katsuki Sekida, *Two Zen Classics: Mumonkan and Hekiganroku* [New York, 1977], 195).

r. The two legendary Tang-dynasty Ch'an eccentrics Han-shan and Shih-te. Han-shan is said to have been a hermit-poet on Mount T'ien-t'ai in Chekiang; his friend Shih-te lived in a nearby monastery, where he worked in the kitchen, enabling him to slip leftovers to his friend. In paintings they are often shown together, laughing wildly, Shih-te with a broom and Han-shan reading from a scroll. At times, the two were regarded as manifestations of the bohdisattvas Manjusri and Samantabadhra.

Bibliography

Akamatsu Shinmyō. *Ōbakushū kōyō*. Tokyo, 1934.

Akamatsu, Toshihide, and Yampolsky, Philip B. "Muromachi Zen and the Gozan System." In *Japan in the Muromachi Age*, ed. John Hall, 313–329. Berkeley, 1977.

Akao Ryūji, ed. *Bankei zenji zenshū*. Tokyo, 1970.

Akizuki Ryomin. *Jūgyūzu, zazengi*. Tokyo, 1989.

Amakuki Setsusan, ed. *Myōshinji roppyakunen shi*. Tokyo, 1935.

Andō Yoshinori. "Chūsei zenshū ni okeru goroku shō no shokeitai." *Indōgaku Bukkyōgaku kenkyū* 48, 1 (December 1998): 161–166.

Atsuo Masamune, ed. *Banzan zenshū*. Tokyo, 1940.

Baroni, Helen J. *Obaku Zen: The Emergence of the Third Sect of Zen in Tokugawa Japan*. Honolulu, 2000.

Bielefeldt, Carl. "Recarving the Dragon." In *Dōgen Studies*, ed. William R. LaFleur, 21–53. (Honolulu, 1985).

Bodiford, William M. "Dharma Transmission in Sōtō Zen: Manzan Dōhaku's Reform Movement." *Monumenta Nipponica* 46, 4 (Winter 1991): 423–451.

———. *Sōtō Zen in Medieval Japan*. Honolulu, 1993.

Braverman, Arthur. *Warrior of Zen*. New York, 1994.

Collcutt, Martin. *Five Mountains*. Cambridge, 1981.

Dumoulin, Heinrich. *Zen Buddhism: A History*. Vol. 2: Japan. New York, 1990.

Faure, Bernard. "The Daruma shū, Dōgen and Sōtō Zen." *Monumenta Nipponica* 42, (Spring 1987): 25–55.

Fontein, Jan, and Hickman, Money L. *Zen Painting and Calligraphy*. Boston, 1970.

Fujimoto Tsuchishige, ed. *Bankei zenji hōgoshū*. Tokyo, 1971.

Fujioka Daisetsu. "Gozan kyōdan no hatten ni kansuru itchi kosatsu." *Bukkyō shigaku* 6, 2 (March 1957): 47–66.

Fujiyoshi Jikai. "Suzuki Shōsan no nenbutsu zen." In *Zen to Nihon bunka no shomondai*, ed. Ogisu Jundō, 311–329. Kyoto, 1969.

———, ed. *Shōsan*. Vol. 14 in *Nihon no zen goroku*. Tokyo, 1977.

Fujiyoshi Jikai and Mizukami Tsutomu. *Ryōkan, Shōsan, Hakuin*. Tokyo, 1975.

Furuta Shōkin. "Dokuan Genkō no shisō." *Indōgaku Bukkyōgaku kenkyū* 2, 2 (March 1954): 376–385.

———. *Zensō no yuige*. Tokyo, 1965.

Gernet, Jacques. *A History of Chinese Civilization*. Cambridge, 1972.

Hashimoto Hiroshi, ed. *Dai bukan*. Tokyo, 1965.

Hirakubō Akira, ed. *Shinsen kōtei Ingen zenshū*. Tokyo, 1979.

Hirano Sōjō. *Daitō. Nihon no zen goroku* series, vol. 6. Tokyo, 1978.

———. *Daitō zen no tankyū*. Tokyo, 1972.

———, ed. *Ungo oshō nenpu*. Kyoto, 1983.

Hirose Ryōkō. "Sōtō zensō ni okeru shinjin kedo, akuryō chin'atsu." *Indōgaku Bukkyōgaku kenkyū* 31, 2 (March 1983): 718–721.

Hurvitz, Leon. "Chu-hung's One Mind of Pure Land and Ch'an Buddhism." In *Self and Society in Ming Thought*, ed. William Theodore de Bary, 451–481. New York, 1970.

Ienaga Saburō et al. *Nihon Bukkyōshi*, vol. 3. Kyoto, 1967.

———. *Zenshū no rekishi*. Tokyo, 1976.

Inoue Yoritoshi. *Kyōtō minzokushi*. Tokyo, 1968.

Ishikawa Rikizan. "Chūsei Sōtō shū kirikami no bunrui seiron." Part 1, *Komazawa Daigaku Bukkyō gakubu kenkyu kiyō* 41 (March 1983): 338–350; part 2, *Komazawa Daigaku Bukkyō gakubu ronshū* 14 (October 1983): 123–155; part 3, *Komazawa . . . kiyō* 42 (March 1984): 82–96; part 4, *Komazawa . . . ronshū* 15 (1984): 152–169.

———. "Mino koku Ryūtaiji shozō no monsan shiryō ni tsuite (1)." *Komazawa Daigaku Bukkyō gakubu kenkyū kiyō* 37 (March 1979): 254–269; part 2 ibid., 38 (March 1980): 191–203.

Ishizuki Shōryū. "Manzan zenji to zenkai shisō." *Indogaku Bukkyōgaku kenkyū* 26 (March 1965): 712–714.

———. "Migo shihō no mondai." *Shūgaku kenkyū* 6 (April 1964): 161–188.

Jiin honmatsuchō kenkyū, ed. *Edo Bakufu honmatsuchō shūsei*. Tokyo, 1981.

Kagamishima Genryū. *Dōgen zenji to sono monryū*. Tokyo, 1961.

———. *Manzan/Menzan. Zen no goroku* series, vol. 18. Tokyo, 1978.

———. "Nihon zenshūshi: Sōtōshū." In *Kōza Zen*, ed. Suzuki Daisetsu, vol. 4. Tokyo, 1967.

Kamakura shi hensan iinkai, ed. *Kamakura shi*. Kamakura, 1956–1959.

Kamimura Kankō, ed. *Gozan bungaku zenshū*. Tokyo, 1936.

Kaneda Hiroshi et al. *Tōmon shomono to kokugo kenkyū*. Tokyo, 1976.

Kawakami Kōzan. *Myōshinji shi*. Kyoto, 1917.

Kimura Seiyū. "Tokugawa shoki ni okeru Rinzai zen no teimei to sono dakai." In *Zengaku ronkō*, ed. Yanagida Seizan, 437–447. Kyoto, 1977.

———. "Ungo Kiyō: sono daigo to nenbutsu zen." *Zen Bunka* 70 (September 1973): 112–117.

Koda Rentarō, ed. *Shidō Mu'nan zenji shū*. Tokyo, 1956.

Kokushi daijiten henshū iinkai, ed. *Kokushi daijiten*. Tokyo, 1988.

Komazawa Daigaku. *Shinsan zenseki mokuroku*. Tokyo, 1962.

Kurebayashi Kōdō. "Shishōron ni okeru Tenkei no shisōteki genryū." In *Dōgen zenji to Sōtōshū*, ed. Kawamura Kōdō and Ishikawa Rikizan, 127–154. Tokyo, 1985.

Lehmann, Jean-Pierre. *The Roots of Modern Japan.* New York, 1982.

Maeda Eun, ed. *Dai Nihon zoku zōkyō.* Kyoto, 1905–1912.

Makita Tairyō. *Minmatsu Chūgoku Bukkyō no kenkyū.* Tokyo, 1975.

Matsukura Zentei. "Daigu Sōchiku zenji no gyōjō." *Zengaku kenkyū* 52 (1963): 40–82.

Minamoto Ryōen. *Tetsugen.* Vol. 17 in *Nihon no zen goroku.* Tokyo, 1979.

Miura, Isshū, and Sasaki, Ruth F. *Zen Dust.* New York, 1966.

Miyazaki Yasuemon. *Yasei Tōsui oshō.* Tokyo, 1958.

Monbushō shūkyō kyoku, ed. *Shūkyō seido chōsa shiryō.* Tokyo, 1977.

Morimoto Sangai. "Ōbaku no nenbutsu zen." *Zen Bunka* 18 (March 1960): 45–55.

Mujaku Dōchū. *Shōbōzanshi.* Kyoto, 1975.

Murase, Miyeko. *Bridge of Dreams: The Mary Griggs Burke Collection of Japanese Art.* New York, 2000.

Nakamura Hajime et al. *Ajia Bukkyōshi: Nihon hen,* vol. 7. Tokyo, 1972.

Ogino Dokuon. *Kinsei zenrin sōhōden.* Kyoto, 1973.

Ogisu Jundō. "Ingen zenji to Ōbakusan." *Zen Bunka* 18 (March 1960): 9–21.

———. *Nihon chūse zenshūshi.* Tokyo, 1965.

———. *Zenshūshi nyūmon.* Tokyo, 1977.

———, ed. *Myōshinji.* Kyoto, 1977.

Oishi Morio. "Ōbaku shingi no kenkyū." *Zengaku kenkyū* 48 (February 1959): 142–149.

Ōkubo Dōshū. "Sōtōshū no seiritsu ni tsuite." In *Zen no sekai,* ed. Aichi Gakuin Zen kenkyūjo, 137–180. Nagoya, 1976.

Ono Kyōsei. "Hakuin Ekaku zenji to kinsei kayō: Hakuin zenga no gasan ni miru kayō (1)." *Zen Bunka* 168 (April 1998): 84–97.

Ooms, Herman. *Tokugawa Ideology.* Princeton, 1985.

Osaka Fushi iinkai, ed. *Osaka Fushi.* Osaka, 1987.

Otsuki Mikio, ed. *Ōbaku bunka jinmei jiten.* Kyoto, 1988.

Rinoie Masafumi, ed. *Ōbaku sanketsu Egoku zenji den.* Tokyo, 1981.

Russell, Terence C. "Chen Tuan's Veneration of the Dharma." *Taoist Resources* 2, 1 (June 1990): 54–72.

Sahashi Hōryū. *Chōkoku no kanwa.* Tokyo, 1983.

Sasaki, R. F., et al. *Record of Lin-chi.* Kyoto, 1975.

Shibayama Zenkei, ed. *Zenrin kushū.* Kyoto, 1962.

Sōtōshū zensho kankōkai. *Zoku Sōtōshū zensho.* Tokyo, 1974–1976.

———, ed. *Sōtōshū zensho.* Tokyo, 1929–1936.

Suzuki Daisetsu. *Bankei no fushō Zen.* First published Tokyo, 1941. Included in *Suzuki daisetsu zenshū,* vol. 1. Tokyo, 1968.

———. *Manual of Zen Buddhism.* New York, 1960.

———. *Zen shisōshi kenkyū,* vol. 1. First published Tokyo, 1943; and vol. 4, first published Tokyo, 1944. Included in *Suzuki daisetsu zenshū,* vols. 1 and 4, respectively.

Suzuki Gakujutsu Zaidan, ed. *Dai Nihon Bukkyō zensho*. Tokyo, 1970–1973.
Suzuki Taizan. *Zenshū no chihō hatten*. Tokyo, 1942.
Takenuki Genshō. *Kinsei Ōbakushū matsujichō shūsei*. Tokyo, 1990.
———. "Nihon zenshūshi (7)." *Zen Bunka* 128 (April 1988): 33–63.
———. "Nihon zenshūshi (8)." *Zen Bunka* 129 (July 1988): 21–47.
Takuan oshō zenshū kankōkai, ed. *Takuan oshō zenshū*. Tokyo, 1929.
Tamamura Takeiji. *Engakuji shi*. Tokyo, 1964.
———. *Gozan bungaku*. Tokyo, 1955.
———. "Gozan sōrin no tatchū ni tsuite." In *Nihon zenshūshi ronshū*, 1: 197–244. Kyoto, 1976–1981.
———. "Hōkei no kenkyū hōhō ni kansuru itchi kenkai." In *Nihon zenshūshi ronshū*, 2: 843–863. Kyoto, 1976–1981.
———. "Kitayama jidai zenrin no shichō." In *Nihon zenshūshi ronshū*, 1: 1075–1096. Kyoto, 1976–1981.
———. "Kenchōji no rekishi." In *Nihon zenshūshi ronshū*, 3: 787–798. Kyoto, 1976–1981.
———. "Nihon chūsei zenrin ni okeru Rinzai, Sōtō ryōshū no idō: rinka no mondai ni tsuite." In *Nihon zenshūshi ronshū*, 2: 981–1040. Kyoto, 1976–1981.
———. "Nihon no shisō, shūkyō to Chūgoku: zen." In *Nihon zenshūshi ronshū*, 1: 1039–1066. Kyoto, 1976–1981.
———. *Nihon zenshūshi ronshū*. Kyoto, 1976–1981.
———. "Rinzaishū Genjū-ha." In *Nihon zenshūshi ronshū*, 2: 865–926. Kyoto, 1976–1981.
———. "Zenshū no hatten." In *Nihon zenshūshi ronshū*, 1: 989–1012. Kyoto, 1976–1981.
Tamamuro Fumio. *Edo Bakufu no shūkyō seido shi no kenkyū*. Tokyo, 1971.
———. *Nihon Bukkyōshi: Kinsei*. Tokyo, 1987.
Tanaka Shigeru. *Kōjiki Tōsui*. Tokyo, 1939.
Tanaka Tadao. *Kōjiki Tōsui*. Tokyo, 1975.
Tōgō Toyoharu. *Shinshū Ryōkan*. Tokyo, 1970.
Toyoda Michinosuke. *Nihon shūkyō seido shi no kenkyū*. Tokyo, 1973.
Tsuji Zennosuke. *Nihon Bukkyōshi*. 7th ed. Tokyo, 1992.
Tyler, Royall. "Suzuki Shōsan: A Fighting Man of Zen." Ph.D. dissertation, Columbia University, New York, 1977.
Watanabe Yoshikatsu. "Ungo nenbutsu." *Shūkyō kenkyū* 49 (March 1976): 85–86.
Yamada Kōdō, ed. *Zenmon hōgoshū*. Tokyo, 1921.
Yampolsky, Philip B. *The Zen Master Hakuin*. New York, 1971.
Yanagida Seizan. "Chūgoku zenshūshi." In *Kōza zen*, ed. Nishitani Keiji et al., 3: 89–102. Tokyo, 1967–1968.
———. *Rinzai no kafū*. Tokyo, 1967.
———. *Rinzai Nōto*. Tokyo, 1971.
———, ed. *Kyōunshū*. Shinsen Nihon kōten bunko, vol. 5. Tokyo, 1976.

——— et al. "Suzuki Shōsan o kataru" (transcript of symposium for NHK broadcast). *Zen Bunka* 70 (September 1973): 62–71.

Yoshikawa Hanshichi, ed. *Arai Hakuseki zenshū*. Tokyo, 1905–1907.

Yu Chung-fang. *The Renewal of Buddhism in China: Chu-hung and the Late Ming Synthesis*. New York, 1981.

Zoku gunsho ruiju kansekai, ed. *Zoku gunsho ruiju*. Tokyo, 1923–1928.

Index

agyo. *See* capping phrases
"*a-hum* koan," 8
Amida, 45, 69, 70
Amitabha. *See* Amida
Arima, hot springs at, 77–80
Awadaguchi, 67

Bakufu: "closed country" (*sakoku*) policy of, 31; and persecution of Christians, 13–14; and Tokugawa class system, 10–11
Bankei Yōtaku (1622–1693), 33, 38, 100, 136n. 126; asserts collapse of Chinese and Japanese Zen, 133n. 100; and three-hundred-year decline of Zen teaching, 131. 61
begging, 39, 61; Banzan's comments on Zen and, 16; Ungo and, 24–25
biographical sources, 95–96; problems with modern biographies, xii
Blue Cliff Record, 127nn. 18, 21
bodhisattva precepts, 61, 139n. 58
Buddhism: Bakufu regulation of, 11–15; main-and-branch-temple system, 12–13; monastic armies, 11; parish system, 13–14; religious census of, 14; Tokugawa patronage of, 18
Bukkokuji, 67, 87, 88, 105, 107

capping phrases (*agyo, jakugo*), 4, 8
"Chao-chou's dog," 8
Chen Tuan, 38

Cheng Ch'eng-kung (1624–1662), 32
Chiden (d. 1709), 61, 67, 79, 87, 107, 116
Chihō, 11, 73–75, 77
Chinshū (d. 1706), 61, 63, 65, 67, 79, 87, 107, 116
Chōon Dōkai (1628–1695), 131n. 61
Christianity, 69, 102, 142n. 91; persecution by Bakufu, 13
"clear-eyed" (*myōgen*), 20, 23
Confucianism, 39; and anti-Buddhist critique, 15–17; as Tokugawa orthodoxy, 15
cosmic play, realm of (*yugyōzanmai*), x, 86

Daigu Sōchiku (1584–1669), 18, 20, 21–22, 23, 29, 30, 35, 39, 49, 98
Daineiji, 99
Daitokuji, 1, 5, 6, 12, 28, 98, 100; persistence of *missan* at, 19, 129n. 60
Date clan, 24
dharani, 34, 47, 88
Dharma brother, 125n. 6
Dharma transmission: debated in Tokugawa Sōtō school, 2–3; "paper transmission," 3; by proxy, 2; from a single teacher face-to-face, 2
dialogues (*mondō*), 4, 9, 134n. 107

161

Dōgen Kigen (1200–1253), xi, 2, 10, 31; and transmission, 2; and Zen practice, 2, 5, 89, 92

Dokuan Genkō (1630–1698), 38; views on independent transmission, 3, 20

Dōkyō Etan (1642–1721), 26

Eiheiji, 5, 12, 100

Ejō, 58

Engakuji, 5; *missan* study at, in Tokugawa period, 129n. 60

enlightenment: of Daigu, 21–22; of Gudō, 26; independent sanction of, in Tokugawa Zen, 20–21; of Isshi, 131n. 67; as manifestation of Buddha Mind, 4; of Shōsan, 132n. 68; of Ungo, 22–24

Esoteric Buddhism (*mikkyō*): in Gozan, 6; and late medieval koan transmissions, 8–9; *manji*, 9; in Ōbaku practice, 33

Fei-yin T'ung-jung (1593–1661), 33

Final Teachings Sutra, 59

five desires, 47

funerals: in late medieval Sōtō, 7; and Tokugawa parish system, 13

furegashira, 12, 55, 57

Genjū-ha, 129n. 37

Gesshū Sōko (1618–1696), 27, 33, 38, 104

Gojō Bridge, 73, 142n. 102

Gomizuno'o (1596–1680), 22, 25, 106

Gozan: Esoteric Buddhism in, 5; and infiltration of *missan* Zen, 10; formation of, 5; and literary Zen, 5; role of Chinese culture in, 5

Gudō Tōshoku (1579–1661), 19, 20, 26, 29, 30, 35, 49, 98, 104

Gyōgan Unpo (n.d.), 18, 59, 69, 71, 77, 91, 104

Hakuin Ekaku (1686–1769), 1, 5, 26

Higashiyama, 75, 142n. 103

Hōganji, 53–58, 101

Hosokawa Tsunatoshi (1643–1714), 69, 71

Hsiang-yen's "Man Up a Tree," 8

Hsü-t'ang Chih-yü (1185–1269), 1

Hui-men Ju-p'ei (1615–1664), 106

Igan Sōtetsu (n.d.), 41, 45, 47, 90–91, 97, 99; Dharma heirs, 147n. 10

Ikeda, 79, 95

Ikeda Mitsumasa (1609–1682), 15

Ikkyū Sōjun (1394–1481), 9, 26, 97, 117, 131n. 61

Ikkyūbanashi, 97

imperial abbacy, 100

Ingen. See Yin-yüan Lung-ch'i

inka, 2, 8, 26

Ise, 67, 142n. 100

Ishikawa Rikizan, 127n. 22

Isshi Bunshu (1607–1645), 19, 20, 31, 33; independent enlightenment of, 131n. 67

Itchū Tōmoku (1522–1621), 21, 23

jakugo. See capping phrases

jigo jishō (self-enlightened and self-certified), 20

kago, 67, 69, 71, 109–110, 141nn. 80, 81

Kamakura Zen temples: and Chinese literary culture, 5; and court and military elites, 5

Kannon, 23
Kao-ch'üan Hsing-tung (J: Kōsen Shōton, 1633–1695), xi, 40, 49, 67, 87, 89, 105, 106–107
Kawajiri, 121
Keizan Jōkin (1268–1325), 7
Kenchōji, 5
Kengan Zen'etsu (1623–1701), 59, 104, 121, 139n. 47
kessei ango, 103; continuity in late Middle Ages, 10
Kichijōji, 49, 98
Kirei Ryōkaku (1600–1691), 35
kirikami, 128n. 25
Kitayama, 85
koan, 1, 29, 98; development in Sung China, 4–5; *mu* koan, 98; *nenbutsu koan*, 33; persistence in seventeenth-century temples, 26–27; secret transmission in late Middle Ages, 7–10; syncretic interpretations of, 8–9
Kōfukuji, 32, 34, 35, 36
Kohō Ryōun (d. 1717), xi, 41, 67, 91–92, 105, 107
Kōriki Takanaga (1605–1676), 59, 89, 102–103, 104
Kōsen. See Kao-ch'üan
Kōtōji, 77, 121, 139n. 44, 148n. 20
Kumazawa Banzan (1609–1691), 15–17, 35; anti-Buddhist policies, 16; condemnation of parish system and priesthood, 15–16; criticism of Zen school, 16
K'uo-an Shih-yüan (active ca. 1150), 118–119

"letting go," 29, 58, 102, 105
Lin-chi lu, 38, 148n. 36
Lotus Sutra, 53, 91, 112

"madman" (*fūtenkan*), 47, 98
Maitreya, 48, 70, 118
Mangen Shiban (1626–1710), 19, 20
manji, 9
Manpukuji, x, 34, 39, 106–107; and Chinese abbots, 37, 135n. 121; Chinese atmosphere at, 37; founding of, 37
mantra, 34
manure, 138n. 31
Manzan Dōhaku (1635–1714), 2, 38; and transmission without enlightenment, 116
Menzan Zuihō (1683–1769), 2, 40, 41; as author of *Tribute*, xi–xii; denounces syncretic transmissions, 9; first to record Tōsui's contact with Rinzai teachers, 40; as a leader of Sōtō revival, xi; and *zazen*, 26
mind-to-mind transmission, 20
missan (secret study of koans): ascendancy in late Middle Ages, 10; and dated Sōtō materials, 129n. 60; earliest examples of, 128n. 23; enters Kyoto and Kamakura Gozan, 10; and Genjū-ha, 129n. 37; influence of Esoteric Buddhism on, 8–9; in late medieval temples, 8; modern study of, 127n. 22; origins in Kamakura period, 128n. 24; persistence in seventeenth-century temples, 19, 130n. 60; protests against, 9–10; syncretic transmissions of, 129n. 33; use of dialogue in, 9
Mitsuzen, 121–122
Mokuan. See Mu-an Hsing-t'ao
Mosuke, 85, 122
mu koan, 98
Mu-an Hsing-t'ao (J: Mokuan

Shōtō, 1611–1684), 49, 92, 106–107
mudra, 34, 36
mushi dokugo (enlightened independently without a teacher), 20, 23
Myōshinji, 5, 6, 7, 20, 21, 23, 24, 25, 98, 100; daimyo affiliation with, 18; and opposition to Yin-yüan, 35–37; revival of Zen hailed by Mangen, 19

Nagasaki, 31-32, 33, 49
Nanpo Jōmyō (Daiō Kokushi, 1235–1308), 5, 31
Nara, 67
nenbutsu, 83
nenbutsu koan, 33, 134n. 107
Nichiren school, 11

Ōbaku geki, 135n. 114
Ōbaku school, 31–32; founding of *sanpukuji*, 32; influence on development of Tokugawa Zen, 38; Tao-che, 32–33; Yin-yüan, 34–37
Ōbaku shingi, 34, 38, 106
Ōbakusan. See Manpukuji
Okayama: anti-Buddhist policies and, 15-17
Osaka, 53, 61, 100, 101
Ōtsu, 66, 67, 71, 110
Ōtsu-e, 69, 141n. 84

pack-horse drivers, 69, 71, 109–110
parish system (*danka seido*), 12–14
pilgrimage (*angya*), 49, 99–100
popular Zen, 27–28; of Shōsan, 29–30; of Takuan, 28–29
precepts, 33, 38; and Isshi, 136n. 123; and Manzan, 38

Pure Land, 36; mentioned in Tōsui's poem, 83; teachings in Ōbaku practice, 33; Tōsui's family adherents of school, 45
Pu-tai (d. 916[?]), 117–119, 152n. 56

rinka: ascendancy in late Middle Ages, 7; formation of, 6–7; koan study in, 7–10; term used by Tamamura, 127n. 18
Rinzai school: Hakuin's revival of, 1; *missan* practice in, 8, 9–10. See also Gozan
Ryōkei Shōsen (1602–1670), 35–37
Ryūchōin, 45, 61, 91, 99

sanpukuji ("three good fortune temples"), 32
Sengan, 53, 61, 91, 107
Sesshū Hōganji Tōsui Unkei zenji (*Zen Master Tōsui Unkei of Hōganji in Settsu Province*), 125n. 7
Shakyamuni, 99
Shidō Mu'nan (1603–1676), 17, 26
Shimabara, 59, 71
Shimabara rebellion, 102
Shingon, 11
shisho, 2
Shōbōgenzō, 2, 5
Shūhō Myōchō (Daitō Kokushi, 1282–1337), 1, 142n. 102
shūmon ninbetsuchō (religious census), 14
Sōfukuji, 32, 33
Sōjiji, 7, 12, 89, 90, 97, 100
Sōtō school: dated *missan* materials in, 129n. 60; and Dharma transmission, 2–3; late medieval provincial expansion of, 7;

legitimacy of transmission compromised, 19; main-and-branch-temple system in, 12; Manzan's "transmission without enlightenment," 116; Ōbaku influence on monastic codes of, 38; popular forms of worship incorporated in, 8–9, 10, 128n. 25; resort to Rinzai teachers in, 19, 131n. 63; Tokugawa revival of, 2, 126n. 6

soy sauce, 143n. 108

straw horseshoes, 70, 141n. 82

Suminokura, 11, 81, 83–85, 113–114

Suzuki Daisetsu: and *missan* Zen study, 127n. 22

Suzuki Shōsan (1579–1655), 19, 21, 39, 49, 98; invokes warrior spirit, 30; merger of Buddhism and worldly activity, 29; popular teachings, 29-30

Tachibana Muneshige (1567–1642), 96

Taigu Ryōkan (1758-1832), ix, 150n. 36

Takagamine, x, 85, 89, 144n. 127

Takuan Sōhō (1573–1645), 19, 30, 39, 49, 98, 100, 117; declines to appoint Dharma heir, 25–26; popular teachings, 28–29

Tamamura Takeji: and *missan* Zen study, 127n. 22; negative assessment of *missan* Zen, 10; and term *rinka*, 127n. 18

Tanaka Shigeru, xii, 105, 150n. 39

Tao-che Chao-yüan (J: Dōsha Chōgen, d. 1662), 32–33, 35, 104; dialogues with Japanese monks conducted in writing, 134n. 104; friction with Yin-yüan, 135n. 115

tatchū, 6

Ten Ox-Herding Pictures, 118–119, 151n. 53

Tendai school, 11

Tetsugen Dōkō (1630–1682), 53, 117, 138n. 29

T'ien-t'ung Ju-ching (1163–1228), 2, 5

three worlds, 78, 112, 143n. 109

Tōkaiji, 28

Tokugawa Bakufu. *See* Bakufu

Tokugawa daimyo: and Zen school, 18

Tokugawa Iemitsu (1604–1651), 22, 28

Tokugawa Ietsuna (1639–1680), 37

Tokugawa Tsunayoshi (1646–1709), 106

tokuhō, 129n. 35

Tōsui oshō den (Biography of Master Tōsui), 125n. 7; text, 121–123

Tōsui Unkei (d. 1683): attitude toward charity, 111; and begging, 58, 74, 98, 101–102; compared with Han-shan and Shih-te, 88; compared with Ryōkan, ix; compared with Saint Francis, ix; contact with Rinzai teachers, 39–40; dating of his birth, 96, 147n. 11; death of, 85–87; as descendant of Dōgen, 89; Dharma transmission from Igan, 51, 90, 99–100; encounters Unpo at hot springs, 77–79; enters priesthood under Igan, 97; and female companion, 113; fixed dates for, 125n. 8; flight from Zenrinji, 59, 61, 105; and Kōriki Takanaga, 103; "letting go" poem, 58; at Manpukuji, 49, 106–107; meets layman Suminokura, 81; as "original hippie," ix; pilgrimage, 98; poems by,

58, 63, 69, 78, 83, 85, 122; possible influences of his teachers, 39; relations with Ōbaku Zen, 107, 116; as sandal maker in Ōtsu, 67; Sōjiji abbacy, 100; study under Rinzai teachers, 19

Tribute to the Zen Master Tōsui (Tōsui oshō densan), x; chronological problems and inconsistencies in, xii–xiii; compared with earlier Tōsui biographies, xii; contents of, 41; inconsistencies in account of post-1657 period, 95, 105–106, 109, 146n. 1; Menzan's aim as compiler of, xi; text, 41–43; and woodblock illustrations, 90

True Pure Land (Ikkō) school, 11

Tsūgen Jakurei (1322–1391): as founder of main Sōtō line in late Middle Ages, 7

Tu-chan Hsing-jung (J: Dokutan Shōkei, 1628–1706), 92, 146n. 158

twin guardian kings (Niō), 30

two-hundred years: as period of decline in Zen transmission, 19–20, 130n. 61, 131n. 64

Ungo Kiyō (1582–1659), 19, 20, 21, 29, 30, 39, 49, 98; enlightenment of, 22–24; and Pure Land practice, 33

Unzan Gūhaku (d. 1702), 59, 79, 104, 121, 122

vinegar, 85

Wan-fu ssu, 33, 37, 106–107

Wu-chia cheng-tsung tsan (J: *Goke shōshūsan*, Tribute to the authentic school of the five houses), 59, 62, 139n. 51

Wu-hsüeh Tsu-yüan (1226–1286), 128n. 24

Wu-men kuan, 128nn. 26, 28

Yanagawa, 45, 59, 96

yin-yang thought: in late medieval koan transmissions, 8–9

Yin-yüan Lung-ch'i (J: Ingen Ryūki, 1592–1673), 34–37, 106–107; arrival in Japan, 34; Banzan's criticism of, 35; difficulties with Bakufu, 34; founding of Manpukuji, 37; Myōshinji opposition to, 35, 36–37; and syncretic practice, 34, 36; Tōsui encounters, 49, 99; (1654) training period described, 35–36

yugyōzanmai. See cosmic play

zazen, 1, 29, 47, 98; in seventeenth-century temples, 26

Zekan, 61

Zen school: begging in, 101; identities of Rinzai and Sōtō fluid till eighteenth century, 3; and imperial abbacies, 100; mind-to-mind transmission in, 20; popular teachings in early Tokugawa, 27–28; ready contact among schools in Tōsui's period, 39–40; as special transmission outside the scriptures, 3; spiritual crisis in, 18–20; (1632–1633) survey of temple affiliation, 8; and Tokugawa daimyo, 18; Tokugawa Zen as key to identities of modern Zen schools, 1; two-hundred-year decline in, 19–20, 130n. 61. *See also* popular Zen

Zenrinji, 59, 89, 148n. 20

Zōsan Ryōki (n.d.), 121

About the Translator

Peter Haskel received his Ph.D. from Columbia University, Department of East Asian Languages and Cultures. He is the author of *Bankei Zen* (Grove, 1985), co-author with Ryuichi Abe of *Great Fool: Zen Master Ryōkan* (University of Hawai'i Press, 1996), and co-editor of the forthcoming *Original Mind,* lectures on the Platform Sutra by the early-twentieth-century Zen master Sokei-an Sasaki. He is currently at work on a translation of the writings of Takuan Sōhō.